PATTON'S PAYBACK

ALSO BY STEPHEN L. MOORE

Battle Stations: How the USS Yorktown *Helped Turn the Tide at Coral Sea and Midway*

Rain of Steel: Mitscher's Task Force 58, Ugaki's Thunder Gods, and the Kamikaze War off Okinawa

Uncommon Valor: The Recon Company That Earned Five Medals of Honor and Included America's Most Decorated Green Beret

As Good as Dead: The Daring Escape of American POWs from a Japanese Death Camp

The Battle for Hell's Island: How a Small Band of Carrier Dive-Bombers Helped Save Guadalcanal

Texas Rising: The Epic True Story of the Lone Star Republic and the Rise of the Texas Rangers, 1836–1846

Pacific Payback: The Carrier Aviators Who Avenged Pearl Harbor at the Battle of Midway

Battle Surface!: Lawson P. "Red" Ramage and the War Patrols of the USS Parche

Presumed Lost: The Incredible Ordeal of America's Submarine POWs During the Pacific War

Relic Quest: A Guide to Responsible Relic Recovery Techniques with Metal Detectors

PATTON'S PAYBACK

THE BATTLE OF EL GUETTAR
AND GENERAL PATTON'S
RISE TO GLORY

STEPHEN L. MOORE

CALIBER

CALIBER

An imprint of Penguin Random House LLC
penguinrandomhouse.com

Library of Congress Cataloging-in-Publication Data
has been applied for.

ISBN 9780593183403 (hardcover)
ISBN 9780593183427 (ebook)

Printed in the United States of America
1st Printing

BOOK DESIGN BY TIFFANY ESTREICHER

For my family, for enduring my desire to preserve history, and to the North African veterans who fought to preserve our freedom.

CONTENTS

CONTENTS

PATTON'S
PAYBACK

PROLOGUE

On a mild, sunny afternoon on the outskirts of Casablanca, Morocco, a tall U.S. Army officer was riding a Thoroughbred charger named Joyeuse when an adjutant reached him with a message: General Dwight Eisenhower had phoned.

The message was terse. The officer, whose men knew him as "Old Blood and Guts," among other less polite nicknames, was to pack his bags and be ready by morning to depart for extended field service in Tunisia.

George S. Patton knew something was up. It was about damn time.

For the past two months he had been largely removed from frontline action. During the Allied invasion of French North Africa, dubbed Operation Torch, Major General Patton had commanded a task force of 33,000 men whose November 8, 1942, landings centered on Casablanca. Within three days his men had battled through fierce Axis resistance and taken the city, resulting in an armistice with the French resident commander, General Auguste Charles Noguès.

By early 1943, Patton had converted Casablanca into a vast Allied supply depot and an entry point for thousands of Allied troops arriving weekly into North Africa. Although his role was important to the war effort, he was a fighter, not a man meant to watch from the sidelines, and he found himself miserable. "I wish I could get out and kill someone," Patton wrote to his wife. During a visit to troops in Tunisia, he wondered aloud where the Germans were. "I want to get shot at," he told another officer.[1]

His chance would come soon enough. The fifty-seven-year-old two-star Army general was a complex man and leader: charismatic, irreverent, impulsive, and inspiring, often at the same time. He was a showman who strutted about with an ivory-handled Colt revolver on each hip as he vented his frequent frustrations with a high-pitched voice.

Patton had been tabbed with planning Operation Husky, the forthcoming Allied invasion of Sicily. While Patton prepared in Casablanca, the major general in command of the U.S. Army's II Corps in Tunisia sent his ill-disciplined forces against Adolf Hitler's battle-hardened Panzers and Field Marshal Erwin Rommel's Afrika Korps infantrymen, but the fighting had not gone as expected for the Americans.

Throughout these actions, Patton had been mired in Morocco, supremely frustrated at being left out of the action. On March 2 his depression grew deeper when he learned that his son-in-law Lieutenant Colonel John K. Waters had been missing in action for weeks. With a heavy heart, he wrote to his wife and daughter that Waters was unaccounted for. To his diary, he confided that he believed his son-in-law to be dead.[2]

He took a break from planning the following day. He and some of his staffers joined a wealthy local to duck hunt on his 10,000-acre farm. Patton shot poorly and instead found more interest in two Roman ruins his group encountered during their outing in an amphibious vehicle. As a boy, he had read of Julius Caesar's conquests and those of other great soldiers like Napoleon and Hannibal. He believed himself to be the reincarnation of great warriors of the past who had fought in famous battles.[3]

On the morning of March 4, he inspected troops of the U.S. Army Third Division, finding them to be undisciplined and unsanitary. During the afternoon he had borrowed the Thoroughbred from General Noguès for a ride through the countryside.

He returned to his office and made a quick phone call to Major General Bedell Smith, one of his friends on Ike's staff, to ask what the move was about. Smith informed him that he might be taking over II Corps. Patton was up for the task and eager to immerse himself in the action. In a matter of hours "Old Blood and Guts" would be transported from the sidelines to the front lines. Here was his chance to push U.S. infantry, artillery, and armored forces in North Africa onto the path of redemption. That night he wrote in his diary that he expected to encounter more trouble working with his British allies than he did in whipping Hitler's German Army.[4]

Before turning in for a few hours of sleep, he scribbled one final line:

God favors the brave, victory is to the audacious!

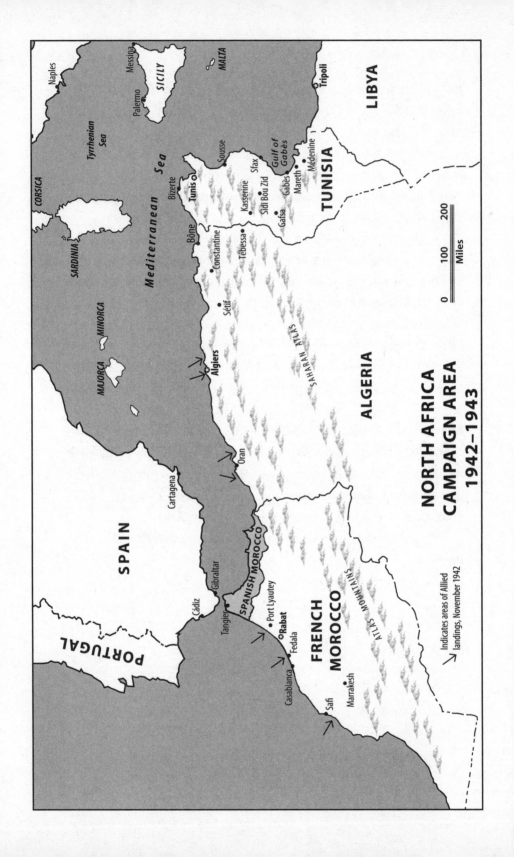

NORTH AFRICA
CAMPAIGN AREA
1942–1943

→ Indicates areas of Allied
landings, November 1942

0   100   200
Miles

ONE

PURPLE HEART TANKER

The ten-ton tank destroyers churned slowly forward, engines whining, four dozen sets of clanking armored tracks grinding the desert sand into clouds of smoky white powder. Technician Fifth Grade Tom Morrison stood in the open-topped rear compartment, one hand clutching the armored shield that surrounded his half-track's main gun. His body stiff from hours of being jostled about, he wiped the dust from his eyeglasses and peered ahead.

His armored force was pushing deeper into central Tunisia, a world little changed in thousands of years. Though embroiled now in the Second World War, over the millennia the land had been ruled at various periods by Romans, Vandals, and the Byzantines before being conquered by the Arabs in the seventh century. In 1881, Tunisia had been invaded by France and had since endured six decades of French control that left little room for nationalist progression.

The remote North African village before Morrison was little

more than sand, rocks, and ruins. The Ousseltia Valley, nestled in an eroded plateau between the rugged Eastern and Western Dorsal—extensions of the Atlas Mountains—still sported crumbling remains of structures that dated to Roman times. Farms were scarce in this region, leaving local Arabs to feed their animals on cultivated cactus patches, bunch grass, and scrub growth that dared to survive in the pebbly foothills. Spatterings of green palm and olive groves added color to the desert hills near the village of Ousseltia, sustained by irrigation from wells hacked through the rocky desert terrain over the centuries.

Inside the fifteen-foot-high ancient rock wall that surrounded Ousseltia were hundreds of freedom fighters dressed in white kepi hats, with blue sashes over white linen trousers and colorful epaulettes topping their blue greatcoats. The desert settlement was being used as a forward operating post for members of the French Foreign Legion, infantrymen from a multitude of countries and cultures whose service had been accepted.

To Morrison, they were just fugitives. Many had joined the Foreign Legion to escape punishment for infractions committed in their homelands. While most spoke heavy dialects in incomprehensible languages, one legionnaire had admitted to Morrison in English that he originally hailed from Chicago, where he was sought by both the police and Illinois crime gangs. He had also delivered a sobering warning: as many as forty-seven German Panzer tanks were lying in concealment in the desert just miles ahead.[1]

To the German and Italian soldiers concentrated throughout the region, Tunisia was worth fighting for. Morrison, possessing little knowledge of the military big picture, could scarcely imagine why American lives were worth losing over these arid hills punctuating the Sahara Desert. But the brain trust of the Axis forces understood that air bases here could put Allied bombers within reach of Italy and portions of Germany. It could also double as a staging area for future Allied offensives into Sicily, the Italian peninsula, and southern France. Adolf Hitler, the Nazi dictator of Germany, had declared North Africa to be the enemy's approach to Europe, a land that "must be held at all costs."[2]

Although Morrison's unit had already seen action in North Africa, he was not apprehensive this day. Over the past several weeks, his tank destroyer unit had been rushed to different areas in Tunisia to counteract enemy tank activity, only to find nothing there. Today was January 19, 1943, and Morrison was celebrating his twenty-fifth birthday thousands of miles from his home in Ohio.[3]

The mechanized fighting vehicle in which he served had come a long way since Little Willie.

Britain had developed the first armored land vehicle in 1915, nicknamed "Little Willie" after an uncomplimentary moniker for the German crown prince Wilhelm. Fitted with imported American tracks, Little Willie saw service only for driver training; by early 1916 a superior replacement—known variously as "Big Willie" or "Mother"—had entered testing. Mother resulted in the first production order for one hundred armored vehicles by Britain, whose first units began seeing action in September 1916. Production workers, under orders to keep their project secret, shipped the first vehicles in crates labeled "tank," since their odd shapes resembled water tanks that could be used for troops in the field. The name "tank" stuck with the new military invention.[4]

The idea of an armored battle car was almost as old as recorded history. The ancient concept had been to provide infantrymen with mobile protection and firepower. In 1482, artist and inventor Leonardo da Vinci drew concepts of a "war car," a land weapon combining armor, mobility, and firepower that was operated by four men turning large cranks to power its wheels. Leonardo's design was not deemed practical, and centuries would pass before a self-propelled armored vehicle would come into being.[5]

Horse-drawn machine guns and artillery pieces were vulnerable to enemy fire in combat. In 1769, French military engineer Nicolas-Joseph Cugnot built three-wheeled, steam-powered vehicles for trials by the French artillery, but little progress was made. In 1855, Britain patented a steam traction engine based on Cugnot's design, but it was never mass-produced.[6]

Evolution of the modern tank progressed in the early twentieth century with the advent of the internal combustion engine and caterpillar tracks. Science fiction writers played a part in influencing design. In the December 1903 *Strand* magazine, H. G. Wells wrote an influential short story called "The Land Ironclads," which described armored fighting vehicles carrying soldiers who fired semi-automatic weapons from reinforced ports. Britain's development of Little Willie and Mother was underway a little more than a decade after Wells's fictional inspiration.[7]

By the concluding years of World War I, British, French, and German tanks had become a vital means of warfare. America's early taste of tank combat, in 1918, came via French-obtained Renault FT light tanks, characterized by poor mechanical reliability and a dreadfully slow speed of 5.5 miles per hour. Dwight Eisenhower was the officer in charge of training tank crews stateside, and a young officer named George S. Patton commanded the U.S. armored forces in World War I. The M1917 Six Ton Tank was licensed for manufacture by the United States, and it remained the key armored vehicle of the American military until the early 1930s, when efforts commenced to develop a new generation of tanks. But aside from experimental types, the U.S. Army procured only 321 light tanks from 1930 to 1939, until new emphasis was focused on development due to the rise of Nazi Germany and Fascist Italy. The Europeans surged forward with technological advances during the arms race of the late 1930s, and by the time the U.S. Army produced its M2 medium tank in the summer of 1939, it was already considered obsolete.[8]

Only 112 M2 tanks were produced that year, as its primary armament—a 37mm gun—was vastly inferior to the 75mm (3-inch) turret gun of the newest German Panzer IV tanks. In July 1940, design commenced on a replacement, the M3 medium tank, produced in America with a 75mm gun for use by the U.S. Army and its British allies. M3 tanks employing U.S. pattern turrets were called the "Lee," after Confederate general Robert E. Lee, while variants using modified British turrets were dubbed "Grant," after Union general Ulysses S. Grant. British troops employed both Grant and Lee variations of the M3 medium tank in North Africa during 1942, but by the time the U.S. First Armored Division deployed to North Africa, it was largely using a new medium tank.

In February of that year, production commenced on the M4, which was quickly named the "Sherman" by the British in reference to another American Civil War general, William Tecumseh Sherman. The British Eighth Army drove the first Sherman tanks into battle in late October 1942 at the Second Battle of El Alamein, where they successfully engaged German Panzer III and IV tanks at 2,000 yards. As the North Africa campaign entered early 1943, the U.S. Army was steadily upgrading its M3 Lee tank battalions with the superior M4 Shermans.

In addition to developing traditional fighting tanks, the U.S. Army's big thinkers advocated divisional anti-tank battalions to challenge enemy armored divisions. Such units would consist of mechanized gun vehicles that were more mobile and capable of handling additional reconnaissance duties. War games held in Louisiana, North Carolina, and South Carolina in 1941 had proven the value of self-propelled anti-tank guns against traditional armored regiments, thus paving the way for additional "tank destroyer" battalions.[9]

Tom Morrison was attached to the 601st Tank Destroyer Battalion, a detachment of the First Infantry Division, which had been officially activated by the U.S. War Department on December 15, 1941. More than half of the original members of this anti-tank battalion were pulled from the ranks of the so-called Big Red One, the Army's famous First Infantry Division. Its original commander was forty-six-year-old battle-wise veteran Major Herschel David Baker, who was raised on military posts as the son of an army surgeon.

At the commencement of World War I, Baker enlisted as a private in the cavalry and later won a commission as a second lieutenant in an officers' training school in France. During the Meuse-Argonne offensive of September–November 1918, he was injured during a gas attack and later received the Purple Heart. Baker was commissioned into the regular army in 1920, serving in various roles prior to the outbreak of World War II. An accomplished horseman and polo player, he was a true showman, loud and brash around his officers but unafraid to wade into a poker game or host a beer party for his battalion. In the 601st's unofficial history, Baker was described as "a two hundred and twenty pound, roly-poly, cherubic looking, foghorn-voiced ball of fire."[10]

In August 1942, Baker (now a lieutenant colonel) and the 601st had set sail from New York Harbor on board the 80,000-ton troopship RMS *Queen Mary* for deployment to England to prepare for combat against the Axis forces in North Africa. The men and their machines were debarked in Africa in November, then moved to Algeria before commencing an eight-hundred-mile trek to Tunisia during December to help make a difference in the desert war against German and Italian forces.

Morrison's armored anti-tank vehicle was named the M3 Gun Motor Carriage, and built on a rear half-track chassis with regular wheels in the front for steering, thus providing the handling of a truck with the capabilities of a tank. Each M3 sported one-quarter inch of face-hardened plate—just enough to ward off small-arms fire to protect its five-man crew. The half-track's main weapon, a 75mm gun, was protected by five-eighth-inch-thick steel rated to stop .30-caliber rounds at 250 yards. The vehicle had only one foot of ground clearance, but it could do 45 miles per hour on level terrain, making it faster than even the lightest tanks. The M3 half-track measured just over twenty feet in length and weighed nine tons. Its front end resembled that of an Army truck, with two front wheels, while the two rear tracks were made of molded rubber over steel cabling with metal guides. The M3's sixty-gallon tank allowed it to travel 150 miles before refueling.[11]

The M3 included a mounted .50-caliber M2 Browning machine gun, while newer M3A1 variants added .30-caliber machine guns mounted along the sides of the rear passenger compartment. Being largely open-air, the half-track offered its crew little protection from the desert heat, blowing sand, and the occasional thunderstorm. Morrison hated riding in the back of his. The occupants were largely unprotected from bursting artillery shells, and driving an M3 came with its own challenges. Staff Sergeant Bill Harper, a twenty-three-year-old East Texas native assigned to C Company of the 601st, found few good points to like about it. Drivers making turns too quickly were subject to throwing a track, and the gun motor carriages had very thin armor. The men ended up calling them Purple Heart boxes, a grim reference to the U.S. Army decoration for combat wounds.[12]

Tank crews, whether manning full Sherman tanks or the lighter tank destroyer variations like Morrison's crew, were eternally challenged in the Tunisian desert. Daily maintenance was constant: cleaning oil, fuel, and air filters; checking and adjusting track tensions to prevent throwing a track in combat; frequent cleaning of guns, ammunition, and optical sights to remove dust and sand; and hand-fueling of each tank from five-gallon jerry cans.[13]

Life inside the tanks was even more demanding. The crews operated in sweltering, confined quarters and were jolted about while on the move, with minimal padding and ample protruding instruments to create bruises and black eyes. When the afternoon desert heat exceeded 110 degrees, the armored vehicle's interior when completely buttoned down could easily reach temperatures 20 degrees higher. Added to the energy-draining heat was the torturous blasting of sand that invaded a man's eyes, mouth, and uniform.[14]

Combat service in North Africa for a Purple Heart box tanker left little to be envied.

———

Morrison had spent the previous year rarely "in the know." Born in the village of Brewster, Ohio, Thomas Elwood Morrison was known simply as Tom to his military comrades, though his siblings called him Elwood. He was finally accepted into military service in May 1942, although he had been rejected the year before due to poor teeth. (He had lost two teeth while working as a railyard pipefitter following high school.) Morrison had started his Army career in radio training at Fort Bragg, but by the time he shipped out overseas in late 1942, he was attached to the First Infantry Division. His 601st Tank Destroyer Battalion destroyers were marked with a yellow square emblazoned with a black letter Y. Morrison would learn that German soldiers nicknamed the American battalion the "Black Y Boys" because of their prominent identification mark.[15]

The 601st had an authorized strength of 38 officers and 860 enlisted men organized into a headquarters company, a reconnaissance company, three gun companies, and a sixteen-man medical detachment. Each of the three gun companies had five armored cars, eighteen jeeps, eight M3s, and four newer-model, lighter M6 half-tracks. Each company was split into four platoons, with Morrison's crew officially part of A Company, First Platoon.[16]

His time in the village of Ousseltia was brief. Early the next morning, January 20, his platoon fell in with a procession of armored vehicles along the hard-packed road. Morrison's half-track driver, Sergeant Dick Hammond, drove them forward of the town some five miles before taking up position on high ground at the mouth of the wide valley below. The 601st's Second Heavy Platoon—four heavy destroyers and four 37mm half-track light destroyers (three-quarter-ton trucks mounted with 37mms)—were stationed on lower ground, near Morrison's First Platoon along the road that ran through the valley.

Morrison's platoon was an armored portion of the U.S. Army's Combat Command B (CCB) of the First Armored Division. The CCB had been sent forward to assist French troops in the Ousseltia Valley area in central Tunisia. They faced the German Fifth Panzer Army, under General Hans-Jürgen von Arnim, who intended to prevent the Allies from advancing through the mountain passes of the Eastern Dorsals toward the Tunisian coast. The American forces—some 3,400 men and four dozen armored vehicles—had been pushed forward to greet von Arnim's Panzers.

The First Platoon used the last hour before daybreak on January 20 to partially camouflage its tank destroyers from the daylight threat of attacks by German aircraft. Morrison dug a deep foxhole from which he had a commanding view of the desert valley once the sunlight began flooding the terrain. Then he took time to marvel at the beautiful green valley, rich with olive groves, large haystacks, and a sprinkling of little Arab houses. "A more peaceful scene one could not ask for," he recalled.[17]

Morrison's crew passed the day snoozing near their M3, reading books, and playing cards until dusk. He did not see any officers during the day: they were occupied at an observation post set up in between the two platoons' gun positions. His platoon had a new commander, twenty-five-year-old First Lieutenant Lawrence Eliot "Lawrie" Marcus, who had stepped into the position after the platoon's previous leader, Captain Robert Steele, was killed by a sniper on Christmas Eve while the unit was assisting French forces near

Pichon. Marcus was a Harvard graduate who hailed from Dallas, Texas, where his Jewish family's retail fashion business, Neiman Marcus, continued to thrive even during wartime.

Marcus concerned himself with keeping tabs on the reported Panzers, and he sent Recon Company jeeps and command tracks up and down the road near Ousseltia during the afternoon. The advance American force was set to counter elements of the Fifth Panzer Army, under the direction of wily Field Marshal Erwin Rommel, popularly known in the press as the "Desert Fox." The valley remained quiet until dusk began to settle, when Morrison heard a nervous call from a 601st sentry.[18]

"Enemy tank approaching!"

Sergeant Hammond's half-track crew dropped their books and stood to see a German tank rumbling slowly toward them some three hundred yards away. Morrison stared in disbelief. Suddenly the German tank erupted with a fiery blast and sent a round screaming toward the American position. The shot hit nothing, but the battle was on.

Everyone scrambled into their machines, and all the gunners in the First Heavy Platoon opened fire. At the relatively close range, some of their shots began hitting the German tank, but their 37mm rounds only bounced off the heavy armor of the enemy tank. The German commander began backing his vehicle down the road and fired off a flare. Morrison was shocked to see other flares erupt from both sides of the road. In an instant the large haystacks below suddenly became enemy tanks that had been brilliantly disguised throughout the day.[19]

Every tree in the valley turned into a tank as Morrison watched. German shells screamed by, followed by the sight of a distant blue flash a split second later. To him, all of the German tanker fire appeared to be concentrated on his First Platoon's hilltop position.[20]

The Panzers began maneuvering around the left flank of the hill, but in the fading light Morrison and his crew struggled to find a target. The entire hillside was bursting with explosions and the valley below was lit up like a bunch of blue fireflies. Noting the German tanks coming around on his left flank, Master Sergeant Cyrus Cobb yelled at his half-track commanders to pull back. The First Heavy Platoon fell back approximately one mile and paused only long enough to once again come under heavy fire from German tankers. Cobb then ordered his tanks to fall back even farther to a command post that had been established about a mile away.[21]

Bill Harper of the 601st was among the M3 crews forced to fall back as the infantry and tanks fired. "It was getting pretty rough. I found out real quick they were shooting real bullets," said Harper. "They had us outnumbered and outgunned. The Germans were good soldiers. We just didn't have any experience." Lieutenant Lawrie Marcus could see German tanks advancing over the hill, pausing occasionally to open fire. Their shells exploded all around the 601st's position. Marcus realized the Tenth Panzer Division his men were facing was aggressive and determined and possessed superior numbers. Second-in-command of his platoon, Marcus passed orders for his outmanned tank destroyers to fall back. In his mind, he rationalized the call: *Is it better to stand still and pop off a few rounds and get hit yourself and be out of the picture? Or is it better to retreat and come back and fight another day?*[22]

As the First Heavy Platoon was falling back about a quarter mile down the road, other American units were left exposed in the sudden German assault. The Second Heavy Platoon was caught completely off guard. Among the 601st observation post men left on foot in this area was Lieutenant Wilcher Conway "Bill" Stotts Jr., a former student at the University of Arkansas who had joined the U.S. Army shortly after the attack on Pearl Harbor. With Stotts was Sergeant Daniel Doney, a twenty-five-year-old from Lowell, Massachusetts.[23]

In the rush to escape the oncoming Germans, a handful of men manning machine guns were left behind, including Stotts and Doney. Another man at the 601st command post who was cut off in the action was Marcus, who found that the advancing German tanks were supported by a strong infantry detachment. The tank destroyer men operating outside of their battalion's half-tracks were in danger of being overrun by the *Panzergrenadiers* before the American guns could establish a proper defensive.

Marcus had crawled 150 yards under machine-gun fire to reorganize his troops and direct 75mm gunfire back at the Germans. Once the fight became so intense that his 601st battery was forced to fall back, Marcus was caught in an unenviable position, seeking cover between the flying shells of both the Germans and the Americans. His capture seemed likely, so Marcus ripped out sections from his field notebook that contained confidential data and with some difficulty ate the pages. Then he used his mess spoon to dig out a shallow foxhole in a hillside to ride out the night.[24]

Before dawn, dozens of Germans established a mortar and command post just yards from his shallow hideout. Marcus steeled his nerves, deciding it was better to die than be captured. He stood and began walking slowly through the enemy's midst, deciding that if he moved slowly he would not be suspected of being an enemy. It took all the nerve he could muster, but he strolled calmly to a nearby cactus patch, then down into a gully.

Tom Morrison's tank crew remained far behind the main night action area for some time as the chaos ensued. Cobb's First Platoon tank destroyers were withheld from firing for fear that they might accidentally hit retreating portions of their own Second Heavy Platoon falling back. Cobb's platoon finally fell back to the village of Ousseltia to join a British antiaircraft unit, forming a semicircle that faced the valley.[25]

Morrison felt his battalion was defensively positioned well enough to make a solid last stand. But his excitement turned to dismay when twenty-four-year-old Lieutenant Frederick Colquhoun Miner from Seaford, Delaware, led the remnants of his A Company of the 601st to their defensive position. Miner was livid, cursing out his fellow tankers for deserting his company while under fire. At least fourteen men of the 601st had been taken prisoner of war; others, like Lieutenants Marcus and Stotts, remained unaccounted for in the din of battle. Miner's A Company tankers were as furious as he was, believing they had been deserted under fire. Around 0100 on January 21, Miner ordered Cobb's tanks to roll forward to support a group of French Legionnaires who were trying to pull out under fire.

Morrison's group pulled up at a crossroads and began firing on German tanks as they crested a hill. It was impossible to ascertain hits in the darkness. The Germans tanks, firing from the crest of the hill, lobbed their shells over the American M3s. But the enemy gunners quickly compensated, and explosions began erupting in front of Morrison's tanks. One round of armor-piercing shells landed so close that its explosion lifted the front of Morrison's half-track. "That's close enough," said Sergeant Hammond, who turned his half-track around and pulled back.[26]

The firing of the American tanks allowed the French foot soldiers to slip away from the German advance. One M3, commanded by Sergeant Michael Dragon, refused to start when the order was passed to fall back, so his crew set off an incendiary grenade in one of the gas tanks and hiked out. The German tanks refused to follow the Americans in their retreat, so the 601st passed the remainder of the night in the area. By daybreak a heavy fog had set in. Morrison's tanks followed a platoon of medium tanks from the First Armored Division that was trying to make contact with the Germans. Enemy fire soon disabled two of the medium tanks, and the other two crews opted to fall back.

The survivors who retreated back on foot through the lightly armored M3 platoon were disgusted. One of Morrison's platoon leaders tried to offer them assistance. "Hey, you guys want to come aboard and ride with us?" he called.[27]

"The hell with you!" one tanker yelled. "You paper armored bastards! All you're good for is to draw fire!"

After daybreak, there were few German targets for the Americans to fire on. Morrison's tank crew resorted to blasting anything that looked like it might hide a gun. Dick Hammond spotted something moving in the distance and told his gunner, "Level on that Arab house out there." Morrison's crew aimed and fired, hitting the corner of the house, where a German gun crew was taking refuge. The concussion killed all four gunners, although Morrison was unaware of that fact until his platoon moved forward two days later.[28]

The first serious combat action against German Panzers for Morrison's half-track crew had ended in failure. The multiday action had cost the 601st five men killed or missing, and nineteen men taken prisoner of war. Four members of the tank destroyer battalion left behind on foot remained alive by the morning of January 22, but their ordeals in evading the German Army had been harrowing.

Lieutenant Bill Stotts and Sergeant Dan Doney had remained hidden behind a bush in a ravine until daybreak on January 21. Throughout the night, they could see German sentries with machine guns. Fortunately, the Germans withdrew from the area around 1000 that morning, and Stotts and Doney began a long trek across the plain. That afternoon they met with a battalion of French Foreign Legion soldiers and felt some relief after receiving candy, water, and crackers. That feeling was short-lived, as German forces opened fire the next morning and pinned down the French with mortars and machine-gun fire.[29]

A small ravine offered the only possibility of escape. Stotts and Doney were advised by the French they could make a break or stay and surrender. They opted to flee by sticking to the riverbed to escape the firefight. They were aided en route by indigenous mountain soldiers of the Moroccan goumiers (referred to as "goums" by the Allies), auxiliary units attached to the French Army of Africa. The Moroccan goums helped the two stranded Americans slip past the nearby German supply road into the nearby mountains. Stotts and Doney endured an agonizing climb through the mountains with their goum guides. The next day they reached a French headquarters post, where they were overjoyed to join two other men from their unit who had escaped.

It was Marcus, in company with Captain Benjamin Apthorp Gould Fuller from Milton, Massachusetts, who had each endured their own hardships in evading German troops for two days. Marcus had survived in the desert without water and with only four lumps of sugar and two small pieces of candy that happened to be in his pockets. When the quartet was escorted back to their tank destroyer battalion, Marcus learned from a comrade that they had been written off as killed in action. "They told me they were already about to divide up my baggage, but I got there in time to save my cigarettes," Marcus later recalled.[30]

The action with the German Panzers in the Ousseltia Valley had been a rude introduction to the Desert Fox's forces. Some had perished, others had been captured, and four had narrowly escaped capture. It left tankers like Tom Morrison, Ben Fuller, Bill Harper, and Lawrie Marcus yearning for vengeance.

TWO

"LLOYD'S VERY LAST RESORT"

Major General Lloyd Ralston Fredendall was a popular officer with wartime reporters, thanks to his accessibility and propensity to offer worthwhile quotes. The short, stocky intellectual often tossed out phrases designed to boost American morale. "I always knew my boys could handle themselves all right," Fredendall said on December 13, after his forces had pushed into Tunisia. In an hour-long chat, he credited the Germans with being sharp but added, "They have taught us a few things but we sure showed them some new tricks, too." The general tossed out morsels of optimism to please stateside readers: "We are beginning to get the measure of the Germans and I know that with proper support we can lick them."[1]

While approachable and sharp to the press, Fredendall was increasingly being viewed by his own army as a man of just the opposite traits—prone to remaining a great distance from any real action and at times almost incoherent. A case in point was the set of instructions he offered on the afternoon of January 19 as events escalated for his First Armored Division in the Ousseltia Valley. From the safety of his fortified II Corps command post, Fredendall issued the following instructions to Brigadier General Paul Robinett, head of the First's Combat Command B (CCB) forces:[2]

> *Move your command, i.e., the walking boys, pop guns, Baker's outfit and the outfit which is the reverse of Baker's outfit, and the big fellows to "M," which is due north of where you are now, as soon as possible. Have your boss report to the French gentleman whose name begins with "J" at a place which begins with "D," which is five grid squares to the left of "M."*

Intending to confuse any eavesdropping enemy forces, Fredendall effectively bewildered his own army. Robinett's group eventually deciphered their corps commander's message to mean that 3,400 infantrymen, dozens of tanks, and Herschel Baker's 601st Tank Destroyer Battalion were to report to French XIX Corps general Alphonse Juin at Djerissa, in the vicinity of Maktar. Robinett's CCB would join other battalions of the U.S. Army's First Infantry Division for scattered fighting during the next several days in the djebels (mountain ranges or hills) of Tunisia. In that time Robinett was further plagued by orders from Fredendall that contradicted the local French command, prompting CCB staff to conclude that it was "an excellent example of lack of coordination in the high command."[3]

By January 24 the battles had claimed more than two hundred American casualties, and the French had suffered nearly 3,500 troops taken as prisoners of war. In contrast, fewer than forty German soldiers had been captured. That day the supreme Allied campaign commander, General Dwight David Eisenhower, gave command of the entire Tunisian front to Lieutenant General Sir Kenneth Arthur Noel Anderson of the British First Army, including French and American units. Some 67,000 British and American troops of the

First Army were thus joined by the 32,000 men of the U.S. Army's II Corps, under command of Major General Fredendall.[4]

Throughout the confusion and piecemeal deployment of First Infantry battalions, Fredendall had remained safely tucked away at his command post, some one hundred miles from the front lines. He might have been far from the fighting, but he was no stranger to army life. He was born in 1883 at Fort Warren, an Army post near Cheyenne, Wyoming, where his father, Ira Livingston Fredendall, was serving during the late years of the Indian Wars. The elder Fredendall had been sheriff of the town of Laramie but served with the Army during both the Spanish-American War and World War I. Thanks to his father's connections, Lloyd was able to secure an appointment from his Wyoming senator to the United States Military Academy at West Point, New York.

But young Fredendall struggled with trigonometry and analytic geometry, and was dismissed after his first semester. Although he was reappointed to the academy the following year, he ultimately dropped out a second time due to his poor grades. Fredendall then attended the Massachusetts Institute of Technology from 1903 to 1904; at MIT he brought his skills up enough to pass the officer's qualifying exam in 1906. He received his commission in the U.S. Army on February 13, 1907, as a second lieutenant in the infantry branch.[5]

During his early years, Fredendall served both stateside and in overseas assignments that included Hawaii and the Philippines. In August 1917 he was shipped to the Western Front with the Twenty-Eighth Infantry Regiment, but he held noncombat instructor positions in France. By the end of World War I, he held the temporary rank of lieutenant colonel based on his record as an efficient administrator and trainer.

Following the Great War, Fredendall held a variety of staff and training duties, climbing to the two-star rank of major general by

October 1940. His army career had been safe, rooted more in the theory of combat versus the reality. Yet Fredendall's reputation as an excellent teacher of troops aided his continued rise in the opening months of World War II. General George Marshall, the U.S. Army chief of staff, recommended his friend to Lieutenant General Eisenhower for a major command in the Allied invasion of North Africa, code-named Operation Torch. Blue-eyed and sandy-haired, Fredendall was cocky and youthful-looking, prompting Marshall to remark, "You can see determination all over his face."[6]

Fredendall had commanded the largest of three task forces for Operation Torch in November 1942. Altogether, some 220 ships had transported more than 107,000 men across the Atlantic to arrive off the shores of North Africa to make simultaneous landings in the areas of Casablanca, Oran, and Algiers. The Oran and Algiers landings had included First and Thirty-Fourth Infantry Divisions, the First Armored Division, and the First Ranger Division. The army forces landing at Casablanca were commanded by General George S. Patton, and his force included the Third and Ninth Infantry Divisions and the Second Armored Division.[7]

Following the Torch landings, Fredendall served as the de facto military commander from his headquarters in the Grand Hotel of Oran. He issued orders headed by "II Corps—In the Field," although such a title drew jeers from his troops enduring desert life under primitive conditions. By January 1943, Eisenhower had assigned fifty-nine-year-old Fredendall to command the U.S. Army's II Corps forces for their advance into Tunisia against German and Italian forces, with the U.S. troops serving under Lieutenant General Anderson's British First Army.[8]

Among the more seasoned staff officers attached to Fredendall's II Corps was Lucian K. Truscott Jr., newly promoted to the rank of major general. Truscott had been involved in helping to create an American commando unit that became known as the First Ranger Division during 1942, and he had commanded 9,000 troops during the landings in Morocco during Operation Torch in November. "Small in stature, loud and rough in speech," Truscott said of Fredendall, "he was outspoken in his opinions and critical of superiors and subordinates alike." Truscott found the II Corps commander to be "inclined to jump at conclusions which were not always well founded."[9]

Truscott believed that Fredendall disliked the British, particularly General Anderson, had no confidence in French forces, and thought little of many of his American subordinate commanders. "He rarely left his command post for personal visits and reconnaissance," Truscott recalled, "yet he was impatient with the recommendations of subordinates more familiar with the terrain and other conditions than was he."[10]

Possessing a hard-driving manner, Fredendall slept little. His staff found him many nights either reading or sitting cross-legged on the floor, playing solitaire. A strict disciplinarian, the major general shunned solid advice as earnestly as he avoided being present on the front lines.[11]

Fredendall's command post for the Tunisian campaign drew even more ridicule than his former posh headquarters in Oran. On the eastern border of Tunisia's western neighbor, Algeria, Fredendall made his new headquarters nine miles southeast of the ancient walled city of Tébessa. He and sixty-eight staff officers set up shop in a sunless, frigid ravine known as Speedy Valley. Inhospitable and primitive it might have been, yet it was still far from the flying bullets and exploding shells of the front lines. The valley quickly became known unofficially as "Lloyd's Very Last Resort" and "Shangri-La, a million miles from nowhere." Fearing German air strikes, Fredendall immediately put engineers to work with jackhammers and pneumatic drills to bore subway-like tunnels and underground complexes beneath Speedy Valley's rock walls.[12]

When General Eisenhower later visited "Lloyd's Very Last Resort" and conducted a troop inspection, he found II Corps soldiers to possess "a certain complacency" while also noting a lack of training and experience on the part of their commanders. "It was the only time during the war that I ever saw a higher headquarters so concerned over its own safety that it dug itself underground shelters," Ike later wrote.[13]

———

Operation Satin was the code name given to the first big Allied offensive plan to push across southern Tunisia toward the coastal town of Gabès, 260 miles south of the capital city of Tunis. The drive was intended to prevent two large German army forces from uniting, with the American II Corps handling the charge while General Anderson's British First Army was afforded the chance to hammer the stretched-out German military. The II Corps push would be headed by the First Armored Division, affectionately known as "Old Ironsides."[14]

The man tapped to lead Operation Satin, Major General Orlando Ward, quickly found that he was not held in high regard by Lloyd Fredendall. A veteran of World War I, fifty-one-year-old Ward's graying hair had once been red enough to earn him the nickname "Pinky." His innovations in artillery techniques had afforded him a steady rise through the U.S. military ranks, and by March 1942, Ward was only the second officer to command the First Armored Division. It consisted of tanks, artillery, infantry, tank destroyers, and a full array of maintenance, medical, supply, and engineering battalions, all divided into separate combat command brigades.

Ward and Old Ironsides were held in mobile reserve during mid- to late January, to be deployed for counterattacks against Axis forces in lower Tunisia. Ward's division was soon scattered into three parts by various orders, as combat units were shuffled to Ousseltia without his even being consulted. He considered it to be a "dribbling commitment" of his division, noting that the II Corps commander,

Major General Fredendall, "does not look with favor on matters I suggest."[15]

In the wake of the Ousseltia fight, Ward was called to Speedy Valley to meet with Fredendall. The First Armored Division commander recommended attacking Maknassy, a key Eastern Dorsal pass nearly a hundred miles from the current action, to put American troops within striking distance of German forces. Although Fredendall was in favor of the Maknassy proposal, he ordered Ward to first make a raid from the staging point town of Gafsa on the Axis post at Sened Station, an Italian-held stronghold located midway between Gafsa and Maknassy. Ward worried that such a move would alert the Germans to his plans for seizing Maknassy, but Fredendall waved away his concerns, telling Pinky to "knock the shit out of the Italians at Sened Station."[16]

Some 2,000 of Ward's troops did just that on January 24, taking the Sened Station village crossroads post in a matter of hours. They rounded up nearly a hundred Italian prisoners and left as many dead, prompting Lloyd Fredendall to gloat over his great victory. Pinky Ward was less optimistic, fretting over his First Armored Division being scattered across a hundred miles of terrain while the Germans were now well aware of American targeting of the key town of Maknassy, fifty miles due east of Gafsa. He noted in his diary days later that his entire staff was "completely disgusted with the high command as inefficient and meddlesome."[17]

Ward's second-in-command, Lieutenant Colonel John Knight Waters, was equally unimpressed with Fredendall. A 1931 graduate of the U.S. Military Academy, Waters had met his future wife, Beatrice Patton, while attending West Point. John and Bea were married in 1934, and he became part of the family of Major George Patton, an officer known for his brash leadership. To Waters, Patton was a man of limitless knowledge, "warm within but gruff on the exterior."[18]

Equally bright and handsome, Waters had been able to win the affection of both Bea Patton and her father by abiding by the general's initial crotchety demand. When Waters asked Patton for permission to marry his daughter, Patton refused, saying, "I don't know who you are. You haven't proven yourself." During the year following his graduation from West Point, his duty station in Fort Myer, Virginia, allowed him to become better acquainted with Patton, who eventually consented to the wedding.[19]

Waters's new father-in-law had been born to serve a soldier's life. George Smith Patton Jr. was only seventeen when he sought his own appointment to West Point, but his collegiate career commenced at Virginia Military Institute, which his father and grandfather had also attended. Patton eventually secured a nomination to West Point, where he was forced to repeat his plebe year because he had failed mathematics. He graduated in June 1909 and was commissioned as a second lieutenant in the U.S. Army's Fifteenth Cavalry. Patton represented the Army in the 1912 Summer Olympics in Stockholm, where he finished fifth in the pentathlon, and became the military's first master sword instructor.

Patton's dedication as a hard-driving leader was recognized early by his superiors. In 1915, while he was assigned to border patrol duty with the Eighth Cavalry in Sierra Blanca, Texas, his firearm accidentally discharged in a saloon. He traded it for an ivory-handled Colt single-action Army revolver that would later become an iconic part of his image. Patton pursued Mexican rebel Pancho Villa through much of Mexico in 1916 and was credited with shooting three of Villa's men, earning him the title of "bandit killer."[20]

Promoted to captain in 1917, George Patton took an interest in tanks during World War I. In little more than a year he had advanced two ranks to lieutenant colonel and served with distinction in European tank warfare. He was eventually pinned with the Distinguished Service Cross after being wounded in an attack on German machine guns.

In the fall of 1919, Colonel Patton arrived at Camp Meade, Maryland—halfway between Baltimore and Washington—home of the U.S. Army's tank corps. There he met a lieutenant colonel five years his junior named Dwight "Ike" Eisenhower, who was in charge of training tankers. Ike had spent World War I stateside, teaching others to fight under men like Patton. Within weeks of meeting at Camp Meade, Ike and Patton found a common passion in changing military doctrine. Both men believed that tanks should be used as an independent fighting force rather than as infantry support vehicles.[21]

The Eisenhower and Patton families lived next door to each other at the camp, and the men's friendship continued to grow. Together, they worked on tank regulations and drill manuals, predicting that tanks would play a greater role in future wars. In May 1920, Patton's "Tanks in Future Wars" article in the Army's *Infantry Journal* warned that armored vehicles simply grafted on infantry, artillery, or engineers would be "like the third leg to a duck." He instead argued that the tank, "for the fulfillment of its destiny, must remain independent."[22]

Six months later, Eisenhower's own article in *Infantry Journal* pointed out that true trench warfare was likely a thing of the past. He recommended that each infantry division should replace a fifty-seven-vehicle machine-gun battalion with a company of fifteen tanks. But his superior warned Ike that such thinking was wrong and dangerous and could lead to his own court-martial.[23]

Such criticism only tightened the bond between Patton and Eisenhower. Aside from drilling and training their men, the two found time to enjoy poker games, dinner parties, and even such sport as finding out how long they could fire a .30-caliber Browning machine gun before its barrel overheated. At times their robust personalities landed the pair in heated shouting matches over trivial matters, but their respect for each other endured. They parted ways in late 1920 when the War Department folded the Tank Corps into the infantry branch during peacetime reorganization, but their paths would cross again.[24]

Patton dropped from his wartime rank of colonel back to his permanent rank of captain. He returned to the cavalry, feeling some despair through the 1920s as his military career advanced slowly in peacetime. By 1934 he had been promoted to lieutenant colonel and was transferred to the Hawaiian Division to serve as G-2 (intelligence officer). He returned to cavalry duty in 1938, having attained the rank of colonel. His work with the Third Cavalry impressed Army chief of staff George C. Marshall enough that the latter considered Patton to be a prime candidate for promotion to general.[25]

After Germany invaded Poland in 1939 and World War II broke out in Europe, Patton was finally afforded the opportunity to emphasize armored forces in the U.S. Army. In the spring of 1940 he served as an umpire for Third Army maneuvers near Alexandria, Louisiana. Patton was critical of the roles in which tanks were utilized in these games and soon enough he received the opportunity to change things. In July 1940 he was sent to Fort Benning to command the new Second Brigade of the Second Armored Division.[26]

While training his brigade, Patton was promoted on October 1 to the one-star rank of brigadier general and quickly took over the entire Second Division. He trained his mechanized division relentlessly, moving them at such a pace through Florida that he received national attention. In a February 14, 1941, *Time* magazine article, Patton was praised for his persistence. The story claimed that he was known "to dash leg-long into a creek, get a stalled tank and its wretched crew out of the water and back into the line of march, practically by the power of his curses."[27]

"Patton is by far the best tank man in the Army," Marshall echoed. "I realize he is a difficult man but I know how to handle him." Blunt and profane, Patton "loved to shake members of a social gathering by exploding a few rounds of outrageous profanity," Eisenhower remembered.[28]

During the buildup toward America's entry into war in 1941, Eisenhower moved through a series of top-level staff positions in rapid succession. As a colonel serving as chief of staff for the Third Army in September 1941, Ike was invited by Brigadier General Patton to join him with the Second Armored Division, which had adopted the nickname "Hell on Wheels." But when the U.S. Army commenced a new round of training games in Louisiana that month, Ike and George were still on opposing teams. In good-natured jest, Patton offer his men a $50 reward for the capture of "a certain s.o.b. called Eisenhower."[29]

The Louisiana maneuvers were intended to correct some deficiencies that had shown up in war exercises held in Tennessee in late June. The maneuver area in the Bayou State covered more than 13 million acres of forests, swamps, rice fields, and countryside. The two opposing armies were the Red, Lieutenant General Ben Lear's 160,000-man Second Army, and the Blue, Lieutenant General Walter Krueger's 240,000-man Third Army. During preliminary exercises held during August, Patton made one mistake he would not make again in Europe: refusing to deploy an armored regiment to protect a bridge vital for his armored forces to recross a key river.[30]

The main phase of the Louisiana maneuvers began on September 15. Patton's Second Armored Division was attached to Lear's Red Army. The forces under Krueger and Eisenhower won the war game battle by surrounding Lear's forces, attacking Patton's gasoline dumps and supply lines, and finally pinning the Red Army against the Red River. Lieutenant General Lesley McNair, chief of Army Ground Forces, decided that Krueger's Third Army had won the first phase of the simulated war.[31]

The second phase of the Louisiana maneuvers opened on

September 24. This time Patton's armored division was teamed with his old pal Ike and the Third Army. It was his chance to shine. The Blue Army was to advance and capture Shreveport, but Lear's Reds had "destroyed" more than nine hundred bridges, crippling their chances. Patton charged south toward the coast, crossing into Texas and moving more than two hundred miles in twenty-four hours. His tankers even purchased gas from local Texas dealers, allowing his force to drive into Lear's rear echelon.[32]

Patton's boldness and dogged advancement of his tank forces earned the respect of reporters and of many of his constituents. Lieutenant Colonel Omar N. Bradley, escorting two senators to observe the maneuvers, considered him the daredevil of the 1941 war games. He found that Patton broke old-fashioned rules, utilizing "dazzling speed and surprise" to run his division roughshod over the enemy. "It was clear to anybody in the U.S. Army with the eyes to see that we had on our hands one of the most extraordinary fighting generals the Army had ever produced," Bradley remembered.[33]

In regard to Patton's character, Bradley found him to be fiercely ambitious and always impeccably dressed. "He was unmercifully hard on his men, demanding the utmost in military efficiency and bearing," Bradley wrote. "Most of them respected but despised him." He considered Patton to be "the most earthly profane man I ever knew" and wondered if the general's salty language was compensation for a noted character flaw, "a voice that was almost comically squeaky and high-pitched, altogether lacking in command authority."[34]

Patton's own son-in-law Johnny Waters served under him for a time at Fort Benning, Georgia, where he developed a deep appreciation for the general's desire to use armored tanks aggressively. "He was fire and brimstone about it," said Waters. Patton advocated positioning his tanks behind an enemy's rear areas, advancing hard to pound them until their front collapsed. "That was General Patton's theory," Waters stated. "He would hold them by the nose and kick them in the ass."[35]

Just months after the Louisiana maneuvers, America entered World War II.

———

By January 1942, Patton had been given command of I Armored Corps, and the following month he established the Desert Training Center in the Coachella Valley region of California. His fiery personality and reputation for being a leader who loved bouncing around with his tankers on maneuver while shouting succinct orders were noticed by the press. In its February 23, 1942, issue, *Time* magazine reported that General Patton was variously known to his men as "Flash Gordon" and "Old Blood and Guts" while he trained his armored division relentlessly in the deserts of southeast California and western Arizona, where the temperature inside tanks caused soldiers to sweat off pounds at an alarming rate.[36]

On July 30, Patton was summoned to Washington, where he learned he was to go to London to help Lieutenant General Dwight Eisenhower plan for the invasion of North Africa. Their Operation Torch aimed at capturing French Morocco and Algeria, both portions of the African empire of Adolf Hitler's puppet Vichy French regime. The landing, set for the second week of November 1942, saw Patton leading the Western Task Force, consisting of 35,000 soldiers and 250 tanks. Patton's wife, Beatrice Banning Ayer "Bea" Patton, recalled that her husband wrote to General George Marshall saying that he would leave the beaches of Africa as either a conqueror or a corpse.[37]

On October 21, as the invasion of North Africa neared, Patton and Rear Admiral Henry Kent Hewitt, who would command the naval forces in the campaign, met with President Roosevelt in the White House. Patton was dressed to fit the occasion, including a slick steel helmet bearing two stars on the front and a pair of ivory-handled Colt pistols on his hips. Patton hoped to make an impact in the meeting but found the president full of small talk about naval issues. When Patton tried to press the necessity of getting troops ashore because the fate of the war hinged on their success, Roosevelt merely replied, "Certainly you must."[38]

Disturbed that his brief meeting with the president had not offered deeper discussion on military tactics, Patton noted in his diary that night, "A great politician is not of necessity a great military leader."

Patton also met that day with his old friend, General John Pershing, under whom Patton had served during the pursuit of Pancho Villa.

"You took me to Mexico in 1916 and gave me my start," said Patton.[39]

"I can always pick a fighting man, and God knows there are few of them," said Pershing. "I am happy they are sending you to the front at once. I like generals so bold that they are dangerous. I hope they give you a free hand."

Pershing admitted to feeling hurt that he had been relegated to sideline work in World War II—never mind the fact that he was in his eighties. He reminisced on how Patton had killed some of Pancho Villa's men with his ivory-handled Colt. When Patton stated that he was taking the same pistol with him to Europe, Pershing said, "I hope you kill some Germans with it." As they parted ways, Pershing squeezed Patton's hand tight and said, "Goodbye, George. God bless and keep you and give you victory."

The following day, Patton saw his wife for the last time in what would be many months. She accompanied him to the airport, wearing a black hat topped with a red bird. As they said their good-byes, Bea recalled that "my eyes were as red as the bird."

On October 23, Patton boarded the cruiser *Augusta* for the voyage across the Atlantic and enjoyed the comfort of a double bed in the captain's cabin. On November 8 the troops began arriving in North Africa. Patton went ashore with his staff on Sunday, November 9. As his soldiers poured off their landing craft near Fedala, Morocco, the fiery and flamboyant major general strode the beaches, profanely shouting orders to straighten things out and get supplies and men moving inland.[40]

Casablanca fell within days, and Patton negotiated an armistice with French general Auguste Charles Noguès. On December 1, meeting with General Eisenhower at his Algiers headquarters, he was disappointed to learn that he would not be given command of U.S. Army forces in North Africa. Left dreaming of war, Patton took nine members of his staff on a boar hunt days later in Morocco's Middle Atlas mountain range. Using a twelve-gauge Belgian shotgun, Patton killed two boar with slugs and an African jackal with buckshot. Afterward he took the chance to survey the British Army's lines in Tunisia with Lieutenant General Kenneth Anderson.[41]

Patton also had the pleasure of encountering his son-in-law Johnny Waters, who was engaged in fighting German artillery forces near Medjez-el-Bab on December 12. Patton was close enough to the action to hear "the whistle of the fragments" from one artillery shell. He found that Waters's tank battalion had only eighteen of fifty-seven tanks still in service after days of fighting and that three of Waters's captains had been killed. "He himself had a bullet hole through his clothes, the bullet having stuck in his web belt," Patton wrote. "He looked very well, had matured, and had much more self-confidence than I had seen him display, although he has always had confidence."[42]

As the general passed time with his son-in-law, he was surprised to hear some of Waters's tanker comrades comment on how pleased they were to see their first general officer in twenty-four days of frontline service. "It is a sad commentary on our idea of leadership," Patton bitterly noted in his diary.

Patton departed Tunisia less than impressed with his British superior, General Anderson, who was struggling with a supply problem. "Anderson is just good enough to not get relieved," he wrote to Bea. "I should not be surprised to see the Brit 1st Army get driven back." Patton was further disgusted that Anderson's headquarters was located a full hundred miles from the front lines. "Too far by 95 miles," he wrote.[43]

Johnny Waters was equally irked by the location of General Fredendall, hidden away an equal distance from any real fighting in Tunisia. When called to Speedy Valley to offer frontline intelligence to the general in early 1943, Waters found him in his bunkered headquarters. "There's no reason in the world he couldn't have been only 5 or 10 miles behind us," recalled Waters, "or come forward for his information."[44]

While Waters remained stationed near the front lines during late January, his father-in-law spent the month attending various planning meetings in Casablanca. Eisenhower's Allied Forces in North Africa had barely crossed into the borders of Tunisia, while the British Eighth Army, under Lieutenant General Bernard Law Montgomery, was driving German general Erwin Rommel's Army Group Africa steadily west. Attacking from El Alamein, Montgomery seized Tripoli, Libya, Rommel's main supply base, by January 23, forcing Rommel to withdraw to the Mareth Line, a thirty-mile east–west chain of concrete fortifications aimed at keeping invaders out of Tunisia.

While the action played out to the east, Patton passed the time inspecting troops, slogging through meetings, and attending dinners— far removed from combat. The nagging feeling that the war in Tunisia was passing him by was almost more than he could handle. "God, I wish I could really command and lead as well as just fight," he confided in his diary on January 28. Within weeks this desire came closer to realization as Patton was informed that he had been tapped to plan the upcoming Allied invasion of Sicily, code-named Operation Husky. When asked by Eisenhower's chief planner what he thought of capturing Sicily, Patton replied, "I have always been lucky and I am going to need all I have." To his diary he admitted that he failed to see "what real value we will achieve" by taking Sicily.[45]

Far closer to the action, Lieutenant Colonel Waters remained disheartened by the fact that Major General Fredendall had allowed his First Armored Division to be split into three widely scattered groups. The II Corps commander more often directed Old Ironsides than did its commanders. Within two weeks Johnny Waters would have even greater reason to be frustrated with the high command who dictated his every move from the far-removed region of Speedy Valley.

THREE

THE DESERT FOX'S REDEMPTION

The Desert Fox was wearing down by late January 1943.

Field Marshal Johannes Erwin Eugen Rommel looked older than his fifty-one years. His hairline was receding, and his face was bronzed and weathered from relentless exposure to the desert sun. Earlier in the war, Rommel had distinguished himself as commander of the German Seventh Panzer Division during the 1940 invasion of France, solidifying his reputation as one of Adolf Hitler's favored commanders. In February 1941 he had been appointed commander of the new Deutsches Afrika Korps (DAK), consisting of two Panzer divisions, and promoted to *Generalleutnant*, in charge of supporting Italian forces in Libya.

During the next two years, Rommel—a decorated veteran of World War I—gained immortality in North Africa by imposing his will on his Allied enemies. His supreme achievement was the defeat of the British at Gazala in May–June 1942, followed by the seizure of Tobruk. He earned the respect of friend and foe alike with his mastery of mobile and courageous desert warfare tactics, a feat that earned him the "Desert Fox" sobriquet from British journalists.

One young German soldier with the rare opportunity to share his company on a daily basis was his nineteen-year-old personal driver, Rudolf Schneider. Raised in the rural eastern Germany village of Stauchitz, Schneider had studied at the German Institute for Tropical and Subtropical Agriculture in Witzenhausen prior to the war. Drafted into the army after his eighteenth birthday in 1941, he was shipped to North Africa in early 1942 after completing basic training. Once he was in Libya, Schneider's knowledge of British and American vehicles, garnered at agricultural college, proved valuable enough to earn him a posting to the *Kampfstaffel*—Rommel's reconnaissance/bodyguard force of nearly four hundred soldiers.[1]

Schneider was chosen because he knew the English language and could operate the military equipment. He was also adept at memorizing landscapes, vital in a desert where long driving distances provided little more than visions of stones and sand. Schneider believed that Rommel had no fear, a trait that he and his fellow soldiers respected. The young *Kampfstaffel* driver found that not all of the Desert Fox's junior officers shared this respect, as Rommel was confident enough in his own decisions to not bother asking for their advice.[2]

As a young man driving a general, Schneider was intimidated at first. "He was not a man for small talk, not with me or anyone," he said. "If he asked a question, he wanted an answer, brief and concise. If you talked too long, he would tell you to shut up." Schneider carried a photo of his girlfriend, Alfreda, who had promised to wait for him for marriage after the war. One of the few times Rommel made small talk with his driver, he asked if Schneider had a girlfriend.[3]

"I do, Herr General," Schneider replied.

Married more than two decades, Rommel replied simply, "I hope only one."

Another person even closer to the Desert Fox was twenty-six-year-old Oberleutnant (Senior Lieutenant) Heinz Werner Schmidt. He became Rommel's aide-de-camp and advisor in March 1941 and had been at the field marshal's side through the North African conflicts. Although Schmidt had previously commanded a heavy weapons company, Rommel may well have selected him for having been born in South Africa to German parents. "It was months before he called me anything but the formal *Leutnant*," said Schmidt. Eventually, Rommel began asking him more personal questions and calling him by his first name. "It was almost strange, after a long acquaintance, to find the impersonal General actually human," said Schmidt.[4]

In the country south of Gazala, Schmidt once participated with Rommel in a little desert sport: hunting African gazelles with a service rifle and a light tommy gun. Rommel's car, driven by Rudy Schneider, was accompanied by Schmidt's car with an Italian captain in the rear seat. The chase continued for a long distance in spite of the dangerous terrain, pitted with foxholes. "The mad tempo of the chase became a danger to life and limb," recalled Schmidt. "What if Germany's top general in Africa broke his neck in a senseless pursuit of a buck?" The Desert Fox's staffer realized his boss was possessed with a hunting spirit and thrilled by the chase. Schmidt was much relieved by the time the battered staff cars returned to camp with fresh gazelle meat.[5]

The field marshal was often challenged with more lethal situations in North Africa. During the defeat of the British along the Gazala line in May 1942, Rommel's command post came under fire by British tanks. Shells burst all around, splintering the windshield of his command vehicle. Rudy Schneider was peppered in the stomach and hand with shrapnel, but his wounds were insufficient to remove him from combat. After two weeks of bloody fighting, Rommel's Afrika Korps forced the Eighth Army to retreat, and the Germans followed quickly with the seizure of Tobruk.

For Schneider, even more important than this key victory was the capture of ample British stores. He had lived for months on heavy black bread and foul-tasting Italian rations but now was able to suddenly enjoy fresh fruit and vegetables, even strawberry jam. Even more exciting to Schneider than the good food was the seizure of Allied vehicles, field guns, and tanks, giving the *Kampfstaffel* drivers the pleasure of racing through the desert in captured vehicles that still bore their original markings.[6]

Oberleutnant Schmidt returned to Germany on leave during the summer of 1942. When he returned in August, he was given the chance to fight in command of a battalion of Special Group 288 with the Ninetieth Light Division. When he next met with his former boss, Schmidt found the field marshal's face to be visibly thinner. He appeared ill from "twenty months of continuous mental and physical strain in the desert."[7]

Four months after securing such key victories as Tobruk, the Desert Fox's good fortunes ran out when pitted against Field Marshal Bernard Law Montgomery's British Eighth Army at the Second Battle of El Alamein in October and November 1942. Suffering heavy losses of tanks and personnel, Rommel was forced to retreat through an anti-tank defensive position about fifty kilometers west of El Alamein. Schneider could not believe it when his men were ordered to withdraw. Rommel's Panzerarmee Afrika had suffered about half of his men killed, wounded, or captured by year's end, and some 450 tanks and 1,000 guns had been seized or destroyed.[8]

During the next three months, Rommel's forces would fight smaller skirmishes in a retreat across the spine of northern Africa that extended some 1,400 miles by January 1943. Morale continued to sink as supplies ran thin, compelling Rommel to occasionally feed his men by machine-gunning desert gazelle. Rudy Schneider recalled his last fight with the British being just west of Tunis at Sidi

Ali el Hattab, where the Germans managed to seize six British prisoners of war. Informed by their commanders that it was forbidden to shoot them, Schneider and his comrades shared their rations with the captured Englishmen.[9]

The British POWs were shocked to see that the Afrika Korps soldiers had only stale black bread, and stated, "You live like dogs." Lacking toilet paper and even coffee, the German soldiers had resorted to making tea by boiling water and adding leaves from trees. *Seeing the state we are in, they simply can't understand why we continue to fight,* thought Schneider.

To further his dire straits, Rommel's main supply base at Tripoli was seized by Montgomery's Eighth Army on January 23. Fortunately, the onset of heavy winter rains then caused the Allied pursuit to begin bogging down. The Desert Fox retained hope of saving his remaining men by joining forces in Tunisia with General der Panzertruppe Hans-Jürgen von Arnim's Fifth Panzer Army.[10]

Rommel firmly believed that neither Libya nor Tunisia could be held, as the added presence of the American army in North Africa ensured "there was no longer any chance of ultimate victory in that theater." In summation, the Desert Fox felt "we were bound to lose in the end. Tactical skill could only postpone the collapse." Hitler found Rommel to be too pessimistic, and Italian dictator Benito Mussolini remained intent on retaining control of Libya. He insisted that the Italians should be in charge of the war in Africa, to which Hitler agreed that the Italian high command in Rome—Comando Supremo—should be in charge of both Italian and German forces.[11]

Rommel's health declined during the demoralizing retreat, as he suffered from headaches, insomnia, and exhaustion. "Severe rebuke from Rome because we're not holding out any longer against the enemy pressure," he wrote to his wife of twenty-five years, Lucia Maria Mollin Rommel, on January 22. Three days later he wrote his "dearest

Lu" of the torments he faced. "I'm so depressed that I can hardly do my work." At midday on January 26, Rommel received word that Hitler was recalling him to Germany for rest and recuperation. His Panzerarmee Afrika would be redesignated the German-Italian Panzer Army under the command of an Italian, General Giovanni Messe.[12]

By the end of January, Rommel's German units numbered barely 30,000 combat soldiers, 129 tanks, 382 anti-tank guns, 1,411 machine guns, and only one-sixth of his original artillery strength. But German reinforcements were arriving in Tunisia from Europe to the tune of roughly 1,000 men per day, and nearly 50,000 Italian troops were included in his army. As the Desert Fox reached the Tunisian border, some of his lieutenants who had viewed him most recently as a broken man noted that Rommel began showing renewed signs of aggression.[13]

Rommel, whose operations in Africa were controlled by the Italian Comando Supremo, was also under the direction of German field marshal Albert Kesselring, who had been appointed *Oberbefehlshaber Sud* (Commander in Chief South). Tarnished after his defeat by the British at El Alamein, Rommel wished to redeem himself by uniting with von Arnim's Fifth Panzer Army to smash through the inexperienced American lines controlled by Major General Lloyd Fredendall, rush through Kasserine Pass, and seize the major Allied supply hub at Tébessa. At a Luftwaffe air base at Rhennouch, midway between Tunis and Mareth, Rommel met with Kesselring and Arnim to present his plan. General von Arnim, the son of a Prussian general, resented the Desert Fox's heroic image, making the planning meeting a frosty affair.[14]

In the end, Rommel's plan was approved, although it was scaled down from one major offensive thrust through the Tunisian mountains into two separate attacks. Arnim's Fifth Panzer Army would strike first with the code name Operation Frühlingswind (Spring Wind or Spring Breeze) by sending two Panzer divisions through

Faid Pass near Sidi Bou Zid. Frühlingswind was designed to weaken the Americans by destroying some of their elements with a force that included more than two hundred Mark III and Mark IV tanks, plus a dozen Tigers. Rommel's Panzer Army Africa, including the Afrika Korps, would execute Operation Morgenluft (Morning Air) by striking farther south through Gafsa. Including reinforcement from Arnim's army, Rommel would have 160 tanks. Kesselring defiantly declared the two-pronged operation to be intended "for the total destruction of the Americans."[15]

The Desert Fox, who had become more of a fugitive than a feared leader in recent months, now had hope of departing North Africa with the chance to redeem his pride. Field Marshal Rommel had reason to be optimistic with the new dual-thrust offensive against Gafsa and Faid Pass.

German armored forces were not to be taken lightly. The two chief tanks were the Panzerkampfwagen III (PzKpfw III) and the Panzerkampfwagen IV (PzKpfw IV) medium tanks, which had entered mass production in the late 1930s. Known popularly to the Allies as the Mark III and Mark IV tanks, they were referred to by German tankers as the Panzer III and Panzer IV, or *Panzer drei* and *Panzer vier*. From a distance, the vehicles were difficult to tell apart, other than the PzKpfw III having six bogie wheels versus eight on the PzKpfw IV.[16]

Heavily armored, the Panzer III was capable of 25 miles per hour on roads and 12 miles per hour when operated off road. Each crew consisted of five men: a commander, a gunner, a loader, a driver, and a radio operator who also operated the bow machine gun. The main gun on early models was a 3.7cm (1.45-inch) cannon—capable of an effective firing range of 328 yards and a maximum range of 5,997 yards—while the PzKpfw III models manufactured from June 1940 sported a larger 5cm (1.97-inch diameter) main gun. By contrast, the

Mark IV model tank had a slightly slower road speed, a mass of 25 tons, and a short-barreled, howitzer-like heavy 75mm (2.95-inch) main gun. The PzKpfw IV was intended to be a support tank for Mark III divisions, with the Mark IV to be used against enemy anti-tank guns and fortifications.

The most recent tank added to Rommel's arsenal was the Panzerkampfwagen VI Ausführung H, which had been nicknamed "Tiger" by Austrian-German automotive engineer Ferdinand Porsche. The enormous 54-ton Tiger sported heavier armor, maintained a faster road speed than the Mark IV, and featured a massive 88mm (3.46-inch) main gun, and the earliest models were still coming off the German assembly lines as Rommel and Montgomery clashed in the northern Africa deserts. German estimates were that the Tiger's 88mm gun would penetrate the differential case of an American M4 Sherman tank at 1.3 miles and the turret from 1,800 meters (1.1 miles). In contrast, the M4 Sherman's 75mm gun would not penetrate the Tiger frontally at any range and needed to be within 100 meters to achieve a side penetration against the Tiger's 88mm upper-hull superstructure. The first Tiger tanks to enter the North Africa campaign had gone into combat against British forces by early December 1942.[17]

The tankers under Rommel and von Arnim were ready for action in late January 1943 as Operations Frühlingswind and Morgenluft prepared to kick off against the Allies. Lieutenant Kurt Wolff, a tank commander for Fifth Panzer Regiment, had already seen his fair share of action in 1942 against the British. "Every day is a revelation," he wrote of warfare in the deserts of North Africa. "My eyes burn from the clouds of dust and dirt that the tracks kick up."[18]

During the German victory at Tobruk, Wolff's tank regiment had performed admirably. In the heat of such battles, he had to shout to be understood amidst the howling of tank engines and bursting of shells. In the aftermath, Wolff and his comrades enjoyed the British spoils of war: apricots, peaches, cigarettes, chocolate, beer, corned beef, and ham. Huddled around a captured gramophone, they played popular English tunes while smoking cigarettes from Virginia. Six months later, soldiers yearned for loved ones back in their homeland and ate only the scarcest of rations after countless miles of retreating into Tunisia.[19]

As Kurt Wolff and his fellow Panzer commanders prepared for a renewed offensive against the American military forces, they had no knowledge that U.S. major general Lloyd Fredendall was already doing his part to ensure their success by splintering his II Corps forces to protect multiple Tunisian mountain passes. Field Marshal Rommel's desire to drive the Allies back across the border and capture their vast supply dumps had the Afrika Korps poised to strike.

One of the key objectives was Faid Pass, a narrow east–west mountain pass located thirty miles north of Maknassy. Through it, Highway 30 ran from Kasserine in the west to Sfax on the east coast of Tunisia. Running through razorback ridges, Faid had been seized by the Allies in December and was currently held by more than a thousand French troops. During the early morning hours of January 30, German tanks from General von Arnim's Twenty-First Panzer Division rolled forward, ready to hit the French soldiers with a powerful three-pronged attack.

FOUR

FAID PASS SETBACKS

Filthy, exhausted, and disgusted by his own stench, Harley Reynolds clutched his rifle as he bounced around in the back of a troop hauler. Chalky dust clouds rose like geysers in the wake of dozens of military trucks as the convoy snaked through a high pass in the Atlas Mountains. As they neared Faid Pass, the rising desert djebels and rocky landscape reminded infantryman Reynolds of similar terrain he had encountered during U.S. Army maneuvers in southeastern Pennsylvania during the summer of 1942.

Springtime was approaching, yet the night air was frigid as the procession halted for the night near one of the Sahara Desert mountain summits. Reynolds and his company used two-man pup tents for warmth. Each man placed his shelter half on the rough ground, covered himself with a blanket, and then pulled another shelter half over the top to protect against light frost. The aroma of two men sharing such close quarters after they had been on the move for days without a shower made Reynolds yearn for the cold, fresh air.[1]

His Big Red One division had been relatively idle in recent weeks, but young Harley Reynolds's introduction to war and death in North Africa had been swift. Solidly built at five-foot-eleven and nearly 180 pounds, Private First Class (PFC) Reynolds had gone ashore on November 8, 1942, with Weapons Platoon B Company, Sixteenth Infantry Regiment, of the First Infantry Division. He started the day humping ammunition and finished it in charge of his machine-gun crew.

Reynolds's First Platoon landed before dawn on Arzew's east beach and moved swiftly up a mountain to the French-held town of La Macta. At the edge of town, his squad was greeted by a French civilian who came out of his house bearing an old 20-gauge shotgun. Without warning, the man fired his shotgun, striking PFC Frank Fugera in the knee. Medic Arthur Tozar dragged Fugera to a roadside ditch to tend to his wounds, but shock and blood loss claimed Fugera's life as they lay pinned down by artillery fire.[2]

Reynolds was enraged by the loss of his close friend. Enemy machine-gun fire soon pinned his squad down near the La Macta road. Artillery shells screamed overhead in pairs. "Get shooting!" shouted Platoon Sergeant Edward Pastuszynski toward Harley's gun crew. As bullets thumped into the ground all around them, Reynolds realized his gunner had frozen up. *First time under fire, and this guy can't even move!* thought Reynolds.[3]

Still angry over the loss of Fugera, Reynolds grabbed the gunner's feet and yanked him away from the machine gun. He jumped behind the gun and took over. Bullets whizzed by overhead and a close burst hit the top of the sand dune nearby, stinging Harley's face with flying sand. Another man, PFC Ivy V. Bradshaw, a husky twenty-three-year-old farm boy from Biloxi, Mississippi, was beside Reynolds in a flash, acting as his assistant gunner. From that moment on, Bradshaw became Harley's new best friend and assistant gunner.[4]

Sergeant Pastuszyński, affectionately known as "Sergeant Patty," had climbed into a tree near the sand dunes to help direct the fire of his gunners. The same burst of enemy machine-gun fire that had kicked sand into Reynolds's face offered him some brief dark humor. As the bullets clipped through the tree branches, Patty lost his grip and crashed down from his perch. Wiping the sand from his eyes and suppressing a grin, Harley spotted a fresh threat. A pair of German motorcycles with mounted sidecars were racing up the road with their mounted machine guns blazing.

Reynolds and Bradshaw swung into action. Sighting along the barrel, Reynolds opened fire when the Nazi motorbikes were a hundred yards away. His burst caused the leading motorcycle to swerve up into a nearby sand dune and overturn. The second bike kept coming. Harley's machine gun ripped the hard-packed road in front of it, forcing the driver to veer hard left and lose control. The motorcycle hit a road embankment and became airborne as it burst into flames. *Hollywood could not have done the scene any better,* thought Reynolds.[5]

A rifle squad that swept the area later reported to Reynolds that his machine-gun fire had killed four of the Axis bikers. The Allied advance on November 9 was successful, and by 1330 the town of La Macta had fallen to the Big Red One. In the wake of the first fighting, reassignments were made in the platoon. Harley Alvin Reynolds was named the new gunner for his squad, and Bradshaw became his new permanent assistant.

Now, nearly three months later, Harley was blooded and cocky. The youth from rural Pennington Gap, Virginia, sported a mustache in defiance of battalion regulations against facial hair. Harley reckoned he could do so, since he had seen plenty of British troops in North Africa with beards and mustaches. When he was ordered to shave, he protested his case all the way to the Sixteenth Regiment commander, Colonel George Taylor.

"Son, why are you refusing to shave that mustache?" Taylor asked.[6]

Reynolds explained how his family proudly displayed a photo of his great-grandfather in their living room. "He is in uniform and he wore a mustache all the time he was fighting in the Civil War," said the young soldier. Reynolds spelled out that he wished to show his pride by fighting with a mustache in the same fashion as his ancestor.

The colonel pondered the protest for a moment and then barked, "Private First Class Reynolds, get the hell out of my office, and I never want to see you back in here again. Never!"

Reynolds offered a quick thanks and retreated, happy to retain his facial hair.

By January 30, Reynolds and his machine-gun squad were stationed near the front lines in Tunisia. His First Battalion of the Sixteenth Infantry Regiment had moved under armored escort with the Seventh Field Artillery Battalion across the Atlas Mountains and established a forward base at Faid Pass, in the foothills of the eastern arm of the mountains. It was an excellent position for the Allies to push east toward the coast, split the Axis forces in southern Tunisia from forces farther north, and cut the supply line to Tunis.

From his vantage point, Reynolds witnessed the action that ensued as German forces descended upon Faid Pass. General von Arnim's Twenty-First Panzer Division struck the pass in a three-pronged attack on January 30 and quickly overwhelmed the French forces positioned there. The French pleaded with Major General Fredendall's II Corps for help, and by midmorning General Anderson passed orders for Fredendall to restore the situation at Faid.[7]

Fredendall had planned to drive on Maknassy with more than 2,000 troops in a matter of hours, so he was reluctant to cut many troops loose to assist. At 0930 he ordered the First Armored Division's

Combat Command A (CCA) under Brigadier General Raymond Mc-Quillin to counterattack Faid Pass. Part of CCA headed east along Highway 13, only to be attacked en route by German Stukas—Junkers Ju 87 dive-bombers—and then by misdirected American fighter planes. McQuillin's forces bivouacked for the night seven miles short of Faid Pass. His attack began at 0700 on January 31, although he had been warned that the Germans had placed 88mm antiaircraft guns above the western approaches to the pass.

For the second straight day Harley Reynolds found his machine-gun squad too far from the action to make any serious impact. He was close enough to hear the distant roar of artillery and tanks. Luftwaffe bombers and fighters harassed the troops throughout the day, but Harley's B Company was spared casualties. His brothers-in-arms from two other Sixteenth Infantry companies were less fortunate. Five officers and sixty enlisted men were killed, wounded, or captured in the fighting near Faid Pass on January 31.

The brunt of the Axis assault commenced at 0710 against Second Lieutenant Dale Pearce's G Company, which was entrenched to defend the pass and supported by elements of H Company. Both units were overwhelmed by superior enemy forces. The survivors made it two and a half miles through hellacious mortar, machine-gun, artillery, and small-arms fire. The Sixteenth Infantry soldiers who fell fought to the bitter end.

Chester Maksymowicz, leader of G Company's Second Platoon, received intelligence that German forces were moving in from the left and rear of his position. When word finally came to evacuate, the U.S. soldiers were fighting their opponents in hand-to-hand combat. German 88mm artillery shells filled the air overhead to the point that the Sixteenth soldiers dubbed the area "88 Street."[8]

As the G Company soldiers scurried toward safety among the rain of 88mm shells, Corporal James Butler implored his cousin, Private Joseph Conway, to also retreat.

"No," said Conway. "Leave me hand grenades and I will stay here. I would only slow up the withdrawal of the platoon." Seconds later a German shell exploded atop Conway's foxhole, mortally wounding him in the back and head.[9]

Another from G Company who gave up his life during the retreat was Corporal Robert Fullown. As a German tank advanced, he stood, walked toward it, and announced, "I'll either blow it up or knock it out of commission." Fullown had no sooner uttered these words than a German machine gunner laced his chest with bullets.[10]

Men from H Company were equally valiant in their final actions. Thirty-one-year-old Staff Sergeant Habard Gladhill from Maryland continued firing his rifle and shouting orders to his .30-caliber water-cooled machine-gun crew as the Germans advanced. An 88mm shell exploded almost directly on his foxhole, severing Gladhill's right hand at the wrist. Shrieking in agony, he rose to seek first aid but was riddled by a German machine gunner. Nearby, Corporal Thaddeus Thomas, a twenty-two-year-old Pennsylvanian, scrambled out under fire several times to repair severed communication lines running between his gun positions and the Sixteenth's observation post. Thomas was finally felled by a mortar shell that exploded within five feet of him, ripping his stomach so severely that he bled out within a half hour as the fight continued. Both Gladhill and Thomas would later be posthumously awarded Silver Stars.[11]

The Germans at Faid Pass were too well entrenched for the approaching American tankers and infantrymen. In less than ten minutes, nine Sherman tanks were wrecked and blazing along Highway 13 near the pass, and some tanker crews were taken prisoner. Major General Pinky Ward, second-in-command of the U.S. First Armored Division, scheduled another attack against Faid Pass on the afternoon of February 1. The two infantry battalions sent forward were again greeted by heavy tank and artillery fire. By day's end, the First Armored had suffered 210 casualties, and more than 900 French defenders were dead or missing.[12]

———

Oberleutnant Wilhelm Reile understood the task at hand. Having been a staff officer with the German Tenth Panzer Division since the start of the war, he was seasoned and cool. Only half of his division was now stationed at the town of Sbikha, where it remained a formidable force, tasked with breaking into the Ousseltia plain and driving south to Pichon. "The terrain was flat, with no cover, and was dominated by enemy fighters," said Reile. "In the west, where the front was, were high mountains."[13]

On February 1 a Tenth Panzer Division command jeep carrying Major Wilhelm Burklin and Major General Wolfgang Fischer set out from the division command post to reconnoiter the local terrain. Oberleutnant Reile and unit commanders gathered in the afternoon for a command conference, but dismal news arrived. The command jeep struck a mine in a poorly marked Italian minefield, killing three of the four occupants outright.

When news of the tragedy reached the divisional command post, Reile felt the assembled commanders were paralyzed with shock. Among those instantly killed, Fischer was considered by Reile to be "the best kind of comrade, even a fatherly friend." Burklin lost both legs and one arm and spent his final minutes scribbling out a farewell note to his wife, Ruth, as another officer held out a small notebook.[14]

Fischer, Burklin, and the other victims were buried in a German military cemetery near the Tunis airfield two days later. General von Arnim offered a eulogy during the ceremony. A cool wind blew down from the desert mountains as General Kesselring stepped forward to give some final words. General Fischer's son added his tribute to the solemn proceedings. Two German fighters swept low over the airfield and three volleys of rifle fire shattered the silence before the graves were closed.[15]

Friedrich "Fritz" von Broich—a forty-six-year-old veteran cavalryman who had already earned the Knight's Cross and the German Cross in Gold—was promoted to *Generalmajor* and named commanding officer of the Tenth Panzer Division. Taking on General Staff major Josef Moll as his new operations officer, General von Broich took steps to counter the latest threat from the American II Corps. He had intelligence that U.S. troops were moving north from the Gafsa area toward Sidi Bou Zid. Due to shortages of fuel, ammunition, and transport space, Arnim was forced to split his troops. He decided to send a limited force toward the southern sector near Sidi Bou Zid to strike the grouping Allied forces. The "Spring Wind" (Operation Frühlingswind) envisioned by Field Marshal Rommel was about to blow.[16]

─────────

The defeat at Faid Pass was an embarrassment. American infantry and armored division leaders pointed fingers at one another for being inept. From Speedy Valley, Lloyd Fredendall continued to distantly issue confusing orders. His directives sent troops marching to various points. Before they could arrive, Fredendall countermanded with other orders sending them to a different location. Adding to this frustration, on January 31, German Stukas attacked loaded troop trucks of the 168th Infantry Regiment, which were moving from Gafsa to Sened Station, an important crossroads located twenty-eight miles east of Gafsa. The Luftwaffe raid left more than fifty men killed or wounded.[17]

Fredendall was determined to capture the Axis-held post at Sened Station, and his determination sparked another disaster on February 1. Eighty trucks of the Second Battalion of the First Armored Division blundered down Highway 14 into German-occupied territory and became pinned down less than a mile from the cross-roads. Mortars and machine guns destroyed seventeen of the vehicles before an afternoon infantry charge, supported by tank and artillery fire, allowed the Americans to take Sened Station and 152 prisoners of war.[18]

Fredendall ordered his Combat Command D of Pinky Ward's division to push forward on February 2, and they did, taking a ridgeline six miles east of Sened Station by noon. The ground was held only for hours before a vicious assault by Stuka dive-bombers and the appearance of Panzer tanks caused a general panic among soldiers of the Second Battalion of the 168th Infantry. Hundreds of U.S. soldiers retreated back down Highway 14, and by dawn of February 4, CCD had pulled back to Gafsa, abandoning Sened Station for the second time in ten days. American losses exceeded three hundred troops in a matter of days.[19]

Major General Fredendall's II Corps had given up Faid Pass and Sened Station. American commanders began doubting one another. The British commander General Anderson lost confidence and General Eisenhower began having deep reservations as to whether Fredendall was capable of leading II Corps. His efforts to take Maknassy had also failed. The front remained fairly quiet for the next week as American leaders sought to reorganize themselves and make a better showing.

Technician Fifth Grade Tom Morrison's only real challenge during this period had been suffering through the persistent cold weather and occasional snow showers. His platoon, part of the First Armored Division's Combat Command B (CCB), had been pulled back from the valley on the first of February and was put into bivouac near Maktar. Lieutenant Colonel Herschel Baker's 601st Tank Destroyer Battalion had seen no serious action since its encounter with German Panzers weeks earlier in the Ousseltia Valley on January 20. Other units of Baker's 601st were consolidated by February

14 as CCB prepared to move out to participate in heavy action that was breaking out near Sbeitla, located to the east of Kasserine Pass.[20]

While Morrison's group had largely sat idle, Fredendall's II Corps began receiving replacement troops during the second week of February to help replace the seven hundred casualties his army had suffered in the past month. Some of the battalion commanders found their new infantrymen to be poorly trained, lacking even the basic skills of shooting BARs (Browning automatic rifles) or bazookas. While frustrated commanders set to work with on-the-job training in the desert, the U.S. Army's high command prepared for the next German advance.

General Eisenhower and his staff met at the Hotel St. Georges in Algiers on February 10 to debate the best command structure. Allied intelligence pointed toward Axis supply chain difficulties, and that the Allies held superior numbers of tanks, artillery pieces, and battalions (fifty-five to forty-two) in Tunisia. Various counterattack plans were drafted in the event of a German offensive, but Eisenhower and his brass failed to consider that Kesselring and Rommel might act as aggressively as events would soon unfold.[21]

During the same time, the key leaders of the U.S. First Infantry Division, the Army's oldest division, were holding their own council of war in a French farmhouse in the Ousseltia Valley. Heading the discussion were the two flamboyant leaders of the Big Red One, Major General Terry de la Mesa Allen and Brigadier General Theodore "Ted" Roosevelt Jr., his deputy. Allen, whose ancestry included both Anglo and Spanish military heroes, was nicknamed "Terrible Terry" by war correspondents. Although a struggling academic, Allen was a born soldier. During World War I he earned the Silver Star on the Western Front, where he was wounded by a bullet through his jaw. He had developed a close friendship prior to World War II with both Generals Eisenhower and George Patton. Famed war correspondent Ernie Pyle found Allen approachable, picturesque in his speech, "wonderfully profane," and "the only general outside the Air Forces I could call by his first name." Roosevelt, son of the twenty-sixth U.S. president, Theodore Roosevelt, was a colorful character who was well respected by his soldiers. He walked with a permanent limp, aided by a walking stick, from wounds sustained in World War I. He had a booming voice like a foghorn. At age fifty-five, Ted Jr. was equal parts World War I hero, explorer, writer, and politician, a man who had returned to military service in 1941 as America edged closer to being pulled into World War II.[22]

Allen and Roosevelt conducted their meeting with French officers and forty-nine-year-old Brigadier General Paul Robinett, the short, feisty head of the Big Red One's Combat Command B brigade. Robinett found the meeting to be disorderly, with all leaders trying to talk at once. "We can't win a war with a debating society," he noted. Like his superiors, Robinett was frustrated with just how strung out the divisions of the First Infantry were within Tunisia, and he had shared that sentiment with Major General Fredendall.[23]

Major General Pinky Ward, leader of the U.S. Army's First Armored Division, had driven from his headquarters outside Sbeitla days earlier to confer with Fredendall at his distant Speedy Valley command center. Ward felt insulted to have his armored command fragmented with four main units around the Gafsa area. Brigadier General Raymond McQuillin, a gray-haired commander who was nicknamed "Old Mac," was in charge of Combat Command A (CCA) at Sidi Bou Zid. McQuillin's infantry forces, supported by the Ninety-First Field Artillery and the First Battalion of the Seventeenth Field Artillery, were charged with covering Faid Pass. Robinett's CCB, including the majority of Tom Morrison's 601st Tank Destroyer Battalion, was stationed at Maktar to cover the French southern flank with 110 tanks. Farther south at El Aioun was Ward's CCC, while his CCD was stationed to the west at Bou Chebka, near the Algerian border.[24]

Ward was further frustrated on February 11 when Fredendall issued an order entitled "Defense of Faid Position." The general dictated the positioning of units down to individual companies, largely ordered to occupy two prominent hills within sight of the pass. The general's knowledge of the Faid area was primarily obtained from a map, and his subordinates quickly realized that a swift-moving German attack could prove deadly. "Good God," exclaimed Colonel Peter Hains III, commander of Ward's First Armored Regiment, when he saw Fredendall's plan.[25]

Following the general's orders, engineers began laying out barbed wire and mines across the front to be held by Ward's CCA. The key pass at Faid was flanked by two significant hills, Djebel Ksaira on the south and Djebel Lessouda on the north. The front near Ksaira—ten miles southeast of Djebel Lessouda and east of Sidi Bou Zid—was fortified with nearly 1,700 troops of the Third Battalion of the 168th Infantry Regiment, under Colonel Thomas Drake. His troops faced north toward Highway 14 and Faid Pass.[26]

Brigadier General McQuillin's defensive forces at Djebel Lessouda were under charge of Major General George Patton's son-in-law Lieutenant Colonel John Waters. The executive officer of the First Armored Regiment, Waters had some nine hundred troops to guard his mountain position: a company of fifteen tanks, a four-gun field artillery battery, and Major Robert Moore's Second Battalion of the 168th Infantry Regiment, Thirty-Fourth Division.

On February 12, as his troops fortified their positions in the vicinity of Lessouda, Waters was visited by Generals McQuillin and Pinky Ward. Waters found the First Armored Division leader to be dispirited. Ward complained that his division had been taken away from his control by Fredendall, leaving him only a medical battalion at his disposal. "I have no command," said Ward. "I can't tell you what to do."[27]

Intelligence officers believed that any German attack would most likely come some forty miles to the north, aimed at the Ousseltia Valley or the French forces stationed near Pichon. Waters was skeptical. He had just returned from a reconnaissance mission, and he believed Axis force activity was increasing across the Eastern Dorsal.

"General McQuillin, let me ask you a question," said Waters. "Suppose tomorrow morning I wake up and find that I'm being attacked by an armored division coming through the Faid Pass?"[28]

"Oh, Waters, don't suggest that," McQuillin scoffed.

Waters and his men continued digging into the Lessouda hills. While his men effectively did little more than wait for a German attack, one specially trained II Corps battalion was making the most of its opportunities in Tunisia.

FIVE

"WORKED OVER BY RANGERS"

L ieutenant Colonel Bill Darby was itching for action. Circling high above him like giant steel vultures were thirty-three lumbering C-47s. It was Sunday, February 7, and each troop transport aircraft was queued up over the Algerian air base, awaiting its turn to land. In their bellies were thousands of tons of special equipment and more than four hundred elite warriors—handpicked members of the U.S. Army's First Ranger Battalion. In a matter of days, the so-called Darby's Rangers would have the chance to prove their value in stealth operations against Axis forces.

Thirty-two-year-old William Orlando Darby hailed from Fort Smith, Arkansas. He had been serving as a staff officer in Northern Ireland when plans began swirling for the U.S. Army to create its own commando-type fighting unit to mirror that of the British Army. In late May 1942, Brigadier General Lucian Truscott recommended the formation of an all-volunteer American commando unit, which was quickly approved by the U.S. War Department. Truscott selected the name "Rangers" to designate this unit in reference to Rogers' Rangers, an irregular force under Major Robert Rogers that had fought on the French and Indian War frontiers. Rogers' Rangers had been popularized in American literature and most recently in the 1940 film *Northwest Passage*, starring Spencer Tracy and Robert Young.[1]

In early June 1942, Major Darby—a handsome, dark-haired former artilleryman—was selected to form this newly approved Ranger battalion in Northern Ireland. His men would be attached to the British Special Service Brigade for training, but Darby was encouraged to infuse American military doctrines and tactics as much as possible. Promoted to major on June 1, Darby was elevated to lieutenant colonel just eighteen days later, after his appointment as commander of the Rangers.

Darby had quickly selected a tall and lean New Yorker, Major Herman W. Dammer, to serve as his executive officer. Together, the pair interviewed more than 2,000 volunteers and selected 29 officers and 575 men, ranging in age from 17 to 35, from the Fifth Army's infantry, artillery, cavalry, quartermaster, and engineering divisions. By June 15, Major Darby's staff had already weeded out 104 of the volunteers and sent them back to their units.[2]

One of the new recruits, PFC Thomas Sullivan from Vermont, survived a weeding-out process that included a physical exam, an interview board before officers, and ten days of testing, including speed marches, calisthenics, and jiujitsu practice. In his diary, Sullivan described Darby as "a real soldier all the way." Another new Ranger, twenty-year-old Minnesota native Donald Frederick from the Thirty-Fourth Infantry Division, noted that volunteers failed to make the cut for a wide variety of reasons: "They either had flat feet, couldn't run and got exhausted, or they were too heavy, had bad eyes or bad teeth or something." Some of the selected men were further eliminated for being unable to complete a five-mile run to their base after departing their transport train.[3]

The balance of Darby and Dammer's men—selected for their natural athletic ability, physical stamina, intelligence, and elite combat skills—moved forward with advanced Rangers training while officer boards moved out to look for more good men from the Army's armored and infantry divisions. Darby's battalion was formally activated on June 19, 1942, at Carrickfergus, Northern Ireland, some twenty miles north of Belfast. By late June the original Ranger companies had been moved to Northern Ireland for intensive conditioning and training under the British commandos.

Darby's Rangers were put through endless challenges: speed marching with heavy packs and gear in mountainous regions; ascending and descending steep bluffs; learning to traverse streams, swamps, and heavy forest; bayonet practice; scouting work; attacking enemy pillboxes; hand-to-hand combat and wrestling; and sleeping in small tents in the elements. Borrowing from ancient Scottish games, the Rangers even engaged in groups of men carrying heavy logs and tossing them about without letting them hit the ground.

Bill Darby was rightfully proud of the chosen men who had endured months of training and had already proven themselves in combat. A small group of his men had participated in the August Dieppe Raid with other Allied commandos, and his Rangers had fought fearlessly during the November landings in North Africa. As the C-47s began touching down on the steel-matted runways in Algeria, he was confident the pioneering attack techniques of his First Ranger Battalion would make a difference for II Corps against enemy forces in the Tunisian campaign.

Among the few already with Darby as the other Rangers spilled from the planes was his battalion's popular photographer, Staff Sergeant Philip Stern. The twenty-three-year-old New Yorker had worked freelance prewar for top publications such as *Life*, *Collier's*, *Look*, *PM*, and the *Saturday Evening Post*. Phil had even done a stint working from a Hollywood office in 1941 before he entered the Army

65

Signal Corps to continue his photography in the U.S. military. While posted in the United Kingdom during the summer of 1942, Stern learned of the formation of the First Ranger Battalion and the need for someone to document the unit. "Seems some high-ups want a photographic record of the First Ranger Battalion," Stern noted in the small wartime journal he secretly maintained.[4]

Once attached to the Rangers, Stern and his camera captured the men as their training progressed through Scotland. During their off time, fellow Rangers urged him to join them in their tents to recount tall tales of Hollywood personalities he had photographed before the war. Corporal Jim Altieri, a twenty-three-year-old Philadelphia native formerly with the First Armored Division, felt that Stern never let them down. "He either was the most sought-after photographer in Hollywood or he was the world's best liar," said Altieri. During exercises, Stern was often running alongside the Rangers, loaded with a pack of film and supplies, with several cameras bouncing around on his neck. The short, stocky photographer soon became popularly known by his fellow Rangers as "Snapdragon"—the sobriquet pinned on him by First Sergeant Donald Torbett during their training period.[5]

Snapdragon's journal entries for February 7 document the emotion as the Rangers put boots on the ground in northern Algeria. The Youks-les-Bains airfield where they landed was located just seventeen miles from the giant Allied supply depot and II Corps headquarters at Tébessa. "The boys pour out, laughing and raising hell generally," wrote Stern. "The mortar squads roll out of the planes with their carts and ammo. The riflemen, machine gunners, and officers touch their feet to the ground again and feel at home. Colonel Darby scampers around to all companies, greeting them and checking up on personnel."[6]

Tom Sullivan, proud to have survived the months of training and early actions of the First Ranger Battalion, was among them. While his special service could not be detailed to family members, Tom hinted to his younger brother Joe in a letter written from North Africa, "Try to see 'Commandos Strike at Dawn' if you want to see the type of work we do." Stepping off his C-47 after a three-and-a-half-hour flight, Sullivan noted, "Algiers looked beautiful."[7]

The prospect of fresh Ranger action in Tunisia excited him. "What's up now, we don't know," reads one of Sullivan's North Africa diary entries. "An offensive is in the wind."[8]

═══

Staff Sergeant Les Kness was just as eager as Sullivan and Snapdragon Stern to get back into combat. He had already become one of the battalion's more respected leaders, even if he had only made the Rangers roster thanks to some trickery on the part of his younger brother.

Lester Elwood Kness hailed from Audubon, Iowa. He was born July 14, 1919, the fourth of six children of Austin "Brick" Kness and his wife, Bessie Estella Anderson Kness. His mother had died in 1923 soon after the birth of her sixth child, son Arnold. Brick was left to raise three boys and three girls while making only $2 per week as a custodian at Audubon High School. Years later, Brick's second-oldest son, Marvin Eugene "Mike" Kness, was a senior in high school, earning $39 per month as a member of the Iowa National Guard. Mike and older brother Les, then a sergeant with the Iowa Guard, were both pulled from Audubon in February 1942 to join the Red Bull Division of the U.S. Army in Louisiana, from where they were shipped to Northern Ireland for further training.[9]

The brothers soon tired of the monotonous drills. When they caught wind from some officers that Lieutenant Colonel Darby was recruiting an all-volunteer unit called the Rangers, the Kness boys jumped at the chance. The screening process was tough. Mike was accepted, but he was crestfallen to learn that older brother Les was among those rejected in the weeding-out process.[10]

In his new role as a clerk for Darby's Rangers, Corporal Mike

Kness remedied the situation by typing his brother's name and serial number into the newly formed company rosters as part of his own E Company. In the chaos of interviewing and turning down so many volunteer recruits, the sleight of hand was never discovered. The brothers moved forward with Ranger training in Northern Ireland, content to be serving side by side in the same company through training. Although Mike would be shuffled into another company, he and Les watched out for each other through the arduous drills and maneuvers they endured. When one brother struggled while swimming a frigid river, the other was there to lend a hand. When one was challenged hauling a heavy load up toggle ropes in the cliffs, he could count on brotherly support to get him through.[11]

Mike Kness learned that as Rangers they were "trained to go in quietly, do as much damage as possible, and get out." By the time Darby's battalion was going through training in Scotland, Staff Sergeant Les Kness had become a section leader for First Lieutenant Max Schneider's E Company. As such, he was in charge of eleven men: an assistant section leader, a Browning automatic rifle man, seven riflemen, and two scouts.[12]

Kness eventually tapped Corporal Lester Cook to be his BAR man. When the pair met at Carrickfergus during the formation of the Rangers, they learned they had both served in the National Guard in their home state of Iowa. Cook and Kness hit it off and became inseparable thereafter. Right out of high school, with a boyish face and weighing only 97 pounds, Cook had joined the National Guard, then enlisted in the Army in February 1941 at age eighteen. He had since added some pounds during his service time as a rifleman with the Thirty-Fourth Infantry, but he still looked younger than his true age. When a posting was made for Ranger recruitment, he jumped at the chance. "I was bored to tears," said Cook. "I didn't know what a Ranger was, but I volunteered."[13]

Cook and the Kness brothers pushed through the rigors of training without much problem. Regardless of how difficult the conditioning drills were, their leader, Lieutenant Colonel Darby, was always present. Much of the training was at night. "We became very good at night fighting," said Cook. Darby also impressed Cook as one who led by example, taking part in the conditioning runs alongside his enlisted Rangers.

The skills of Les Kness were noticed, and he was one of seven officers and twelve sergeants tapped for temporary duty on the Isle of Wight to observe the Second Canadian Division prepare to take part in a British and Canadian raid on the German-occupied port of Dieppe during July. President Roosevelt, learning of the planned attack from British prime minister Winston Churchill, insisted that American troops be included. The small group of Rangers slated to participate were referred to by Lieutenant Colonel Darby as "the chosen few."[14]

The planned Dieppe Raid was pushed back, and by the first of August 1942 the First Ranger Battalion moved to Argyll, Scotland, for amphibious training operations with the British Royal Navy and then on to Dundee for practice in attacking pillboxes and coastal defenses. It was at the Achnacarry training base in central Scotland that Les Kness struck up a strong friendship with another E Company Ranger, First Sergeant Warren Evans, a powerfully built six-foot-three-inch native of South Dakota. Evans, who had attended South Dakota State on a football scholarship, was also an impressive baritone singer, and he had long held the nickname "Bing" in reference to the popular singer Bing Crosby.

Evans spent his downtime with Les Kness and his younger brother, Mike, who seemed to always tag along. The elder Kness and Bing Evans enjoyed boxing. Evans found that although Kness was shorter than he was by nearly a half foot, "he had arms that hung down to his knees. He kept me out there with his long arms and would give me a pretty good beating."[15]

Les had become a hardened fighter long before joining the Rangers. Dark-haired and blue-eyed, the Iowa youth was not overly imposing at five feet ten inches but he was broad-shouldered and powerfully built, with strong legs well suited for the forced marches Darby's Rangers endured in training. Added to his rugged frame was an innate quickness, an ability to strike like lightning with both his hands and feet. Growing up dirt-poor in rural Iowa, Kness had been ashamed to admit that at times he was forced to scrounge for burned toast and spoiled oranges in the waste bins behind restaurants. He had lost some of his permanent teeth at an early age, and he was quick to react to any teasing about his smile with his fists.[16]

During their free time in the summer of 1942, the Kness brothers and Evans hit the pubs in the nearby Scottish town of Fort William. "Les and I enjoyed ourselves and fought anybody," said Evans. "Every place we went, Les would start a fight and then leave me with it." Kness insulted British soldiers or anyone feisty enough to fight, and Evans would quickly find himself in the middle of a first-class brawl.[17]

The rough-and-tumble life of being a Ranger fit the close friends well. Weeks into the training in Scotland, however, their tight bond was challenged when Evans was promoted to battalion command sergeant major. Because of his promotion, Evans was not allowed to participate in the Dieppe Raid when it was finally put into motion. In his place was Les Kness, freshly promoted to E Company's first sergeant to replace Evans.

As one of the "chosen few," Les Kness and fifty other Rangers accompanied British commandos when they embarked for Dieppe on the night of August 18. Some units made it ashore to successfully destroy the German coastal artillery battery west of town. But the landing flotilla carrying other commandos, including some of the Rangers, came under assault by German "E-boats," similar to American PT boats. "Shells that looked like little yellow balls were floating through the air, just beautiful," said Kness. "It was like the Fourth of July."

Marveling at the display, he suddenly realized he was the last man still standing and took cover in one of the ship's gun turrets. Kness was not among the fifteen Rangers who made it ashore at Dieppe; they became the first American ground soldiers to see action against the Germans in occupied Europe. Several were killed and another was captured during the raid, but the group that had taken the German battery had executed a model commando assault. Surviving Rangers like Les Kness who had gained valuable combat experience found enhanced stature among their peers.[18]

In November 1942, when his Rangers took part in Operation Torch in North Africa, Darby and his special forces battalion was called on to capture two coastal defense batteries that dominated the landing beaches at Arzew, a port town near Oran. Embarking in landing craft, Darby led half his men against the larger, inland Batterie du Nord, while Major Dammer led the remainder against Fort de la Pointe's battery. By 0400 on November 8, only hours after the landings had commenced, both enemy batteries were in Ranger hands.

Photographer Snapdragon Stern went ashore with Darby's force in North Africa and continued to serve alongside his fellow Rangers into 1943. His brilliant images of the Rangers attacking the port town of Arzew and subsequent conditioning training in Tunisia would grace the pages of many wartime magazines, such as *Stars and Stripes*.

One of the Rangers who stood out to Stern, Kness, and others was a slender British Army captain serving as a chaplain for the British Special Service Brigade. Sporting horn-rimmed glasses and a toothy smile, Father Albert Basil had so impressed Darby during their training days in Scotland that he was invited to join the battalion as an ad hoc member for its invasion of North Africa. Basil endeared himself to the Rangers, who knew that rough language and dirty jokes did not faze him. "He'd heard all and still laughed at the dirty jokes and bawdy remarks," remembered one Ranger. "However, a blasphemy from which he cringed, spiritually, mentally, and physically, was the usage of the Lord's name in vain."[19]

Father Basil was among the four-hundred-odd Rangers hustled from the C-47 cargo planes in early February as the battalion arrived in Algeria. It was only fitting that their entrance was greeted by raiding Luftwaffe warplanes. "Just as the last truck of C Company pulls out of Youks-les-Bains Airfield, Jerry bombers start plastering the joint," Stern noted in his diary. Antiaircraft fire blackened the sky as two-and-a-half-ton personnel trucks strained their engines to escape the falling bombs.[20]

Staff Sergeant Les Kness was seated with Iowan buddy Les Cook as their E Company was hauled out from the airfield. As they bounced along in the back of the truck, Cook opened a red tin of Prince Albert tobacco and packed his pipe full. The pipe was Cook's trademark. Since most smokers in the Rangers preferred cigarettes, he found being in the minority in this case paid dividends. "I had a barracks bag full of tobacco," Cook said.[21]

Darby's Rangers were trucked into Tébessa. There they marveled at the massive Allied supply dump and the picturesque North African town, equally composed of more modern civilian homes and the crumbling ruins of ancient Roman structures. While his men set up a temporary camp, Lieutenant Colonel Darby went to General Fredendall's headquarters for a briefing on the current II Corps situation.

There he was told about the mission. His men were to give the impression that Allied strength in central Tunisia was greater than was actually the case. "Night missions with fast movement, darting, pinpricking raids, and heavy firing of weapons were to be our job," said Darby. Tasked to capture prisoners and inflict heavy losses on his enemy with fewer than five hundred men under his command, Darby believed that his men had the chance to stand out to the Army's high command if they accomplished this mission.[22]

After three days near Tébessa, the Rangers were trucked under cover of darkness to the town of Feriana. Then it was on to Gafsa, the southernmost anchor of the American front, about seven miles west of the Axis-held heights of El Guettar. During the afternoon of February 10, Darby held a conference among his officers to outline plans for his Rangers to make several raids against enemy positions. The first would be against Sened Station, a railway junction and supply depot located near Sened Pass—one that was reportedly occupied by elite Italian soldiers of the Bersaglieri of the Centauro Division. That morning Darby had led a small patrol there on a reconnaissance mission to gather intelligence.[23]

He decided to send in roughly half of his battalion that night: A Company under Lieutenant Leonard Dirks; E Company under Captain Max Schneider; F Company under Captain Roy Murray; and the mortar platoon from Headquarters Company. "We're gonna throw the commando book at them—bayonets, knives, grenades—the works!" Murray told his company after the meeting. "They've got to know they've been worked over by Rangers."[24]

Les Kness learned from Captain Schneider that the two-hundred-man assault force would be hauled by trucks roughly twenty miles to a French outpost on the edge of the Allied lines. Each Ranger was to be stripped for speed, carrying only one canteen of water, half a shelter for daylight camouflage, one C ration, and no entrenching tools. Following the company briefings, the men took the opportunity to write short letters back home or catch a nap. Some gambled to ease their tensions.

As the Rangers lined up to board their trucks that evening, Technician Fifth Grade Jim Altieri of F Company was told by First Lieutenant Walter Nye to take over the squad of a sergeant who was running a high fever. Altieri, who had often railed about taking initiative, felt he had little choice. To refuse to accept responsibility at such a critical time would be the same as cowardice, he thought.[25]

Truck engines whined during the predawn hours of February 11. Half of Bill Darby's Ranger battalion was transported through inky blackness along the winding dirt road that led toward Sened Station. The cold desert air and swirls of dust filled the nostrils of the two hundred elite soldiers as they clutched their weapons and bounced against the steel sideboards of their troop carriers.

An hour later the trucks halted near a small stone-walled fort held by French troops. Darby and Dammer were already there. The men formed into squad columns and moved out silently in the long Ranger stride they had learned in Ireland and Scotland over eight miles of rugged terrain in order to arrive four miles from their objective by dawn.[26]

Les Kness and his Easy Company Rangers completed the swift hike without event, although BAR man Les Cook took his share of teasing during the night advancement. If there was barbed wire within one hundred miles of the Rangers in North Africa, Cook was razzed that he was the only man to get tangled in it at night.[27]

Just before dawn the men broke out their shelter halves and used brush cover to remain silently hidden. Second Lieutenant Bing Evans of A Company used field glasses to watch every move of the enemy, four miles away, and scope out the surrounding terrain. In spite of their best efforts to stay concealed, local Arab tradesmen wandered into the Rangers' encampment to trade for cigarettes, gum, and candy. Lieutenant Colonel Darby, afraid of disclosure, had his men put the Arabs under guard until after the attack jumped off in darkness.[28]

The Rangers waited until nearly midnight before preparing to move forward. Corporal Don Frederick worried that the desert was still bathed in the brightest moon he had ever seen. *You don't go on a raid when the moon is bright as day,* he worried. By the time the moon set, it was just past midnight.[29]

Stealth and silence would be vital as they neared the enemy outpost. They camouflaged themselves by smearing their faces and hands with dirt. Dog tags were taped together to prevent any clinking sounds. "We would jump up and down in front of the guys beside us, so we could check one another for any loose rattle of equipment and quieten it," said Les Cook. "We turned our wristwatches over to hide the glow of the face and made sure our shirt sleeves covered them."[30]

Kness had the men of his platoon don brimless knit caps instead of steel battle helmets. Each man's back was marked with a piece of white tape that could be seen in the dark, lettered X, Y, or Z to help companies maintain formation. Kness's E Company was Y, A Company was lettered with a Z, and F Company was X. Their orders were to kill anyone without tape on his back or wearing a helmet.[31]

Darby gave the order to move out, and the men proceeded at a fast pace, winding through steep draws in the darkness, climbing over rocks, ravines, and boulders. As the altitude slowly increased, breathing became more challenging. As they neared their objective, Kness's E Company took the center ground, with A Company to his left and F Company on the right flank. About six hundred yards from the Italian post, the ground was less treacherous and the pace of the Rangers increased from a fast march to a near run. The final assault would be a quick ascent up a steep hill. Atop the half-mile-long ridge ahead lay the heavily fortified Axis encampment, containing an estimated one hundred Italian soldiers. There was no sign of the enemy as they advanced across the darkened plain until a nervous Italian sentry abruptly opened fire from 150 yards away. Bing Evans was pleased when the enemy's gunfire was, as predicted, too high, allowing his men to continue advancing.[32]

At 0120 the order to charge was given. When the sergeant of E Company's First Platoon yelled, his men began to run. But the Second

Platoon, led by two newer officers, was sluggish. Les Kness jumped into action. He began hollering at the men until they took off at a dead charge, with Kness running right alongside them over the hill.[33]

The Rangers caught Italian soldiers streaming out of their tents. Darby had his men sprint the last fifty yards while firing their guns, yelling, and making all the noise possible to rattle their opponents. When the Italians began to respond with intense counterfire, Jim Altieri told his F Company squad to drop to the ground and crawl forward on their bellies.[34]

The initial element of surprise allowed the Rangers to cut down many of their opponents with rifle fire, but Italian machine guns and a 47mm cannon roared to life. As Don Frederick advanced with F Company, a cannon shell beheaded a Ranger near him. The BAR man closest to him was still setting up his automatic rifle when an enemy bullet caught him in the knee and incapacitated him.[35]

Kness's platoon was pinned down by the deadly enemy fire. He could see nearby F Company Rangers lobbing grenades toward the Italian cannon. Each time the enemy fieldpiece flashed, Kness fired into it, even though he was unsure whether his bullets were doing any good. Technician Fifth Grade Owen Sweasey, with PFCs Edwin Dean, Joseph Dye, and Jacques Nixon, led the way for Kness's platoon. Acting as scouts for their squad, Sweasey's quartet charged through gunfire with fixed bayonets into a machine-gun nest, killing the personnel and capturing the weapon to allow their comrades to advance.[36]

The Rangers of A Company found themselves in point-blank combat. Bing Evans, leading the company's Second Platoon, raced through the Italian camp with a .45 in one hand and a knife in the other, using both. An enemy soldier charged him. Evans was so surprised that he was too paralyzed with fear to swing his gun into action. But his adjacent runner, Tommy Sullivan, killed Evans's attacker with a gunshot to the chest.[37]

As Jim Altieri charged through the Italian camp, he jumped into a slit trench and found himself face-to-face with an enemy soldier. The trench was too narrow to bring his rifle to his hip to fire. Altieri pulled his commando knife and thrust it deep into the Italian soldier's gut over and over. As his opponent's body sagged and slid to the ground, Altieri reeled and vomited.[38]

Captain Murray's A Company silenced another enemy gun as the assault evolved into grenade tossing and hand-to-hand fighting. Within twenty minutes, when things calmed down, Darby's men had killed at least fifty opponents, wounded many more, and had begun the process of taking prisoners. He called to Captain Schneider, on the other end of the ridgeline, to see how many Italians his E Company had taken. "I think I have two, sir," Schneider replied.[39]

The field radio reception was poor, so Darby asked for a repeat. At that moment the two E Company prisoners attempted to run, compelling Schneider to open fire. He picked up the walkie-talkie and told his commanding officer, "Well, sir, I *had* two prisoners."

By 0200 the remaining Italian soldiers of the Tenth Bersaglieri Regiment—there were only eleven—were taken captive. Wounded Rangers were hauled to the rear of the Italian camp for First Lieutenant William "Doc" Jarrett to administer first aid in the early morning blackness. Although his force had surprised its enemy and demolished the camp, Darby still found their situation to be "ticklish." Only one of his men had been killed and another eighteen wounded. But with only two and one half hours left before dawn, the nearest positions of real safety were the mountains twelve miles away.[40]

Darby formed his men into two columns. He directed Dammer to lead the first column of able Rangers on a speed march back toward their origination point, where II Corps trucks would be waiting. Sergeant Kness moved to the base of the hill they had assaulted and began counting his men to make sure everyone had made it out alive. He helped with two of the more severely wounded, Corporal Garland Ladd of F Company and Joe Dye of his own company, the latter badly injured during his assault on the machine-gun nest. Ladd and Dye were unable to walk. Kness injected both Rangers with morphine and then started back with them and another five able men. Because Kness and his men were assisting the eighteen wounded Rangers, their procession soon fell far behind the balance of Darby's force. Les Cook helped a Ranger who had been blinded by the concussion of an explosion.

Kness's small group was further slowed by a wounded Italian prisoner his men had taken. In short order the sergeant realized the enemy soldier was moving too slowly and threatened to hold them back. Kness was under orders to leave no prisoners behind who could potentially alert other Axis forces to the direction in which his Rangers were retiring.[41]

With the survival of his wounded men in jeopardy, Kness could not afford for the prisoner to slow them down. He turned to one of his Rangers who spoke good Italian and told him, "Tell him he'd better keep up, or we will have to kill him!"

One of the Rangers ordered the Italian to get moving, but the prisoner refused.

Kness then passed the order to kill the prisoner.

"I can't," protested his Italian-speaking Ranger.

"Why?" asked Kness.

"Because I know everything he's saying!"

It was a painful situation for Kness, but orders were orders. The prisoner was quickly eliminated. Darby's faster columns finished the twelve return miles just prior to dawn and found the waiting truck column. Doc Jarrett and first aid men gave morphine to the badly injured and sprinkled sulfa drugs on their wounds. Kness's slower column did not return until the evening of February 12. He and his men tended to the wounded as they hid in the hills during daylight. When German planes passed nearby, the Rangers covered themselves in the desert brush. Jeeps and trucks dispatched from headquarters re-trieved the straggling soldiers after dark and hauled them back to the French outpost.

Darby's men were offered hot broth and bread by the French sol-diers, who helped maintain guard over the ten POWs hauled in by the Rangers. The energized soldiers swapped stories of their close brushes with death at Sened, passing the time until II Corps troop trucks arrived after dark to haul them back to Gafsa for much-needed rest. Jim Altieri wished he could curl up, sleep for years, and try to forget the gory experience he had somehow survived.[42]

"Slaughter," Tommy Sullivan noted in his diary. "It's ours." He had escaped injury, although a fellow A Company Ranger, Sergeant Mervin Heacock, had been badly wounded. The forced march back from Sened Station left Sullivan weary and grumpy. His commander, Bill Darby, was elated with the Sened Station performance, noting that "the results of the raid exceeded all expectations." Per Bing Evans, "It was the very type of mission we were trained for."[43]

Darby's men were allowed to sleep well into the late morning hours of February 13 before being treated to a hearty lunch of steaks. That afternoon they were surprised to see Major General Lloyd Fredendall himself pull up with his command staff, having driven all the way from Speedy Valley to honor the Rangers. The companies were formed in a clearing between two rows of olive trees with the stone walls of an old fortress standing behind them. Darby was front and center, flanked by Major Dammer and Captain Howard Karbel, the battalion adjutant.[44]

A dozen officers and men from A, E, and F Companies were called forward to be decorated for valor. Karbel read aloud each citation, written in the past twenty-four hours, as each man stepped forward to have General Fredendall pin a Silver Star on his chest. From Kness's company, Captain Schneider and the four enlisted men who had overpowered a machine-gun nest were singled out for their valor. The other company commanders, Captain Murray and Lieutenant Dirks, along with five of their enlisted men, received Silver Stars.

Snapdragon Stern photographed the ceremony. He was surprised when Fredendall announced that two more awards, not on the formal agenda, would be presented. Dammer was awarded a Silver Star, and then Darby was stunned to hear his own name called. He stood at stiff attention as the general pinned on his medal, which was greeted by a thundering roar of approval from his men.[45]

Once the shouting died down, the Ranger commander advised his men they could go back to their business of killing more Germans and Italians. He shared with them that captured Italian soldiers from Sened Station had referred to his Ranger force as "Black Death."[46]

After Fredendall's staff had departed, Darby announced, "I'm damned proud to command this battalion." As though fourteen Silver Stars handed out immediately following combat were not enough, the lieutenant colonel surprised his Rangers by announcing four battlefield commissions. Leonard Dirks, commanding A Company, was promoted to the rank of captain, while three sergeants— Les Kness, Bill Musegates, and Walt Wojcik—were advanced to the officer's rank of second lieutenants.

Nine months prior, Les Kness had missed the cut to become a Ranger. Given a second shot at the coveted special operations battalion, thanks to a bit of muster roll trickery by his brother Mike, he was now among Darby's elite. From a battalion of nearly five hundred men, he was one of only twenty-two who had participated in both the Dieppe and Sened Station raids. And as of February 13, 1943, Kness was one of only four Rangers who had been promoted into officer's rank based on combat valor.

SIX

SPRING BREEZE FURY

John Waters was apprehensive as the fire of the rising desert sun illuminated the dust behind Faid Pass. There was already evidence of trouble brewing. The previous evening, February 13, the lieutenant colonel had sent a patrol to scout ahead toward the pass, fully expecting a report back that the Germans would soon attack his position. But his men had stopped three miles short of the mountain, where they reported only a faint rumble from the direction of the pass.[1]

Waters had warned his Second Battalion commander, Major Bob Moore, of that fact before taking his rest. After a few hours of sleep, he rose at 0400 on Valentine's Day, 1943, and climbed to the lookout position atop Djebel Lessouda. His 900 men of Combat Command A were stationed on and around Lessouda, prepared to counter any German advance through Faid Pass. A steady fifteen-mile-an-hour wind was blowing through the desert, kicking up walls of dust that helped obscure any movement near the pass.

The windstorm prevented Waters from seeing or hearing anything unusual, but he soon had other indications something ominous was happening. He had just returned from his observation to his tent when he received a call from Colonel Pete Hains, who was stationed miles away in the CCA command post at Sidi Bou Zid. Hains asked Waters what was going on near him. "There is an awful lot of firing out there in front of you now," stated Hains.[2]

"I can hear some shooting far out there," replied Waters. But the dust storm, kicked up by high winds, prevented him from seeing anything. Another two hours would pass before the battle reached his men, but by 0650 Waters was aware that Faid Pass was under attack by German Panzers.

———

Generals Eisenhower and Fredendall had done little in the days prior to prevent the deadly onrush of German troops sweeping toward Johnny Waters.

Eisenhower had received his fourth star on February 11, becoming only the twelfth full general in U.S. Army history. The following day the new general made his second visit to Tunisia, driving from Algiers with his command convoy. Ike's Cadillac sedan, in company with eleven other command vehicles, often turned heads because of its driver. Thirty-four-year-old Kay Summersby, an attractive brunette and former model, was a British Mechanised Transport Corps driver assigned as Ike's personal chauffeur and secretary. Although Kay was engaged to a U.S. Army officer of Fredendall's staff, she and the general were friendly enough with each other to start rumors of an affair.

Summersby wheeled Ike's Cadillac convoy up the gravel road into Speedy Valley shortly after lunch on February 13. Pneumatic drills chattered as engineers continued to drill through solid rock to deepen the underground command post of Lloyd Fredendall. The major general arrived in the early afternoon, having just returned from pinning medals on Darby's Rangers at Gafsa. He was beaming with excitement at the success of his Rangers as he greeted Ike. Fredendall and Eisenhower were joined by Lieutenant General Kenneth Anderson, the British commander, to review the Allied troop dispositions. Anderson's British V Corps was posted to the north, the French in the center, and Fredendall's II Corps in the south. Any Axis push through Gafsa or Faid Pass was considered to be a likely diversion, and Eisenhower consented to the current disposition of forces.[3]

Anderson was summoned back to his headquarters in northern Tunisia the late afternoon of February 13. Eisenhower whittled down the size of his convoy and departed from Speedy Valley at 1800 for further inspection of his forces in Tunisia. Kay Summersby remained behind for the time being, afforded the chance to spend time with her fiancé, Lieutenant Colonel Dick Arnold. Ike moved forty-five miles southeast to observe the American airfields at Thélepte and Feriana before driving another forty miles northeast to visit the First Armored Division command post at Sbeitla.[4] There, he was briefed by Major General Pinky Ward on the disposition of his First Armored forces on the two hills at Faid Pass. Another officer informed Ike that the placement of the CCA forces around Faid Pass left them isolated, with no ability to mutually support one another. Eisenhower remained thoughtful but silent on the issue, pressing his tour of the area forward by traveling on with Ward thirty-five miles east to Sidi Bou Zid at 2300 on February 13.[5]

At the Sidi Bou Zid command post, Brigadier General Raymond McQuillin and Colonel Pete Hains briefed Eisenhower on the two CCA forces they had stationed near Faid Pass. John Waters had 900 troops covering Djebel Lessouda, while another 1,700 men from the 165th Infantry Regiment, Thirty-Fourth Division, under Colonel Thomas Drake were clustered at Djebel Ksaira. Eisenhower directed McQuillin's engineers to lay more minefields in the morning to protect Sidi Bou Zid but did little more to help protect these 2,600 men. Intelligence reports on February 13 indicated an imminent attack from Arnim's Fifth Panzer Army but did not specify where such an assault would occur. By the time Ike's motorcade headed away from Sidi Bou Zid in the early morning hours of February 14, the CCA forces stationed near the key pass were hours away from experiencing their enemy's fury.

———

Twenty-year-old Baldur Köhler was awakened long before dawn on February 14 for a breakfast of coffee, preserved bread, and marmalade. His rank, *Panzer Oberschütze*, indicated he was a senior enlisted man who displayed above-average aptitude and proficiency as a *Funker für gepanzert Kraftwagen* (radio operator) of a PzKpfw III. Raised near Frankfurt, Germany, Köhler had tutored under his father in electrical appliance repairs, and after being conscripted into military service in March 1942, he had been trained as a radio repairman. A veteran of previous North Africa actions in the Seventh Panzer Division, Köhler was now a member of Kompanie 5, Abteilung II, of the Tenth Panzer Division's Seventh Regiment. The previous evening his tank crew had cleaned their air filters and guns, prepping for action in which they expected to catch the Americans thinly spread and ill prepared for quick response to the German charge.[6]

Operation Frühlingswind, "Spring Breeze" or "Spring Wind," began to blow long before dawn on Valentine's Day. The Tunisian plain was whipped by a howling sandstorm blowing in from the northwest. German soldiers covered their faces and pressed forward into the western mouth of Faid Pass.

Major General Heinz Ziegler, General Hans-Jürgen von Arnim's chief of staff, commanded the Spring Breeze forces. To his right lay Djebel Lessouda and to his left was Djebel Ksaira. More than one hundred tanks, including a dozen of the new Tigers, creaked forward with half-tracks and infantry vehicles at 0400 through the sandstorm. Hundreds of infantrymen followed the tanks down Highway 13 toward the hills near Faid Pass. At 0630, Ziegler directed his tankers to move through the Eastern Dorsal pass onto the plain and attack.[7]

The red orb of the sun was just filling the area with light as the pressing German force kicked up massive dust clouds. Radio operator Köhler, stationed at a machine gun in his tank's bow, was surprised when his armored company turned off the main Faid–Sidi Bou Zid road and started north toward Djebel Lessouda. As the dawn sandstorm broke, his tank commander began firing rounds toward the hill as American counterfire erupted near them.

The first American infantry squad encountered was wiped out three miles from Faid, and the Tenth Panzer Division in its first hour of action destroyed advanced tanks from Colonel Hains's First Armored Division. Shortly after 0730, Ziegler sent eighty tanks and trucks north to encircle Djebel Lessouda, while another group angled south toward Sidi Bou Zid.[8]

By late morning Köhler's Panzer division was rumbling past abandoned U.S. artillery pieces, trucks, and military equipment. He was pleased to see columns of black smoke and dust clouds were rising from the direction of Sidi Bou Zid and to the south. His comrades had succeeded in catching the American forces completely by surprise.

———————

Wirt Cunningham was fighting off sleep shortly after daybreak. Rated technician fifth class, the scrawny six-foot-four-inch seventeen-year-old was in command of a 105mm howitzer anti-tank gun mounted on a half-track. His Battery B of the Ninety-First Field Artillery included six of the self-propelled guns. Under command of Captain Warren Bruce Pirnie, Cunningham's batteries were positioned near Djebel Lessouda to protect Lieutenant Colonel Waters's CCA soldiers.

Cunningham had lied about his age to enter the U.S. Army in 1940 while he was still shy of his sixteenth birthday. Life around his rural hometown of Steubenville, Ohio, had been tough, and young Cunningham envisioned working with horses as part of the U.S. Army's cavalry. Wirt was well into his military commitment by the time he understood how mounted cavalry had been converted to fully mechanized field artillery during the 1930s. *Was I disappointed when I found out there wasn't a cavalry with horses,* thought Cunningham.[9]

At daybreak on February 14, the action came swiftly for Cunningham. The hundred men of his Battery B—coupled with some 225 U.S. infantrymen—were not prepared for Major General Ziegler's assault. Cunningham heard a battalion guard announce that German Panzer tanks and thousands of foot soldiers were advancing on them. *The desert between Faid and Lessouda is just swarming with tanks, infantry, and Lord knows what,* thought Captain Pirnie. Surveying the scene, Cunningham spotted a main Panzer force bearing down to his right front and two Mark IV tanks coming parallel to his position.[10]

Scarlet-and-white flashes erupted from the German tanks. Pirnie ordered his six howitzer crews to begin firing from the pile of a hundred shells that had been stacked before each gun the previous night. At first things looked good. Cunningham loaded an armor-piercing round into his gun and it made a direct hit on the lead tank's track, knocking it off its bogie wheel. As the German tank commander opened the hatch to his turret, Cunningham's crew sent a high-explosive round into the hatch cover. The second Mark IV crew slowed to see what had happened to the first tank. The Ninety-First Field Artillery howitzers repeated the process, disabling and destroying the second German tank with the same type of rounds. "No one got out of either of those tanks," said Cunningham.[11]

His crew labored to pour out round after round of ammunition, switching to shorter range with each firing. Pirnie's howitzer crews switched from powder charge 7 down to charge 3 within two minutes. The fact that they had knocked out two German tanks was of little consolation. Pirnie's half dozen artillery crews were now mere distractions, like plastic barrels placed before a charging bull. More tanks rolled forward and began landing hits on the Ninety-First's position. Captain Pirnie sent an urgent radio message to Lieutenant Colonel Waters, stationed on Djebel Lessouda behind him: "We can't hit them! They've gotten in under us!"[12]

"Move back to where you can," Waters ordered.

Pirnie passed the word to fall back, and panic immediately set in. "It was a rat race, everybody for himself, tearing like crazy," the captain recalled. High-caliber German shells exploded all around his howitzer crews. Half-track commander Wirt Cunningham was annoyed when three men from his anti-tank crew fled. But he was determined to slug it out with the Panzers.[13]

As the main Panzer column began landing shells perilously close to his 105mm, Cunningham cranked up his vehicle and moved a couple hundred yards. He fired several shells at the main German column, moved positions, and then fired again. The Ninety-First Field Artillery had established its position where it was benefited by a four-foot rock dike. Cunningham continued to move his howitzer from position to position, firing at the German tanks while the balance of his unit's men retreated toward safety.

Pirnie credited Cunningham's solo firing effort with causing the German column commander to stop briefly to assess the size and situation of the force firing against them. This hiatus allowed PFC Dale Jones and dozens of other Ninety-First Field Artillery soldiers to escape with their lives. "We got chewed up pretty bad," said Jones, who was in charge of a 37mm half-track. His crew would fight again another day, but many of his comrades were less fortunate.[14]

Four of Captain Pirnie's howitzers were captured or destroyed, and twenty-nine of his artillerymen were captured by the Germans. Pirnie was finally forced to abandon his own half-track after intense enemy machine-gun fire destroyed his anti-tank gun shield. The heavy steel plate withered until it reminded Pirnie of a piece of aluminum foil that had been crumpled and straightened out repeatedly.[15]

By the time Cunningham was down to only twenty rounds of antipersonnel shot, he figured it was time to save his own skin. The Germans had overrun the dike and were capturing his comrades. Cunningham fired up his jeep-drawn gun and headed for the hills away from the German column. En route, he picked up Captain Pirnie and two members of his own howitzer crew, Tom Arnold and Sam Ray.

The foursome moved miles away from their first encounter with the Germans, fleeing across the plain. The Ninety-First Field Artillery men took cover in a wadi (a dry ravine or channel) and dug in, camouflaging their howitzer. Pirnie decided to wait for darkness to make his next move.

———

Other artillery units suffered against the onrushing German Panzers. Battery A of the Ninety-First Field Artillery, stationed closer to Sidi Bou Zid, fired until a number of its men were killed or wounded. As tank shells, artillery, and machine-gun fire swept through the town, the surviving artillerymen collected their own casualties and moved their howitzer pieces toward safer ground.

Sergeant Hubert Edwards and his comrades of the Second Battalion of the Seventeenth Field Artillery fared little better. Raised on a 350-acre tobacco farm in rural North Carolina, Edwards had his parents sign for him to join the service in 1939. His closest friend in his Battery B, First Sergeant Robert Keeler, also hailed from North Carolina. En route to North Africa on their transport ship, Keeler had tagged Edwards with an unusual nickname. Edwards was one of the few men not disgusted with the menu on the British vessel. Three times a day for thirteen days they were served dried fish, dried goat meat, and boiled potatoes. After a week of eating the same courses, Keeler pronounced the English cuisine to be "garbage" and shoved his plate away. "If you ain't gonna eat those potatoes, give them to me," said Edwards. "I'll eat them!" Everyone in the outfit snickered as the skinny Tarheel shoveled down the potatoes. "From that point on, they called me Garbage," said Edwards. "Nobody in my unit ever knew my first name."[16]

Keeler, Garbage Edwards, and their howitzer crew fired their 1917 Schneider 155mm howitzer with a vengeance on the morning of February 14. Edwards was soon soaked in sweat from both the tension and the rising desert heat as he helped slam ninety-eight-pound shells into his fieldpiece. His crew continued to lower the elevation of their howitzer as the Germans drew closer, forcing them to use smaller-numbered powder charges as the range decreased. By the time his crew was down to using a number one charge, Edwards could actually see the projectile when it left the gun.

Shells from German artillery and Panzers disabled many of the Seventeenth Field Artillery's pieces until Edwards and his crew were forced to retreat on foot toward friendly concentrations. During the same period a platoon of A Company from the 701st Tank Destroyer Battalion was also overrun and captured. Edwards would find that fate was not as kind to many of his Seventeenth Field Artillery comrades.

Corporal Edward Deaton was awakened on Valentine's Day and told to start firing. A native of Troy, North Carolina, Deaton was a member of Battery F of the Seventeenth's Second Battalion. His battery officer, First Lieutenant James Bickers Jr., ordered his crew to begin pumping out rounds as fast as they could.

Within minutes the Germans were so close that Bickers ordered his crew to pull their howitzers by jeep to a safer firing position. But advancing Panzers and swooping Luftwaffe planes attacked so steadily that the American crew never had sufficient time to reposition their weapons. Many of their trucks were smashed by Stuka bombs, and heavy tank shells "sealed the deal," per Deaton. He, Bickers, and a dozen other survivors of their Battery F were forced to race for cover behind a tiny knoll on the rocky plain.[17]

Deaton found that the protective rocks were not much higher than the top of his head. In this perilous position, Lieutenant Bickers saw bursting bombs and heard zinging rounds of machine-gun bullets that he at first assumed were also coming from the dive-bombers. To his dismay, he soon realized the bullets were being fired from two directions, from friendly and enemy tanks. For the first hour Deaton peered over the knoll and assured his companions, "Everything is going to be all right." But the German advance was so swift that he soon looked over the knoll to find German Panzers a mere 150 yards away.[18]

Bickers was soon faced with a young German soldier with long blond hair who rose above his tank's turret and announced, "For you, the war is over." Bickers, Deaton, and a dozen other members of Battery F became prisoners of war. Deaton would survive twenty-six months of captivity and emerge with one prized keepsake, a white handkerchief on which one of his fellow POWs, Ed Murphy, had scrawled a poem in memory of their final fight near Faid Pass. In part, it read:

> We hit the dirt side by side, fired bullets and shells into his
>   front so wide.
> We were trapped—so many died.
> But God above knows how hard we tried.
> Creeping and crawling, bit by bit, the enemy was closer, hit
>   after hit.
> Bodies were falling, still no one quit. Till their machine guns
>   were shoved in our pits.[19]

Hubert Edwards and others of the Seventeenth Field Artillery who managed to scramble to safety counted their blessings. "We lost twelve guns, 35 officers, and 199 enlisted men that day, many of them taken prisoner," he recalled.

The decimation and capture of American artillery crews compelled Brigadier General McQuillin to order in help from the First Armored Regiment. Lieutenant Colonel Louis Hightower, a West Point classmate of John Waters, climbed into a Sherman tank named *Texas*, from which he proudly flew the Lone Star Flag from its antenna. His Third Battalion of Old Ironsides rumbled forward from Sidi Bou Zid at 0730 to assist, but they were doomed from the start.[20]

Hightower advanced with three dozen Shermans, but Stukas began blasting his tanks just two miles north of Sidi Bou Zid. The Twenty-First Panzer Division, sweeping in to join the Tenth Panzer Division, steadily forced the Americans back into the town and chased them beyond it as Luftwaffe planes destroyed the village. The American infantry units positioned on the two hills flanking Sidi Bou Zid proved to be ineffective at providing mutual support or in helping with the debacle unfolding on the plains far below them. Colonel Thomas Drake was atop Djebel Ksaira and soon became frustrated, phoning the command post at Sidi Bou Zid. Drake warned that the American artillerymen were showing signs of panic. He was informed over the phone that the men were merely shifting positions. Drake responded angrily, "Shifting positions, hell. I know panic when I see it."[21]

German 88mm artillery and Luftwaffe attacks turned the Sherman tanks into blazing coffins one by one. The Germans referred to the American tanks by the name "Ronson," after a famous cigarette lighter that fired up every time.

Radio operator Baldur Köhler and his Tenth Panzer Division comrades were vigilant in their attack on the approaching American Shermans. He felt helpless in the beginning, seated in front of a machine gun in the bow of his tank as the first shells were fired from his tank's turret. The order of *"Anfahren!"* crackled through his radio headset, and the Panzers started up, creaking forward from a wadi toward the burning American tanks.[22]

Köhler's Mark III advanced past broken Sherman tanks as excited shouts filled his radio headset that the Americans were running. In the midst of this action, his radio and intercom went dead. His tank commander, an experienced veteran of desert warfare, ducked down from above and shouted at Köhler to fix the problem. His efforts proved to be of no use, forcing his commander to finally pull up alongside another Mark III to relay to their platoon commander that they had lost their radio.

Frustrated at his inability to fix his gear, Köhler began machine-gunning abandoned American trucks until his commander ordered him to cease fire, yelling, *"Feuerpause!"* Köhler did as ordered until he spotted movement behind an American anti-tank gun camouflaged behind a pile of rocks. He opened fire again, peppering the enemy's gun shield with tracer bullets. His tank commander screamed at him only momentarily this time. Perceiving what Köhler's target was, he ordered other Panzer guns to open up until the Allied threat was obliterated.[23]

Lieutenant Colonel Hightower's battalion earned the respect of many German tankers before the superior Panzer vehicles began taking their toll on the American effort. "The enemy fought back hard and tenaciously," recalled Major Helmut Hudel of the Tenth Panzer Division. "Shermans appeared continuously firing from shortest distances, which at times were only five to ten meters. However, they were unable to hold out very long because German tanks were moving in from everywhere."[24]

Hightower's own *Texas* tank crew hit four Panzers before his tank was knocked out. In short order, the longer-range German artillery had decimated Hightower's offensive. "Let's get the hell out of here!" he finally announced. Hightower's men ran nearly a half mile across flat terrain under enemy machine-gun fire before they halted to catch their breath. Only six of his fifty-two tanks survived the retreat.[25]

By 1345 on February 14, half a dozen Tigers were pushing through the rubble of Sidi Bou Zid. By 1705, tanks from the Twenty-First Panzer in the south and those from the Tenth Panzer in the north met two miles east of town on Highway 125. The Americans had been flushed from Sidi Bou Zid in less than twelve hours; the town was now under possession of German colonel Hans-Georg Hildebrandt. Another 2,500 U.S. troops had been left marooned on their two hilltops near Faid Pass as the German tidal wave surged past them. General Fredendall sealed the fate of Drake and Waters's men by refusing to allow them to escape while there was time to do so.

———

By midmorning Lieutenant Colonel Johnny Waters and his infantry commander, Major Bob Moore, were painfully aware of the disaster that was playing out on the desert floor below their vantage point on Djebel Lessouda.

The first German advance on Lessouda was turned back by Moore's infantry, but by noon a second enemy advance pressed up the southern face toward the gulch where Waters's command post stood. Waters put radio calls out for Moore but was unable to reach him. Soon, Waters could see gray-clad soldiers moving through the tuft grass and olive trees below his position.

There was no cavalry coming to rescue Waters's men or those of Colonel Drake on nearby Djebel Ksaira. Mac McQuillin, the CCA commander at Sidi Bou Zid, had already evacuated that town and moved his command post seven miles west toward Sbeitla. At 1400, Drake radioed for permission to pull his men from Ksaira and save them. The request was relayed on to General Fredendall in his underground command bunker at Speedy Valley.

"Continue to hold your position" was the word relayed back from Fredendall.

On Djebel Lessouda, Waters sent his driver up the hill to locate Moore. The soldier staggered back minutes later with a bullet hole in his chest. Waters wrapped him in a bedding roll and administered morphine to ease his pain, but the young man was clearly dying.[26]

Waters directed his assistant, Captain James Fraser, to hide in a nearby wadi until dark before trying to get himself to safety. With his remaining men he moved his command half-track to another wadi and sent another radio transmission to Pete Hains, detailing his situation.

"Pete, I'm going to shut this thing off and go up on the O.P. [observation post]," Waters announced. "They are all around here and looking at me now, but I don't think they have discovered this half-track yet." Waters detailed that he would dismantle the radio and hide the parts in hopes that he could reassemble the radio if he managed to dodge the Germans through the night. His final word was that he planned to hide in a ditch near his observation post until darkness.[27]

Around 1600, Hains sent a final reply, offering his best wishes.

"Never mind about me," radioed Waters. "Just kill those bastards at the bottom of the hill."

Hains promised to do all that he could before the pair signed off, and Hains headed closer to the tank action playing out near Faid Pass.

Lieutenant General Patton's son-in-law had not been long in hiding before he heard the rustling of someone walking up the dry ditch in which he was concealed. For a brief moment he hoped it was Captain Fraser trying to find him. But as he crawled out from an overhang, Waters faced a German infantry patrol led by several Arab scouts. One of the soldiers fired a burst from his burp gun from the hip, and the bullets narrowly missed Waters. He was moved to a mobile headquarters located on the side of the mountain where officers were surveying the battle situation. Fortunately for the lieutenant colonel, his captors were winning the battle at hand and they treated him fairly.[28]

Waters was placed in a motorcycle sidecar and hauled back to a holding camp on the other side of Faid Pass. His interrogations would begin soon enough as his life as a German POW commenced. With the capture of Waters and his command post, Colonel Drake, Major Moore, and their men remained trapped on the opposing hill as nightfall enveloped Faid Pass on February 14.

———————

Four members of the Ninety-First Field Artillery narrowly escaped from the Valentine's Day fiasco at Djebel Lessouda. Captain Bruce Pirnie and three of his artillerymen—Wirt Cunningham, Tom Arnold, and Sam Ray—had spent the afternoon with their jeep-drawn artillery piece camouflaged in brush in the hills about seven miles from the point of their morning encounter. Near dusk, an eight-man German patrol approached the wadi where the four Americans were concealed.

The enemy soldiers halted just fifty feet away and began conversing among themselves. Cunningham had Ray load for him as he opened up and eliminated the patrol with automatic fire. In two consecutive days his actions had helped his comrades avoid death and capture. His solo assault on German tanks the previous day had created a window for many other members of the Ninety-First Field Artillery to escape the massacre. Pirnie would recommend Cunningham for the Medal of Honor for his actions, although the award was later downgraded to a Silver Star.[29]

Pirnie's survivors continued to dodge German patrols throughout the night. "It was damnedest race you ever saw," he said of their flight. He found the desert between Faid and Lessouda swarming with tanks, artillery, and infantrymen. Cunningham was finally ordered to destroy their artillery piece with a thermal grenade, but the quartet's luck held out. Shortly before dawn on February 15, Pirnie, Cunningham, and their comrades made contact with other elements of Bob Moore's battalion.[30]

———

Second Lieutenant Les Kness was frustrated by the inability of his battalion to reach the key passes to assist with the Valentine's Day fight. Scuttlebutt on enemy positions reached his E Company of the First Ranger Battalion on a regular basis. Although his men remained vigilant near Gafsa, Kness could simply not find action.[31]

Kness was finally tapped by his company commander, Captain Max Schneider, to take out an eight-man recon patrol on February 14. A listening post had reported seeing and hearing enemy movement to their front. Kness marched forward with his team to survey the situation, leaving word with his platoon sergeant to pull out and join the rest of the company if shooting was heard.

Bill Darby's Rangers were left behind to guard Gafsa against enemy advance once the main army forced had pulled out. He stationed his defenses and sentries about their darkened outpost, sending out patrols like Kness's to probe for enemy movements. "The enemy was approaching," said Darby. "But we were not certain when or in what number."[32]

Word was received at the Ranger command post that the enemy was advancing through the darkness in three columns. Darby sent one company forward to engage the enemy troops, but their reports a short while later brought roars of laughter. "The approaching 'enemy' was a herd of two or three hundred camels, kicking rocks as they moved along," Darby recalled.[33]

Les Kness's patrol moved a half mile beyond the listening station that had also reported enemy movement but found nothing. They returned to find that their platoon had pulled out. Darby had ordered his Rangers out of Gafsa to march down the long road toward Kasserine Pass. Kness would spend two hours struggling to catch up with the rest of his company. They neared the town of Feriana on February 15 only to find its citizens in a state of panic as they evacuated their homes.[34]

To Kness, Feriana was "bedlam." To squad leader Les Cook it was "chaotic," with villagers running in every direction. Men, women, and children were on the road, pushing buggies and pulling carts among swirling dust clouds. In addition to the civilians, the Rangers found some five hundred French troops in the process of fleeing Feriana before the Germans could reoccupy the Gafsa area. Captain Schneider had two of his sergeants commandeer two American troop trucks found parked alongside the main road.[35]

As his Rangers began loading onto the vehicles, the French troops came running. Kness ordered his men to push the French soldiers off the sides and back of the truck. The Rangers crammed into the trucks and were hauled into Feriana. Only once they were unloaded were the commandeered vehicles sent back to Gafsa for the use of other soldiers. "Captain Schneider got into a lot of trouble for this, and it is a wonder he wasn't tried for it," recalled Kness.[36]

The following day, Darby's Rangers moved through Thélepte before turning westward toward Dernaia Pass. His men spent the rest of the day holed up in a rocky area; kitchen trucks arrived to feed them and provide a fresh supply of water. The next morning Darby assembled his Rangers and told them that a German Panzer unit was about to cut the highway between them and the Allied lines. "We will have to walk out," Kness was informed by his commander.[37]

The Rangers were heavily armed with anti-tank ammunition, grenades, and even special anti-tank grenades nicknamed "sticky bombs." Covered in a strong adhesive, these grenades could be attached to enemy tanks or other vehicles once armed. Kness informed his men they would have to slip up close enough to physically slap them to the sides or bottoms of the armored vehicles. Darby had boldly encouraged his men to "make one hell of a fight" against Axis tanks. "If we encounter the Germans, God help the tanks!" he had proclaimed.[38]

We wouldn't stand a chance! thought Kness.

Darby's Rangers hiked more than twenty miles to reach their assigned post at Dernaia Pass, a grueling journey through the desert heat for infantrymen so heavily laden with weapons and ammunition. Aside from the stifling heat, there was the real danger of tripping a planted land mine near the Tunisian roadways. Sergeant Cook was adept at sniffing out such dangers. "I don't know how I spotted them," he admitted. "I just had a knack for it."[39]

At one point during the long march, Cook was on the right flank of his Iowa comrade, Lieutenant Kness, when he spotted an abnormality in the rocky soil ahead.

"No, Les!" Cook shouted as the officer was about to plant his right foot forward.

Shaken, Kness thanked his friend and added, "All right, Cook, you lead us through here from now on."

Many Rangers ran out of water by late in the afternoon, but Kness managed to nurse his canteen to the last drop. Even so, his tongue became swollen. His lips cracked and bled from dryness to the point that even talking was painful. After crossing the highway leading to Kasserine Pass, Darby's Rangers moved a mile farther into the small foothills. They passed through the deserted lean-to shelter village of a nomadic Arab tribe.

Several Rangers were parched enough to take their chances with a blood-crusted goatskin filled with water found hanging from a snaggled old tree. Even the bravest could stomach little more than a few sips of the vile liquid. Mike Kness worried that the bag appeared to contain blood. "My thirst didn't bother me as much after that," he said. The grueling forced march through the Tunisian desert was at least a learning experience on future rationing. "Those there cherished water from then on," said brother Les Kness.[40]

The road from Gafsa running past Feriana made a junction between Thélepte and a mountain labeled Djebel Krechem. From this junction one road branched westward toward Tébessa while the other continued north to Kasserine. "Intelligence officers analyzing the terrain and the enemy's capabilities reckoned that the main attack would come through Dernaia Pass towards Tebessa," Lieutenant Colonel Darby related. His four-hundred-odd Rangers were thus assigned covering duty on February 17, detailed to patrol both sides of the main road to Dernaia Pass.[41]

Already frustrated at missing the battles on February 14, Les Kness and his comrades were now resigned to more days of idle scouting and patrolling. In short order they would learn the wily Germans had again foiled the best reckoning of Allied intelligence. The Americans had been stunned with the bold Axis thrust at Faid Pass. This time the alert Ranger patrols at Dernaia Pass were bypassed and the Allies would be surprised again at a different Tunisian mountain pass called Kasserine.

SEVEN

KASSERINE PASS

Lieutenant Kurt Wolff was in high spirits. His Fifth Panzer Regiment had achieved their objective by delivering a smashing victory against the Americans the previous day at Sidi Bou Zid. Now his Fourth Company of the First Battalion was consolidated southwest of the town they had taken over.

All was quiet on February 15. Each Panzer company was widely separated by many kilometers. The American artillery, usually quite active, had been silent during the morning hours. *Everything is almost peaceful,* thought Wolff.[1]

Some soldiers exchanged captured American goods. Others took the opportunity to dash off letters to their loved ones back home. Their Mark III and Mark IV tanks sat baking in the desert sun, idly spaced among clusters of cacti. Wolff knew the relative calm was but a short-term luxury. In midafternoon the lieutenant moved to the back of his company to visit with his commander, who was preparing a cup of coffee. Wolff learned that his regiment would soon advance rather than wait or retreat.[2]

Wolff's Fifth Panzer Regiment, under Oberstleutnant (Lieutenant Colonel) Dirk Stenkhoff, consisted of his tank regiment, reinforced by elements of Panzer Artillerie Regiment 155. The full German force included additional artillery, infantry, and tanks from the Tenth and Twenty-First Panzer Divisions. The fifty tanks of Lieutenant Wolff's First Battalion were under charge of Hauptmann (Captain) Heinz Rohr. Wolff was still visiting with Rohr when the Fifth Panzer Regiment's communication officer appeared with startling news: large clouds of dust could be seen swirling to the west, in the direction of the American forces. The American tanks were clearly on the move.[3]

Wolff dashed back to a personnel vehicle to retrieve his maps as his company commander drew up hasty plans to counter the American force. Wolff soon counted thirty Sherman tanks rolling toward his position, roughly 5,000 meters ahead of his own Panzer unit. *In ten minutes, they will be opening fire on us!* Wolff thought.

His Fourth Company was nearest to the approaching American tanks. For the moment, other German companies were blissfully unaware of the impending danger. Wolff was still getting his tank engine started when Captain Rohr shouted out orders: "Drive straight at the enemy and stop him! The 1st Company will be led into their flank. Do not retreat under any circumstances."[4]

Wolff passed orders to his platoon as they rolled out toward a flat hill overgrown with cactus, his first objective. Ahead of his Panzers lay a level area about eight hundred meters across. Each of the American tanks would have to traverse this area, leaving Wolff's men to hope that their enemy did not recognize the danger and turn away. He was pleased when his company finally reached the hill, at which point he could clearly make out every detail of the U.S. tank battalion.[5]

By this point he estimated the American force to be even larger, numbering perhaps fifty tanks. Behind him lay Sidi Bou Zid, while five kilometers to the east he could see the First Company of his First Battalion just moving forward. The Americans appeared to be aware of only one other German Panzer regiment northeast of the town. Wolff watched the American force push forward to within 3,000 meters of his position before the Shermans stopped. Captain Rohr made it clear that no one was to open fire yet. "Only I will give the order to fire!" he directed by radio.[6]

Finding his First Company to be straggling toward the point where he hoped to ambush the American Shermans, Rohr excitedly called over the radio, "Step on it! Step on it!" For the moment, Wolff's Fourth Company of fourteen tanks could do nothing but await their orders. *Time is passing, and the Americans are still at a halt,* thought Wolff. *Are they uncertain about something?*[7]

Wolff worried that the Americans still held the upper hand if only their leaders could act quickly. At long last, the word was passed to the lieutenant: "Fourth Company, attack!"

An open plain lay before him, but orders were orders. Wolff advanced, ordering his last platoon to veer to the left to reach a favorable position. The German right platoon was first to dash across the broad plain, followed three minutes later by the center platoon. Wolff's own group of Panzers rolled to within 2,000 meters of the American tanks, just a few hundred yards shy of the optimal firing distance.

German artillery opened up on the American tank formation, causing them to begin shifting positions. First Division commander Rohr was pleased, noting that the Americans could not detect his tanks in the bright sun. Wolff's men estimated the distance to the white steel bodies of the enemy and asked excitedly when they could fire. Their shells were already in the firing chambers.[8]

To the lieutenant, the scene before him was more like a training field exercise than actual warfare. His Panzers stood ready to fire and not one of the Shermans had turned a turret in their direction.

As the German artillery ceased firing, the long-awaited orders from Hauptmann Rohr finally reached Lieutenant Wolff.

"Fourth Company, open fire!"

———

Wolff's Fifth Panzer Division faced only what Major General Pinky Ward's First Armored Division could piece together in short order. The rout at Faid Pass and Sidi Bou Zid had created a mass evacuation by II Corps. On Sunday night, Highway 15 became jammed with Army trucks, refugees, and livestock. On orders from British general Anderson, the Allied air bases at Feriana and Thélepte were to be abandoned next. The 3,500 troops began moving out during the early morning hours of Monday, February 15, destroying Allied aircraft with thermite charges in the process.

From his divisional command post in the Sbeitla cactus patch, Ward hastily scrounged a tank destroyer company, an infantry battalion from CCC, and a few artillery pieces. It was midmorning on February 15 when twenty-four-year-old Lieutenant Colonel James Alger led fifty-eight Sherman tanks (mainly M4s) of his Second Battalion, First Armored Regiment, out from Maktar to confront the Germans. Following the medium tank battalion on the flanks were a company of M3 75mm tank destroyers from the 701st Tank Destroyer Battalion, two batteries of self-propelled artillery from the Sixty-Eighth Armored Field Artillery Battalion, and, finally, half-tracks from the Third Battalion, Sixth Armored Infantry.[9]

War correspondent Ernie Pyle had visited the First Armored Division's command post several times but he was in awe of the number of German tanks he could now see rolling forward. In a meeting with Major General Ward earlier that morning, Pyle found him to be confident. "We are going to kick hell out of them today and we've got the stuff to do it with," Ward had pronounced. Shortly before noon a young lieutenant offered to drive Pyle into the heart of the American front to Djebel Hamra to watch the show. From a 2,000-foot crest on the mountain, Pyle and other correspondents gathered with II Corps officers. From their vantage point they could see Alger's tanks heading toward Sidi Bou Zid, thirteen miles distant. Beyond that town lay Djebels Ksaira and Lessouda.[10]

Alger's force of M4 Sherman tanks, crewed by brave but inexperienced men, moved forward at eight miles per hour at 1300 toward Sidi Bou Zid. Lighter-skinned tank destroyers nipped at their flanks like sheepdogs. The leading force created huge clouds of dust that liberally painted the trucks and half-tracks trailing the procession with infantrymen and artillery tubes. The choking dust served to both blind American drivers and make their tanks easy for the Germans to spot and target. It resembled an old-style cavalry charge, with tanks rolling forward in a rough V-shaped formation, with tank destroyers bringing up the rear. Along their path, fourteen swirling German Junkers Ju 87 Stukas swooped in to heckle them with bombs.[11]

Ward optimistically sent word via radio to Colonel Drake's men marooned on Djebel Ksaira to be on the lookout for help. "Be ready to jump on the bandwagon," one of Ward's staffers advised of the inbound salvation force. But, around 1445, Alger's armored division rolled right into the waiting German trap. The Germans expected a larger American force and therefore delayed their attack until all of Alger's meager group was in view. Veteran Mark IV Tigers lay waiting amidst olive groves and opened fire while other Panzers attacked Alger's flanks. German artillery, well placed and ready for the American counterattack, rained down on the American tankers and artillerymen.[12]

To the north, the Americans faced the Twenty-First Panzer Division, while on the southern end of the battlefield the Tenth Panzer Division lay in wait. From his seat atop Djebel Hamra, Ernie Pyle watched the battle through field binoculars. "Brown geysers of earth and smoke began to spout," he later wrote. As the battle grew in intensity, the war correspondent found a "ridiculous impingement of normalcy" amidst the chaos in the form of Arab civilians trying to continue their daily routine of herding camels and plowing fields. "Children walked along, driving their little sack-laden burros, as tanks and guns clanked past them," wrote Pyle.[13]

By 1615, Alger's tanks were fighting the Germans at point-blank range. Captain Provine Winkler's D Company was in the Panzer crosshairs, and his tanks began taking hits. An armor-piercing round exploded in his tank, killing his radio operator instantly. Corporal Robert Newton had been "damned glad" when he was assigned to his army's "elite" tanker division as a 75mm gunner. He was less excited now, suffering from burns to his face, hands, and chest. Two others from his crew had sustained head wounds. Captain Winkler's face was so badly burned by the blast that his eyes were scorched shut. The survivors helped one another from their burning mount, and Winkler was escorted to the next nearest tank to attempt to reach Alger by radio.[14]

As the desperate fighting continued, Alger reported by radio to CCC commander Colonel Robert Stack that the "situation is hard." Moments later a German round clipped the radio antenna from Alger's tank and communication was lost. Around 1645, armor-piercing rounds struck Alger's tank, killing his radio operator. Alger and his surviving crewmen jumped from their flaming tank and raced to take cover.[15]

The sky was filled with multicolored tracers. The German Panzers crashed past the flaming M4 wreckage that filled the desert floor. Only four Shermans from Alger's force survived the chaos. During their retreat west through heavy fire, one of the crews paused long enough to scoop up Captain Winkler, still stumbling blindly with his scorched face. Many of the injured American survivors, including Alger, were overrun and captured by the Germans and would soon join John Waters in a German POW camp.

Kurt Wolff's Fourth Company, First Battalion, Fifth Panzer Division, began scoring hits immediately and the first shells from his company torched three of Alger's Shermans. His heartbeat, which had been pounding in his chest as his tank began rolling, returned to a calmer rhythm as American armored vehicles exploded. The Tunisian landscape was soon bathed in red flames. Charred steel simmered below rising pillars of dark gray and black smoke. In the distance Wolff noted the Fifth Panzer's First Company gaining position and landing deadly shell hits. Within minutes, fifteen burning Shermans lay ahead of him as the German division maneuvered through the American wreckage.[16]

The Germans had waited to open fire until Alger's tank force emerged from crossing its third wadi. A classic tank-versus-tank battle ensued, but the hours-long fight was almost entirely one-sided. By 1740 the surviving tanks of Alger's unit were seen to depart the battlefield. The Tenth Panzer Division reported thirty-nine enemy tanks destroyed or captured, along with seventeen armored troop carriers, numerous guns, and about a hundred vehicles. "At night, the burning enemy tanks gave the appearance of a brightly lit street in a major city," recorded Oberleutnant Wilhelm Reile.[17]

Lieutenant Wolff noted witnessing only one American tank escape the Panzer assault and flee back toward its vanquished leader as the sun set. Amidst the burning wreckage of Shermans blazing around the hills, Wolff found his division commander to be laughing like a boy. He moved from company to company, asking, "Did you ever see anything like it?"[18]

Captain Rohr, commander of the First Battalion of the Fifth Panzer Regiment, was pleased when Field Marshal Rommel arrived overnight as his tankers were being refueled and rearmed. Standing beside one of his victorious tank crews, the Desert Fox explained his plan to Rohr and other officers, adding, "Immediately pursue and then continue to march as far as Algeria!"[19]

Rommel understood the chance at hand. "The inexperienced Americans were steadily battered down by my tankers," he wrote. "Large numbers of Grants, Lees and Shermans were blazing on the battlefield." His men had destroyed the bulk of the American force, leaving the remainder to flee to the west. He urged his Fifth Army to push straight on through the night, keeping his enemy on the run until they could take Sbeitla. "Tactical success must be ruthlessly exploited," he felt.[20]

While Wolff's Panzers had enjoyed their success, other German forces were ill-positioned. Oberleutnant Heinz Schmidt, former aide-de-camp to Field Marshal Rommel, was now second-in-command of the Second Battalion of Special Group 288. "We were excited at the thought of meeting Americans on the battlefield for the first time," he thought. His scout company, detailed to occupy Gafsa, was east of the main valley. By afternoon his troops had felt their way through minefields to find only debris of war. Schmidt's scouts would suffer artillery shelling and attacks by Allied dive-bombers through the next day. The direct conflict he so desired fell instead to other German regiments.[21]

The February 15 ambush of Jim Alger's Sherman tanks was one for the books, in the eyes of Kurt Wolff. "We had destroyed a whole tank battalion," he said. "It was truly a rare day."[22]

———

By 1800 all that was left were four Sherman tanks held in reserve below Djebel Hamra. Alger's offensive had been crushed. Along with the carnage of tanks, some three hundred American soldiers had been killed, wounded, or captured by the Germans. In two days of fighting, U.S. losses were estimated by CCA at 1,600 men, nearly a hundred tanks, fifty-seven half-tracks, and twenty-nine artillery pieces. That evening Pinky Ward, having listened to the battle on the radio, could only report to General Fredendall, "We might have walloped them, or they might have walloped us." In short order, the debacle became clear, and Ward realized his forces could not be rescued. Fredendall finally gave permission for Waters and Drake to try to break free from their two hilltops on the evening of February 15.[23]

The remaining men of John Waters's command on Djebel Lessouda, led by Bob Moore, retreated during the night parallel to Highway 13 toward a crossroads where Major General Ward had posted sentries. As the defeated infantrymen were assaulted by artillery barrages and German gunners, they made their way through the deadly desert. Shortly after sunrise on February 16, Moore was able to count only 432 survivors from his original force of 904 men.[24]

Colonel Thomas Drake and 1,900 men on the slopes of Djebel Ksaira and another adjacent hill, Djebel Garet Hadid, faced a similarly deadly retreat during the afternoon of February 16. He issued the code phrase "Bust the balloon," an order for his men to begin exfiltration. Far away, Major General Fredendall had already dismissed Drake's men over the phone by stating, "We have got to write him off." Disabling their vehicles by shooting up the engines and slashing tires, Drake's men began the march through the desert that night, hauling their wounded out on litters. Shortly after dawn on February 17, Drake's men were approached by a column of trucks some five miles west of Sidi Bou Zid. Machine-gun fire and German vehicles from the Twenty-First Panzer Division encircled the Americans until they were captured in small groups. A German officer shouted to Drake from the turret of a Tiger tank, "Colonel, you surrender."[25]

"You go to hell!" Drake shouted back.

Only a few hundred GIs would manage to cross the desert and avoid enemy captors, reaching Allies lines in some cases days later. Colonel Drake and some 1,400 men—including most of the 168th Infantry Regiment—had been lost, giving the Germans a high number of POWs. Forced to surrender, Drake was taken in a German major's car to the divisional headquarters of the Tenth and Twenty-First

Panzer Divisions. The German general saluted him and said, "I want to compliment your command for the splendid fight they put up. It was a hopeless thing from the start, but they fought like real soldiers."[26]

Drake found little consolation in the praise. His disgust at being captured turned to anger as the Germans allowed local Arab fighters to beat the captured Americans, strip them of their clothing, and pilfer all of their personal possessions. The POWs were then forced to march in columns of four, trailed by three German tanks and armed guards, waiting to strike, bayonet, or shoot any who straggled. The Americans were marched naked and shoeless through the desert, suffering from unbearable thirst, until they were allowed to huddle in the sand. Drake and his men practically froze in the piercing cold of the African night. They were moved the next day to a barbed-wire compound near Sfax, where they slept in the sand in a one-hundred-yard-square compound without sanitation, forced to live like pigs.[27]

―――――――

At 1040 on February 16, General Kenneth Anderson ordered the American II Corps to give up on further counterattacks. The U.S. forces continued falling back some fifty miles toward the Western Dorsal chain. The hope was that the Western Dorsal passes— particularly the vital Kasserine Pass—could be held to stop the German offensive.[28]

Frühlingswind was a sweeping success, and decisions were made quickly for the next step. "There were two possible ways to proceed," said Tenth Panzer Division staff officer Wilhelm Reile. "Either we would continue toward Sbeitla, which meant coming under Rommel's command, or veer off to Hadjeb el Aioun and roll up the front at Pichon." In a meeting with his division commander and General Heinz Ziegler, General von Arnim chose to order his troops on to Sbeitla, the gateway to Kasserine Pass. After Erwin Rommel's staff car arrived at Gafsa on Tuesday morning, February 16, he pushed forward to capture the Allied airfields at Feriana and Thélepte.[29]

Even as Sbeitla fell to the Germans, the Desert Fox was disturbed that Arnim had not fully exploited his successes at Sidi Bou Zid. Rommel did not accept Arnim's pleas that he could not advance much farther due to fuel and supplies becoming questionable. Rommel's desire was to assemble all available Axis forces for a major thrust through Kasserine Pass. As his command vehicle advanced, Rommel passed long columns of Arabs driving pack animals laden with loot. He and driver Rudy Schneider found the locals to be so delighted with their new Allied spoils of war that they presented German soldiers with many chickens and fresh eggs. Rommel noted that the Arabs were bitter toward the Americans who had destroyed their villages.[30]

Rommel hoped that his northwestern thrust through the pass would get him behind General Anderson's British First Army, which he could trap and annihilate at his leisure. He felt the Americans "were showing the lack of decision typical of men commanding for the first time in a difficult situation." Rommel requested of his superior, Field Marshal Albert Kesselring in Rome, that both the Tenth and Twenty-First Panzer divisions be placed under his command to attack the Allied supply depot at Tébessa and the areas north of it. As of February 17, Allied eavesdroppers learned that Rommel had only fifty-two German and seventeen Italian tanks under his command as he urged the push on Tébessa. This bold plan needed immediate action, but his superiors were slow to offer approval. At least one day was wasted while Kesselring and the Italian high command debated. When the go-ahead was finally given, it was given the code name Sturmflut (Hurricane), although the proposal was somewhat watered down from what the field marshal had initially proposed.[31]

Rommel wrote to his wife, Lu, that although he was in his final days as commander of the German Tunisian forces, his health was holding up. He hoped to soon "restore my old vigor." Under Sturm-flut, Axis forces were to push through Kasserine Pass, then head in the direction of Le Kef. Kesselring finally consented that Rommel should press his attack toward Tébessa and sent word on Friday morning, February 19, that he could have two Panzer divisions to sweep forward. It was not the strong encircling of Allied forces that Rommel had desired, but it was something. Rommel had the green light, and he acted accordingly to prepare for the battle of Kasserine Pass. Rommel was ready for the attack and told his aide, "I feel like an old war horse that has heard the music again."[32]

———————

The town of Sbeitla was in absolute chaos by the evening of February 16. The ancient settlement was crowded with hundreds of French colonial troops driven from Faid Pass two weeks earlier, as well as survivors from II Corps' most recent defeats near Sidi Bou Zid. Word that German Panzer divisions were moving west toward Sbeitla created panic as wounded were evacuated from hospitals and loaded onto trucks to rumble west toward Kasserine Pass.[33]

"It was hard to realize, being a part of it, that it was a retreat—that American forces in large numbers were retreating in foreign battle, one of the few times in our history," wrote correspondent Ernie Pyle. "We couldn't help feeling a slight sense of humiliation."[34]

Technician Fifth Grade Tom Morrison's company of the 601st Tank Destroyer Battalion had reached Sbeitla as word of the approaching Germans came down. He was amazed at the size of the Allied ammunition dump, which appeared to cover half a square mile. Morrison knew that trouble was brewing, but the only intelligence coming from his M3's radio was a high-frequency squeal. His tank destroyer battalion pushed far south of Sbeitla and set up a defensive perimeter at nightfall, with all guns pointing outward to be ready for any approaching Axis forces.[35]

Morrison saw artillery and tanks firing in the distance, working over elements of the First Armored Division. Distinctive colors allowed him to distinguish American and German tracers at night. Assigned guard duty until midnight, Morrison was approached by the S-3 (battalion operations officer) and acting commander of his division, Captain Ben Fuller, who had narrowly escaped from the Germans in early January when units of the 601st were overrun in Ousseltia Valley. Fuller planned to take a nap, but he requested that the young tanker wake him if the German tracers that could be seen dancing around both sides of their position should merge together.

Just as he was being relieved of duty at midnight, Morrison found the tracers joining, a sign the Germans were beginning to surround the area. He found Captain Fuller was still awake and aware of the situation. Fuller sent Morrison ten yards forward to continue a watch as outpost guard. Morrison's optimism was ebbing. He had heard that the First Armored had lost a great number of tanks and that the Thirty-Fourth Infantry Division at Fondouk had been overrun.[36]

To his relief, no German Panzers advanced during the night, but a different commotion further shook the young tank destroyer gunner. As the retreat from Sbeitla continued, Army engineers began demolishing installations: a pump house, a railroad trestle, an aqueduct, and even the ammunition dump. An earthshaking roar and brilliant yellow flame erupted across the Tunisian desert. To Morrison, it was "the damnedest explosion I ever saw. It lighted up the countryside like day." Sergeant Stefano Vita warned Morrison that German patrols were likely working the area, so the pair lay prone at their forward outpost, scanning the horizon until day began to break on February 17.[37]

From his First Armored Division command post near Sbeitla, Major General Ward could do little to stop the flight of French and Americans from the town. Brigadier General Ray McQuillin's CCA troops were among those shifting west toward Kasserine Pass until an angry Ward issued orders to McQuillin to halt his retreat and return to his original position. Ward phoned Fredendall in Speedy Valley at 0100 on February 17 to alert the II Corps commander that German Panzers were only three miles east of Sbeitla.[38]

Fearing the German advance, Fredendall took the opportunity to meekly abandon Speedy Valley, leaving his underground bunker project incomplete. His command headquarters was shifted farther north into a primary school building at the Algerian border town of Le Kouif, seventeen miles northeast of Tébessa. The nearest German Panzer was a good eighty miles distant as the American senior commander retreated while ordering CCB troops to shift forward. "Move the big elephants to Sbeitla, move fast, and come shooting!" Fredendall demanded of Brigadier General Paul Robinett.[39]

Ward positioned his armored divisions near Sbeitla during the early hours of February 17. Robinett's CCB was on Ward's right just east of town. Across Highway 13, the remnants of McQuillin's CCA anchored the left, while Colonel Stack's CCC provided a rearguard reserve just west of town. As Tom Morrison's M3 company was setting up position after dawn, he noted four Allied fighters hedgehopping over the dunes. Someone mistakenly opened fire on the friendly planes, causing them to retaliate and spray the tankers with machine-gun fire before the mistake could be straightened out.[40]

The Germans took a casual approach during the morning hours as the Allies retreated westward toward Kasserine Pass. A quarter hour before noon, their attack commenced with Wehrmacht infantry marching forward along Highway 13 and Panzers laying into Brigadier General Robinett's advance CCB forces. Lieutenant Colonel Herschel Baker's 601st Tank Destroyer Battalion was almost immediately embroiled in the action.

The 601st's Recon Company made first contact. Morrison waited as B Company fired several rounds before pulling back. His own A Company half-tracks then each fired several rounds while B Company retreated back through their echelon. The idea was for each company to fire, fall back, and re-form while the other company fired. Morrison believed this to be a good retreat policy, until his company commanders saw roughly three hundred Panzers moving down on them. At that point, B Company simply turned and moved out.[41]

While his count was lofty, Morrison's assessment of the hopeless situation was shared by others. Lieutenant Colonel Baker advanced in front of his tank destroyer platoon and directed their fire while standing exposed in the desert terrain. He and Lieutenant Robert Luthi would both later receive Silver Stars for directing their small force against the leapfrogging Panzer division, although Luthi's B Company M3 was destroyed in the process.[42]

Morrison's A Company fired about eight rounds before things were deemed too hot. His unit retreated behind B Company as the American tankers tossed out smoke pots to cover their exit. As the 601st rumbled back toward Sbeitla, they encountered some fifty tanks lined up outside of town, their guns training on the retreating half-tracks. Fortunately, the tanks proved to be First Armored Division Shermans, whose gunners were ordered to hold their fire as Baker raced through in his command jeep to avert a potential friendly-fire incident.[43]

As the 601st half-tracks retreated toward a rallying point, the unit's S-3, Captain Ben Fuller, acted as a sheepherder. With two M3s carrying command post radio equipment, he moved about the plains to ensure his men made it out safely. Germans tanks approached to within six hundred yards, and his men endured their heavy fire and that of nearby artillery as they fell back. By the time Fuller's track reached Sbeitla, he found the road going south was blocked by rock piles.[44]

An MP warned Fuller that the road to the south from Sbeitla was mined and pointed out a safer route. Four Messerschmitt fighters appeared overhead, bombing the town and strafing the gaggle of American military vehicles. Temporarily abandoned vehicles littered the town as soldiers took cover in the ruins of buildings. As Fuller passed each vehicle, he shouted to the men taking cover to get back in their vehicles, fire at the German planes, and keep moving. He and his first sergeant were forced to abandon their half-track as a pair of Me 109s came in strafing.

Fuller and his sergeant removed the machine gun from their M3 and commenced firing on the low-flying German fighters. As the second Me 109 came in, the sergeant fired a hundred rounds directly in front of it. Fuller excitedly watched the plane start smoking and lose altitude. Dropping to five hundred feet as it banked away, the Me 109 was seen to drop over the hills to the east.[45]

When Fuller's half-track reached the first crossroad out of town, he worked diligently under fire to coach his tank destroyer crews toward safety. As his A Company passed through Sbeitla, half-track gunner Tom Morrison was stunned by the burning and smoldering ruins of buildings. Burned-out trucks, jeeps, and shattered tanks further littered their pathway. French soldiers piled onto the half-tracks as they retreated past the charred town under the strafing Me 109s.[46]

By evening, German and Italian troops had moved into Sbeitla as Robinett's CCB continued westward. For tanker Morrison, his fighting spirit was drained by the time his 601st Battalion halted for the night to guard a key road crossing. His body was weak, racked with fever that a platoon medic soon diagnosed as amebic dysentery.[47]

Morrison would spend the next weeks fighting off the parasitical ailment in a hospital bed. By the time he was fully recovered and ready to fight again, he took in the sorry details of a major conflict he had missed at Kasserine Pass.

─────────

Twenty miles west of Sbeitla, Kasserine Pass pierced the Grand Dorsal mountain range near the ancient village of Kasserine. Only a mile wide, this key pass was flanked on the south by thickly wooded

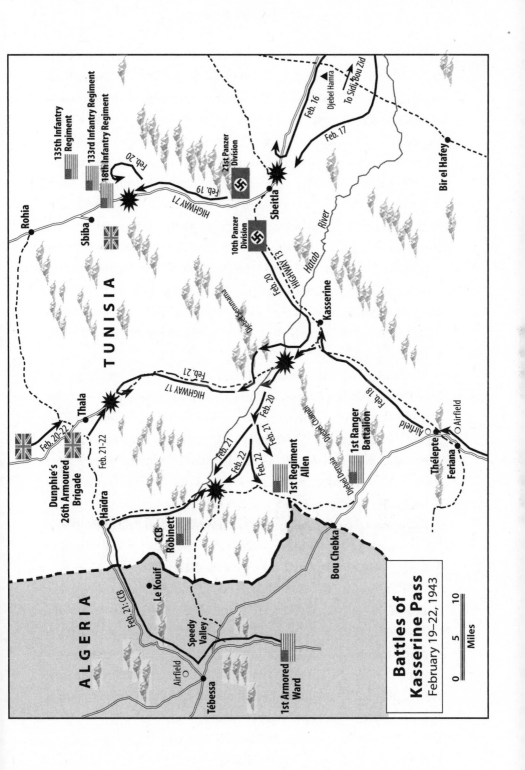

**Battles of
Kasserine Pass**
February 19–22, 1943

ALGERIA

TUNISIA

Rohia

Sbiba

Thala

Haïdra

Le Kouif

Speedy
Valley

Airfield

Tébessa

Dunphie's
26th Armoured
Brigade

Feb. 20–22

Feb. 21–22

Feb. 21: CCB

CCB
Robinett

1st Armored
Ward

Bou Chebka

135th Infantry
Regiment

133rd Infantry Regiment

18th Infantry Regiment

Feb. 20

21st Panzer
Division

HIGHWAY 17

Feb. 19

Sbeitla

Feb. 16

To Sidi Bou Zid

Djebel Hamra

Feb. 17

Bir el Hafey

10th Panzer
Division

HIGHWAY 13

Feb. 20

Hatab
River

Kasserine

Djebel Semmama

Feb. 21

HIGHWAY 17

Feb. 21

Feb. 20

Feb. 21

Feb. 22

Feb. 22

Feb. 22

Djebel Chambi

1st Regiment
Allen

1st Ranger
Battalion

Feb. 18

Djebel Hamra

Airfield

Thélepte

Airfield

Feriana

0   5   10
Miles

5,064-foot Djebel Chambi, Tunisia's tallest mountain. To the north, only 750 feet less in altitude, stood Djebel Semmama. Below the pass lay Highway 13, upon which the battered II Corps troops and tankers had retreated west from Sbeitla. West beyond Kasserine village, the road forked, with Highway 17 continuing north through the pass for another thirty miles toward the hilltop town of Thala.[48]

As Lloyd Fredendall prepared to defend the Western Dorsal barrier, he was left wondering where Rommel would strike next. Kasserine was not the only pass that cut through the mountains, and his forces were simply too thin to cover them all efficiently. Initially, Kasserine Pass was defended only by Colonel Anderson Moore's Nineteenth Combat Engineer Regiment, a 1,200-man unit mainly in place to handle construction versus fighting. The engineers began digging in on February 17 and would spend the next day and a half waiting for signs of the enemy.[49]

The following day Fredendall added a battalion from Terry Allen's First Infantry Division, a four-gun French artillery battery, and some tank destroyers, bringing the collective force stationed at Kasserine Pass to roughly 2,000 troops. On the evening of February 18, Fredendall phoned Colonel Alexander Stark, commander of Allen's Twenty-Sixth Infantry Regiment. He used one of his trademark colorful quips, a reference to a famous Confederate general who displayed great offensive leadership in the 1861 First Battle of Bull Run. "Alex, I want you to go to Kasserine right away, and pull a Stonewall Jackson," said Fredendall. "Take over up there."[50]

Stark's infantry moved through the night and arrived at Kasserine Pass at 0730 on February 19. He found only one platoon positioned on the slopes of Djebel Semmama, with four infantry companies occupying the low ground on the left side of the pass, while an engineer platoon and three companies held the right flats. Stark had little time to organize his forces for a true Stonewall Jackson maneuver before the first German elements began to show.[51]

The Desert Fox had choices to make. By February 18 his forces were stationed just beyond the Roman ruins west of Sbeitla as he contemplated his next move. His moves were directed by the Italian senior command, or Comando Supremo, headed by General Vittorio Ambrosio, chief of staff of the Italian Army. Ambrosio had set the town of Le Kef as the key objective, but Erwin Rommel also wished to push seventy miles toward Tébessa to overrun the vast Allied supply dump located there. Rommel had no regard for Ambrosio's desire to push forward toward Le Kef. "This was an appalling and unbelievable piece of shortsightedness," he wrote. "A thrust along that line was far too close to the front and was bound to bring us up against the strong enemy reserves."[52]

Rommel studied the terrain with his field glasses, peering at the distant peaks of Semmama and Chambi, which marked the narrow bottleneck of Kasserine Pass. He could lead his forces to the left through this pass. He could instead opt to move right along Highway 71 toward the northern objective of Le Kef, which lay some eighty miles away, by traveling along the eastern flank of the Grand Dorsal. He issued his orders at 0450 on Friday, February 19: "Get ready to march immediately." He would hold much of his Tenth Panzer Division near Sbeitla in reserve while sending the Twenty-First Panzer Division north on Highway 71 toward his primary objective of Le Kef. In the meantime his Afrika Korps would drive west and capture Kasserine Pass.[53]

On the morning of February 19, Afrika Korps reconnaissance soldiers were greeted by cold wind, heavy rains, and accurate fire from the American artillery covering the pass. General Karl Bülowius, commander of the Afrika Korps, opened up with heavy artillery fire at 1000, followed a half hour later by his Panzergrenadier Regiment Afrika infantrymen attacking the Twenty-Sixth Infantry on the northeastern side of the pass. This attack made limited progress. At noon, Panzer Battalion Stotten was committed to the fight, but the Americans managed to hold on. Allied reinforcements arrived during the day: more tank destroyers, a small British armored force posted on the road to Thala, and a battalion from the Thirty-Ninth Infantry Regiment, Ninth Division.

Oberleutnant Heinz Schmidt led the Second Battalion of Special Group 288 in an attack on the American right flank at Kasserine Pass. Although his trucks were widely spaced, one was disabled by artillery fire as the Germans approached the foot of a slope. A deep wadi forced his men to detruck and advance on foot into the rugged cliffs. As Schmidt's scouts crested a steep ridge, they were fired upon by an American machine-gun nest thirty yards away. The Germans overpowered the gunners and sent them fleeing, leaving them in control of the high ground.[54]

Schmidt mustered an assault force of three officers and twenty-one men armed with automatic weapons to seize a small bridge on the road below their position. The first U.S. truck that approached the bridge fired on Schmidt's men and roared away as dusk approached. Hidden on both sides of the road, his men assaulted the next truck with machine-gun fire. "The truck swerved off the road and capsized," said Schmidt, whose men seized four American prisoners. In the hours that followed, his scouts held the bridge and continued to take Allied prisoners from both advancing infantrymen and unsuspecting trucks that were riddled with machine-gun fire.[55]

In the late afternoon Bülowius sent the Germans forward again with support from Italian tanks, but they ran afoul of American minefields planted by the engineers. That evening the Germans intensified their artillery pounding of Kasserine Pass and continued to push their infantry forward. Some of the patrols were successful in overrunning solitary U.S. companies, capturing some of the engineers and causing a number of others to retreat toward the rear.[56]

A frustrated Lieutenant Colonel Stenkhoff reported to his commander, "Our tank attack is at a standstill as a result of barbed wire obstacles, mine, and antitank guns, and also because of enemy artillery. Ten breakdowns up to now." Stenkhoff's superior sent word to call off the attack for the evening, allowing his men to regroup, refuel, and resupply with ammunition.[57]

―――――――

At his new command post at Le Kouif, Major General Fredendall was becoming despondent from the troubling news coming in from Tunisia. He made plans to abandon his supply depot at Tébessa, although French general Alphonse Juin urged him to hold on to the key ground, pledging to fight to the end.

Fredendall sent word to General Eisenhower on the afternoon of February 19 that Orlando Ward's First Armored Division was in a bad state of disorganization. "Ward appears tired out, worried, and has informed me that to bring new tanks in would be the same as turning them over to the Germans," Fredendall said. "Under the circumstances, do not think he should continue in command. Need someone with two fists immediately."[58]

Fredendall's chief adversary, Field Marshal Rommel, was more decisive in his moves the following morning. Dawn of February 20 was a cold, wet, and foggy scene as Rommel moved to Kasserine village to inspect the progress of his troops in taking the key pass. Meeting with General Bülowius, the Desert Fox voiced his displeasure that Afrika Korps infantry battalions were sluggish. Rommel knew he had little time left to secure his victory. Montgomery's Eighth Army was still far to the east but approaching the Mareth Line. Finding his Tenth Panzer Division resting comfortably near Sbeitla, Rommel complained that his men were too slow. Division commander Brigadier General Fritz von Broich tried to explain that he was waiting for an infantry battalion to attack first. Rommel, furious that valuable time was being wasted, ordered Broich and other senior commanders to fetch the motorcycle battalion. "I was extremely angry and ordered the commanders to take themselves closer to the front where they could get a proper view of the situation."[59]

Rommel's presence had a positive effect. His German Army employed a rather new weapon, *Nebelwerfer*. These six-barreled mortars fired seventy-five-pound high-explosive rounds that were quickly dubbed "Screaming Meemies" by the Americans for the screeching sounds they created while in flight. The Tenth Panzer Division finally moved in force through the pass, where they were met by a handful of British tanks and American tank destroyers positioned in roadblocks. The outnumbered Allied armored vehicles would prove ineffective in stopping rounds from the German forces.[60]

Stark's forces began to crumble through the afternoon, as many were taken prisoner and others spiked their artillery pieces and retreated. PFC Dominic "Nick" Martello, a twenty-five-year-old from New Orleans, faced frustration that was typical of the members of the Ninth Infantry Division at Kasserine Pass. When Martello had come ashore in North Africa, he was the driver of a half-track armed with 75mm howitzers. Once his vehicle was disabled, he was forced to join the rest of the "dogfaces" of the Thirty-Ninth Infantry Regiment. "The heaviest stuff we had was BAR rifles, so they put us out on the road to shoot at the Germans," said Martello of the Kasserine battle. "But when you have a .30-caliber rifle and a tank coming at you, you're just not going to be able to survive."[61]

Martello's squad was forced to dive into a cactus patch during the hottest action on the afternoon of February 20. He figured he could pull needles from his rear easier than enemy lead. Bullets shredded the cactus above his head, leaving Nick and his men stranded through the late afternoon. One soldier near him was killed and another was hit in the hand with shrapnel. Martello felt fortunate to still be alive, praying to escape once darkness arrived.

By day's end, the U.S. infantry had suffered nearly five hundred killed, wounded, and missing. The Kasserine valley floor was littered with broken, burning tanks and half-tracks. By the following afternoon Rommel's Afrika Korps was solidly in control of the hills on either side of the pass and began pushing through. Once on the western side of the pass, the Desert Fox faced two roads. One went southwest toward the Tébessa supply center, while the other led north to Thala and then on to the town of Le Kef. Rommel's objective in Operation Sturmflut was the town of Le Kef, but he was not enthusiastic about enveloping the British First Army. In the end, the field marshal sent forces down both routes.[62]

Kampfgruppe DAK (Deutsches Afrika Korps) went up the road toward Tébessa, while the Tenth Panzer traveled north toward Thala and Le Kef. By this time, more and more Allied units were being redeployed and came into battle, stiffening resistance. Colonel Paul Robinett's CCB of the First Armored Division gave the Germans a rough time on the Tébessa road. The Axis drive was stalled by accurate tank and artillery fire, and American infantry pushed the Germans back, eventually recapturing some equipment that had been lost earlier. Rommel begrudgingly acknowledged that the Allied counterattack was very skillful.[63]

German forces driving down the northern road enjoyed greater successes against the Allied forces defending Thala. During the afternoon of February 20, Brigadier General Charles Dunphie's Twenty-Sixth Armoured Brigade fought hard on Highway 71, two miles north of Kasserine Pass, but could not match the German equipment. British Crusader and Valentine tanks were outgunned and outranged, and their armor was thinner. Thick black plumes of smoke filled the desert sky as British tanks were knocked out. Dunphie was forced to pull back to a ridge three miles south of Thala, having lost 38 tanks, 28 guns, and 571 men captured. The road to Thala was open after the British resistance crumbled. Field Marshal

Rommel noted, "The action took place at point-blank range, and the enemy soon abandoned his tanks and vehicles and tried to escape on foot over the hills."[64]

Axis forces had suffered their own casualties, although personnel losses were relatively light. Some individual Italian units had been decimated. The main problem for the Axis was a bad shortage of ammunition and fuel. More Allied units were joining the fight, some from as far away as Morocco. Axis advances, once promising, slowed to a crawl or in some cases were stopped cold in their tracks on February 21. That morning Rommel moved forward to Kasserine Pass, where he inspected the destroyed American tanks. "The enemy's plan now appeared to be to fight delaying actions in new positions and to stay on the defensive." The Desert Fox decided to counter this Allied move by pressing immediately on the American and British rear guard.[65]

Nick Martello and his squad from the Thirty-Ninth Infantry Regiment survived the February 20 fighting but were captured the next day. The survivors from his unit tried hiking back toward friendly lines during the night, but their presence was betrayed by local Arabs. Martello was disheartened, but his men had little choice but to surrender once a German tank crew approached them. It was a hard pill for him to swallow after all that his buddies had fought and died for. "When you still have the fight in you but you don't have anything to fight with, how are you going to fight against a tank?" said Martello.[66]

Weighing two hundred pounds at the time of his capture, Martello would emerge from German POW camps twenty-seven months later too malnourished to even walk, weighing a mere eighty-seven pounds.

=====

Bill Darby's First Ranger Battalion was not in position to offer assistance to the II Corps troops under fire near Kasserine Pass. His hundreds of Rangers had been stationed to the southwest at Dernaia Pass, on the hill line west of Thélepte, near the town of Bou Chebka, to handle reconnaissance and intelligence duties along key Tunisian roadways.

At 0800 on February 20, one of Darby's rearguard patrols was approached by two sedans, a truck, and a motorcycle moving along the Feriana–Tébessa highway. The Rangers opened fire, destroying the truck and capturing one of the sedans. The motorcyclist and other sedan fled the scene, leaving three Italians dead and seven captured.[67]

During the early afternoon, Darby's patrols halted another sedan approaching them on the highway. Italian soldiers dismounted the vehicle and disarmed the first Ranger who approached them. Private Carl Lehmann, positioned on a bluff overlooking the road, opened fire and began hitting the Italian soldiers. Other B Company Rangers joined in firing machine guns as the Axis soldiers scrambled for cover. When the smoke settled, Lehmann and his fellow Rangers had taken one wounded prisoner and killed another three Italians.[68]

These first successes were followed on February 21 by the Rangers destroying a German truck with a World War I–vintage 37mm anti-tank gun and capturing two jeeps and a Volkswagen sedan. Eight Germans, seven noncommissioned military policemen and an officer—who errantly believed they were proceeding through a safe zone—were taken prisoner. Phil "Snapdragon" Stern, the Ranger photographer, was part of the patrol involved in this capture. Stern removed a Luger from the German officer, but found he did not have the stomach for shooting an unarmed opponent. "I never saw a guy deflate so fast," wrote Stern. "He turned yellow. His humiliation was lovely."[69]

The loudest prisoner taken from this German procession was a terrified little dachshund that refused to stop barking. "She was the mascot for the Afrika Korps' 10th Panzer Division," wrote Stern.

"Rommel had her named 'Fritzi.'" Although the Rangers were quick to rename her "Nazi Bitch," the mutt became a favorite and was soon being fed American C rations. "After three days of food, sleep, and humane treatment, we indoctrinated her to the Allied cause," said Stern.[70]

Lieutenant Colonel Darby's Rangers remained on station at Dernaia Pass, attacking any Axis vehicles that attempted to pass them by. They also conducted scouting missions into the nearby terrain to attack any Italian patrols. Darby considered his men to be real veterans by this point. "We believed ourselves masters of any situation and were mentally prepared to accept any task," he later wrote.[71]

The occasional brushes with German and Italian vehicles marked the only action for the Rangers during this period. Second Lieutenant Les Kness had a German motorcyclist run up on his Dernaia Pass roadblock, only to turn tail as an American 37mm opened up on him. The lucky rider expertly weaved his way back down the road as Kness noted thirty-seven shell bursts all around his motorcycle. Such pass protection duty left Kness clamoring for real action and pessimistic that his meager forces could repel any major German thrust that might appear.[72]

Kness's Rangers would continue their rearguard actions near Dernaia for the next week, until the Battle of Kasserine Pass was concluded, and Darby's men were relieved by the Sixtieth Infantry.

———

Erwin Rommel studied his maps on the morning of February 21 at his command post near Kasserine village. His army was currently divided between Kasserine Pass and Sbeitla, challenging his ability to simultaneously drive north toward Thala and west toward Tébessa.

His decision was finalized by an intelligence report arriving to him at 1125. Wehrmacht scouts reported that no substantial Allied forces could be found at Djebel el Hamra, a rugged escarpment that lay twenty miles west of Kasserine Pass. Rommel thus ordered his Afrika Korps to push to el Hamra while his Tenth Panzer Division continued on up Highway 71 toward Thala with a main attack. "By deploying troops at several danger spots, I hoped to split the enemy forces far more than our own," Rommel theorized.[73]

General Bülowius surged forward toward Djebel el Hamra on the afternoon of February 21, but German intelligence proved faulty. The pass was fortified with First Infantry troops under Major General Terry Allen and Colonel Robinett, who had eight battalions and a sizable quantity of artillery batteries. Bülowius's forty Panzers and infantrymen were hit by accurate Allied artillery fire as they advanced and were forced to withdraw before dusk. By 1800 the Germans had lost ten tanks to only one lost by Robinett.[74]

Rommel had gone forward to observe this action, continually urging his men to keep their speed up. He moved up to where his advance scouts were pinned down by artillery barrages in a cactus patch. "Confusion was complete," he noted. The Desert Fox was pleased to see a number of British tanks destroyed and moved on in the late afternoon to watch over another engagement involving his Afrika Korps, where he found the American defense to be "very skillfully executed."[75]

Rommel ordered Bülowius to make a sweep to flank the Americans in the south and catch them in the rear. In the darkness and heavy rain that fell overnight, Bülowius and his men became lost, wandering seven miles south of Djebel el Hamra. Two of his grenadier battalions attacked at dawn on February 22 and succeeded in capturing five American howitzers, smaller fieldpieces, and thirty vehicles. The Americans retreated, allowing the grenadiers to take Hill 812.[76]

Once the morning fog lifted at 0900, the German grenadiers were left exposed. Bülowius ordered two dozen Panzers and the Fifth Bersaglieri forward to create a diversion for his trapped infantry, but they soon ran afoul of a thunderous Allied barrage. The artillery-men fired thousands of rounds during the next hours at the bounti-ful German targets: 88mm batteries, tanks, trucks, and infantrymen. Rommel met at 1300 with his superior, Field Marshal Kesselring, and his subordinates—who had landed at Kasserine and had been hauled to the front lines in the Desert Fox's staff car—to assess the situation. "We agreed that a continuation of the attack towards Le Kef held no prospect of success and decided to break off the offensive by stages," wrote Rommel.[77]

By 1400 the Afrika Korps was in retreat. The Sixteenth Infantry retook Hill 812, recapturing every gun and truck lost during the morning and rounding up hundreds of German and Italian POWs in the process. During the same period Field Marshal Rommel led his main attack toward Thala along Highway 71 with his Tenth Pan-zer Division. He expected only Americans north of Kasserine Pass but instead was greeted by a stout British armored division.

Rudy Schneider positioned Rommel's staff car to the left of the highway. General Friedrich "Fritz" Freiherr von Broich was on the right as the Germans churned slowly forward for hours, slowly forc-ing the British to retreat after losing fifteen tanks. As the battle con-tinued into the morning of February 22, the British were reinforced by 2,200 American artillerymen and forty-eight guns, led by Briga-dier General Stafford Irwin of the Ninth Infantry Division. The re-newed Allied force held the Germans in check, and Rommel halted his advance.

Kesselring found the Desert Fox to be physically worn out and psychologically fatigued. His army had only four days of rations left, little ammunition, and fuel enough to travel less than two hundred miles. Kesselring returned to Rome and formally authorized the withdrawal of the Afrika Korps, whose troops began falling back after darkness on February 22.[78]

The Germans suffered more casualties during the retreat. Baldur Köhler, whose Tenth Panzer Division Mark III had taken part in the Valentine's Day slaughter of American Sherman tanks a week before, had been lucky so far. But his good fortunes faded on the afternoon on February 22 as his company joined those falling back. Köhler was atop the turret as his tank was subjected to American artillery fire. Five shrapnel fragments ripped through his back, resulting in severe muscle damage and the loss of full movement of his right arm. Tanker Köhler was taken to an aid station and would be moved through Sicily and Italy before being returned to Germany for further surgery. His part in the frontline action was thus ended in the closing hour of the Kasserine Pass battles.[79]

The Desert Fox had been stopped. His command car headed through Gafsa back to Mareth for him to regroup and assess his losses. In their first extended combat of the war, the Americans had sustained losses of 6,600 killed, wounded, or captured—more than 20 percent of their entire 30,000 personnel engaged in the battles. The German reported the capture of 4,026 Allied soldiers against their own losses of 1,000, including 201 killed in action. At Kasserine Pass, II Corps alone lost 183 tanks, 194 half-tracks, 208 pieces of artillery, 512 trucks and jeeps, plus fuel, ammunition, and rations. Despite such heavy losses, the U.S. Army was the real winner at Kasserine Pass by stopping Rommel's offensive.[80]

The victory had been costly. On the positive side, the American forces had endured their most severe testing ground. They had gained experience and improved their knowledge of weapons and battlefield tactics. But the conflicts near Kasserine Pass highlighted ugly flaws in American leadership, including incompetent and mediocre commanders.

Fredendall's line had buckled, with men fleeing for their lives. Eisenhower's inner circle fretted that the U.S. Army had taken its "worst walloping" and perhaps its stiffest setbacks of ground forces yet in World War II. One staffer recalled that Ike's headquarters "had all the cheer of an empty funeral parlor." Omar Bradley later wrote of Kasserine Pass: "It was probably the worst performance of U.S. Army troops in their whole proud history."[81]

Change was inevitable.

EIGHT

"YOU MUST HAVE A BETTER MAN"

The white powder dusting the rocky plains was the first Sergeant John Nowak had seen in Tunisia. Since arriving in North Africa in December with the 601st Tank Destroyer Battalion, he had endured plenty of cold nights, but the snowfall during the early morning hours was noteworthy for him. The twenty-four-year-old from Ludlow, Massachusetts, had spent his first months in Algeria and Tunisia serving as a .50-caliber gunner on an armored antiaircraft vehicle before joining Lieutenant Colonel Herschel Baker's anti-tank division.[1]

Nowak had since endured his share of strafing from German aircraft while hauling about the desert with the 601st to protect various Allied strongholds. Going into the Kasserine Pass action, Nowak had been transferred from his antiaircraft vehicle to serve as the machine gunner for the vehicle of Lieutenant John Dee Yowell, the Texan commander of the First Platoon. His M3 had handled mainly rearguard duties during the German assault, but Nowak had been close enough to observe the shells from Rommel's tanks and the fires burning in Sbeitla.

As his platoon moved forward on the morning of February 25, Nowak watched the snow disappear rapidly under the rising sun. Rolling through the Kasserine Pass battlefields, he saw considerable wrecked and discarded German equipment and a number of Italians who had been rounded up as POWs. He heard rumors that the Italians carried clean white handkerchiefs for that very purpose, and he was left with the feeling that these troops did not relish fighting nearly as much as did the Germans.[2]

The weeks following the Kasserine Pass battles saw the American II Corps struggling to find solid leadership. Nowak's tank destroyer battalion would take up station in a forest near Bou Chebka for the next two weeks, time spent reorganizing and replacing vehicles and personnel lost in the previous actions.

First Lieutenant Edward Josowitz, one of the officers of Nowak's 601st battalion, wrote that the tank destroyer men spent this time with numerous classes, drills, and ten-minute alerts. Captain Michael Paulick lectured on German mines, while Lieutenant Samuel Richardson took advantage of the idle time by solidly beating "the Old Man to the tune of 2,500 dollars" in a great poker match.[3]

The "Old Man" of the 601st Tank Destroyer Battalion was Lieutenant Colonel Baker, who would be decorated with the Silver Star for his gallantry in the recent Kasserine Pass battle. "The 601st was 'Baker's Outfit' and it was not long before it had taken on much of the Old Man's hell-for-leather personality," Josowitz recalled. Their leader's resolve would see them through great trials in the near future, but for the moment Baker was content to let his men take their rest in the Bou Chebka forest. With the Germans cleared for the moment, the local citizenry made their way into the Allied camp to trade their stashed loot for American goods. "Mattress covers were still worth a thousand francs or two hundred eggs and used, dried, repacked tea leaves had a ready market," wrote Josowitz. "Vino, rough, rugged vino, turned up out of nowhere in fabulous quantities."[4]

In the wake of the Kasserine Pass battles, Rommel's army faded back across the central Tunisian plateau toward the Eastern Dorsal, planning to recapture some of its lost ground from Anderson's First Army and Montgomery's Eighth Army. General Eisenhower was enthusiastic that the Germans had been forced to fall back from Kasserine Pass. He cabled Fredendall on February 22 that he believed II Corps would "play an effective part in driving the enemy from Tunisia." The senior Allied commander followed with a phone call that night to tell Fredendall that the proper time to act aggressively was now. He should counterattack Rommel in the open.[5]

Fredendall offered only a cautious response, stating that he was unaware of Rommel's exact position and that he preferred to spend another day on the defensive. Eisenhower had already been asked by Fredendall to relieve Pinky Ward of command of the First Armored Division. But Ike had received different intelligence that Ward had actually helped maintain order during the II Corps' chaotic retreat. Eisenhower was in a quandary. So he sent orders to hard-nosed Major General Ernest Harmon, who was in Morocco training the Second Armored Division for the upcoming Sicily invasion. Harmon was told to assume command of either the First Armored or the entire II Corps, whichever seemed most appropriate. "Well, make up your mind, Ike," replied Harmon. "I can't do both." Eisenhower could only admit he did not know which was best.[6]

Harmon reached Le Kouif at 0300 on February 23, intending to serve as a chief assistant to Fredendall. The latter had received word from Ike that Ward was not to be replaced, as he had proven himself in the latest actions. Harmon found that Fredendall appeared to be drunk. Taking a note from Fredendall that introduced him as the new deputy corps commander, Harmon proceeded to visit the II

Corps commanders at Thala to take the pulse of the state of the American command in North Africa.

Ike knew that either Ward or Fredendall must go in the wake of the Kasserine disaster. He realized that his II Corps commander was not acting aggressively but instead merely passing orders from his distant command hideout. Fredendall tried to place blame on others: he had already asked Ike to relieve Ward and he complained that he had been hampered by the heavy-handedness of his British superior Anderson. Fredendall had failed on multiple levels: he had lost self-control; he had violated basic principles of command doctrine; and he had ignored the benefit of displaying personal bravery.[7]

During the following days, word continued to trickle in to Eisenhower suggesting his next course of action regarding Lloyd Fredendall. British General Alexander stated to Ike, "I'm sure you must have a better man than that." Brigadier General Lucian Truscott, one of Eisenhower's staff officers, voiced his opinion that II Corps would likely never fight well under Fredendall.[8]

Ernie Harmon's assessment of the II Corps commander, following days of touring the frontline troops, was even more damning. As he headed back to Morocco on February 28, he gave Eisenhower his evaluation of Fredendall. Harmon felt that if Fredendall remained in command, there was danger that his II Corps might disintegrate. "He's no damned good," he said. "You ought to get rid of him."[9]

Major General George Patton was troubled by the news from Tunisia. His first hint at the danger his son-in-law Johnny Waters had faced came during a brief visit he made from Algiers to Lieutenant General Mark Clark's headquarters in Morocco on February 19.

Sipping whiskey over a turkey dinner that evening, Clark related the American rout at Sidi Bou Zid and Kasserine Pass. But he assured Patton that Waters was reported to have gotten out safely. Back in his command headquarters in Algiers, Patton's mood darkened as reports trickled in. "Apparently, John's battalion was destroyed," he confided to his diary on February 22. "I have no news of him." On February 23 he wrote to his wife, Bea, "John's battalion was wiped out but he is thought to be safe. Harmon went up to take command of the 1st A. D. [First Armored Division] and will let me know."[10]

Hoping to ease his fears, Patton took in his first movie in four months, *Road to Morocco*, a 1942 comedy starring Bing Crosby and Bob Hope. Patton continued his planning for Operation Husky, the Allied invasion of Sicily, and took time to inspect the troops training in his region. Visiting the Second Armored Division on February 27, he found them lacking proper disposition, with artillery not properly dug in. "I raised hell," he told his diary. Two days later he visited the Third Division, wearing his helmet and ivory-handled pistols "to impress men with the need of being properly equipped."[11]

The truth about his son-in-law finally hit Patton on March 2, when he received a visit from Ernie Harmon, fresh from his tour of II Corps. Harmon informed him that Johnny Waters had been missing in action since February 14, after German tanks had cut through their position near Sidi Bou Zid. "He stayed on the hill with 150 men to cover the retreat," Patton wrote. "Later Fredendall radioed him to surrender, as he could not be rescued. This was a mistake, but I hope John complied. According to Harmon, Fredendall is a physical and moral coward."[12]

Patton was irritated with the actions of the II Corps commander. "Fredendall never went to the front at all, and tried to make Harmon the goat. Harmon won the battle," he wrote. Patton put in a call to Eisenhower, who informed him that he had wired Waters's wife, Bea, that her husband was missing in action. Patton wrote to both Beas, his wife and daughter, and tried to be uplifting for his daughter. Privately, in his diary that night, he scribbled, "I fear John is dead."

The following day Patton took a break from planning and his

mental anguish to enjoy a duck hunt on a 10,000-acre farm north-west of Port Lyautey. "I shot badly," he admitted. He found more in-terest in two Roman ruins his group encountered during their trek, although their excursion was challenged by their amphibious vehicle becoming stuck. Eight Arabs struggled to pull the vehicle free by rope until they were aided by two American soldiers. "This shows the value of Arab labor," Patton darkly noted.[13]

While Patton tried to relieve his depression in Algiers, events were in motion at high levels that would soon offer him the chance to avenge the assumed loss of his son-in-law. Eisenhower had heard plenty of advice from Allied leaders on the lack of cohesion Freden-dall had displayed. One of his trusted subordinates, Omar Bradley, returned from a tour of the II Corps command in early March and privately told Ike of the situation. "I've talked to all the division com-manders," said Bradley. "To a man, they've lost confidence in Fre-dendall as the corps commander."[14]

Eisenhower knew what had to be done. Senior officers—Harold Alexander and Kenneth Anderson of the British Army, plus Ernie Harmon and Lucian Truscott of the U.S. Army—were demanding Fredendall's immediate relief. Ike's chief of staff, Major General Wal-ter Bedell "Beetle" Smith, returned from his own tour of the front, concluding that Fredendall was either "incompetent or crazy or both." Eisenhower responded by offering the job to three-star lieutenant gen-eral Mark Clark, who declined on the belief that the offer was some-thing of a demotion for him. It left Ike with one other obvious choice.[15]

Patton had just returned from a ride on a large, borrowed Thor-oughbred horse at 1640 on March 4, when he found that General Eisenhower had called for him. He was ordered to be ready to leave in the morning for extended field service in Tunisia. A quick phone call to Beetle Smith, his friend on Ike's staff, informed him that he might be assuming command of II Corps. To his diary, Patton wrote that he

would be "taking over rather a mess, but I will make a go of it."
He wrote that he expected more trouble handling the British than
the Germans, adding a quote: "God favors the brave, victory is to the
audacious."[16]

Here, finally, was the chance for Patton to prove his years of ad-
vocating aggressive tank warfare. During his prewar training of
tankers, he had emphasized two strong principles. First, he believed
his armored forces must "find out where the enemy is, hold him in
front by fire, and get around him." Second, he believed in producing
in his enemies "the fear of the unknown." This meant employing
whatever tactic was necessary, even distracting an enemy to throw
them off base. Patton had once advised, "If you can't think of anything else to do, throw a fit, burn a town, do something!"[17]

Unable to take any of his regular general staff officers with him,
Patton gathered several of his trusted aides, including Captain Dick
Jenson and Lieutenant Alexander Stiller. They headed for the Mai-
son Blanche airfield outside of Algiers, where they were met by Generals Eisenhower and Beetle Smith. Ike informed him that he would
be relieving Fredendall of command and handing II Corps to Patton. Eisenhower told him that relieving Fredendall was "on grounds
that it was primarily a tank show" and that Patton knew more about
tanks.[18]

From Algiers, Patton and his group of trusted aides flew to Constantine, where they met with General Harold Alexander of the
newly created British Eighteenth Army Group. Patton was informed
by his new British boss that his command would answer to Alexander's army group as an independent command. Alexander tasked
Patton with helping Montgomery penetrate the Mareth Line. Patton
was to tie up as much of Rommel's army as he could and secure
Gafsa, about fifty miles southwest of Sidi Bou Zid, as a supply base
for the British Army.[19]

Patton found General Alexander to be "competent" and complimentary. Patton was told Alexander "wanted the best Corps Commander he could get and he had been informed that I was the man." Talks with the British staff continued until 0100 on March 6. After a rest of only hours, Patton was on his way to the II Corps headquarters.[20]

═══

Second Lieutenant Henry "Red" Phillips was repulsed by the smell of death and the haunting sight of charred rubble in Tunisia. On March 1, his Forty-Seventh Infantry Division reached Sbeitla, the ancient desert crossroads midway between Faid Pass to the east and Kasserine Pass to the west. He saw naked bodies of American soldiers, stripped by Arab scavengers, still lying about as grisly food sources for dogs and buzzards. Blackened vehicle remains and scorched tank hulls from the previous month's battles protruded from the desert sand in all directions. *This is a graphic, demoralizing way to start getting serious about war,* thought Phillips.[21]

The recent American losses had prompted II Corps command to move the Forty-Seventh Infantry from Port Lyautey to Tlemcen, Algeria, in early February. Continued hot action in Tunisia forced the regiment to push on to the capital at Algiers, where they were loaded into two-and-a-half-ton trucks for round-the-clock transport to Tunisia as the battles near Kasserine Pass raged.

Arriving at Sbeitla, the Third Battalion of the Forty-Seventh Infantry Division, to which Phillips belonged, was assigned to protect an Allied airstrip west of town. Lieutenant Colonel John Evans, the battalion commander, struggled to find a suitable defensive position for his small force. Phillips could see nothing to keep enemy tanks from moving cross-country around either flank, completely beyond range of his division's largest weapons. The only real security lay in round-the-clock patrolling.[22]

For Henry Gerard Phillips, the southern Tunisia desert was reminiscent of southwestern American terrain. Winter storms had left the local djebels (mountains) barren and jagged from erosion, while the valley floors were deeply cut in places by the dry washes known as wadis. Ancient Roman stone ruins jutted up from the landscape near the Forty-Seventh's freshly established machine-gun positions, barbed wire fencing, and defensive minefields.

Home for Phillips for the next three weeks became foxholes carved out by sweat from the rocky landscape. The recently married lieutenant, not quite twenty-one years of age, was left to ponder his fate for days in such a bleak environment. Born in Portland, Oregon, Phillips was a dashing specimen of a soldier: standing six-foot-two, strong as an ox, with brown eyes and naturally curly auburn hair that led to military comrades inevitably christening him with the sobriquet "Red." Quite the hellraiser as a child, he was allowed to join the National Guard at age fifteen. His mother, Eleanor "Dolly" Johnson Phillips, ignored the fact that her son had lied about his age, silently praying the military might straighten him out. Losing his father, Harry, to a railway accident when he was only thirteen had been tough on young Henry.[23]

Three years after his father's death, Red Phillips lost his mother in a car crash, leaving three orphan children—Red; his older sister, Betty Lou; and his younger brother, Roger—to be taken in by their uncle. But along his life's tough journey, time spent in Marysville, California, afforded him the chance to meet the love of his life, Lenore Luella Lembke, at a local dance. When the Forty-Seventh Infantry was preparing to ship overseas in late 1942, Red decided to marry the petite eighteen-year-old he affectionately called Lee before he deployed. Lee endured a cross-country trip on a troop transport train to join her future husband in New York, one of only two women among hundreds of hormone-driven, alcohol-fueled young men heading toward war. Fortunately, a kindly porter locked the two young ladies away from the masses and brought them food throughout their journey. Once in New York, Lee and Red found that the required blood test would take days. Pressed for time, they hopped another train to Arlington, Virginia, for their wedding. Their kindhearted judge even footed the bill for the services and the couple's hotel room after Phillips suffered the indignity of having his wallet stolen on the train.

Red and his beloved Lee would spend more than two years separated by the war. In North Africa, Lieutenant Phillips was in command of a machine-gun platoon in the Forty-Seventh Infantry Division's Third Battalion. The battalion consisted of three rifle companies—I, K, and L Companies—plus one heavy weapons company, officially M Company. Phillips's M Company—166 men hailing from twenty-nine different states—was further broken down into two rifle platoons and one mortar platoon. The rifle platoons were commanded by Second Lieutenants Phillips and Leonard Rackstraw, while Second Lieutenant Ira Rosenfeld led the mortar platoon. The three officers had been so assigned at Fort Bragg, North Carolina, in August 1942, when each was fresh from Fort Benning, Georgia's Infantry Officer Candidate School (OCS).[24]

As a machine-gun platoon leader, Phillips was in charge of four squads of men, each handling a Browning .30-caliber, water-cooled machine gun to support the battalion's rifle companies. His M company leader was Captain Jim Johnston, an older, experienced North Carolinian who was as equally brave and professional as a leader as he was cunning enough at poker to clean out unsuspecting new players. Johnston had seen his company through its first fighting on November 8, when his men landed at Safi harbor and moved ashore in what proved to be an exciting but bloodless day. Phillips, Rackstraw, and Rosenfeld considered themselves most fortunate in their assignment under Johnston's wing.[25]

Red Phillips and his machine-gun squads were eager for first action in Tunisia, but their weeks near Sbeitla would be stressed by nothing other than occasional aerial excitement courtesy of German Messerschmitts. M Company's defensive position was secured by a minefield laid by a team under First Lieutenant John Calton, a loudmouthed Louisianian who proclaimed, "A snake couldn't crawl through there without your knowing it." The only challenge during the first week proved to be an Arab caravan that wandered into the Forty-Seventh Regiment's area. Per Phillips, "Casualties were limited to a goat, two donkeys, and a camel, but Lieutenant Calton's reputation for mine placement was enhanced."[26]

The Forty-Seventh Regiment would spend weeks holed up in Sbeitla, where Phillips detested having to endure British army rations at times. This meant the issue of tea instead of coffee, and canned steak and kidney pie rather than the usual C rations. "There were tinned packages of their tightly packed and flavorless cigarettes, but contrary to all sorts of rumors, no rum," said Phillips.[27]

The lack of immediate action in Tunisia for Red Phillips and his heavy weapons company was taxing on all, but the chance for their machine guns to see combat would present itself soon enough. Their II Corps was in the process of being reshaped by a fiery new leader.

NINE

PATTON TAKES CHARGE

The dramatic arrival of Major General George Patton and his subordinates left no doubt that life for his II Corps soldiers was about to change. Six armored scout cars and half-tracks, with sirens wailing, roared up at 1000 on March 6 at his new headquarters at Djebel Kouif, a small mining town in Algeria about fifteen miles north of Tébessa. Major General Omar Bradley noted Patton standing in the lead car "like a charioteer. He was scowling into the wind and his jaw strained against the web strap of a two-starred steel helmet."[1]

Old Blood and Guts encountered Lloyd Fredendall still finishing his breakfast. Patton found the outgoing II Corps commander—who was being promoted to lieutenant general and sent back to Memphis to train the Second Army—to be cordial. But he noted discipline and proper dress to be lacking and Fredendall's "staff in general poor." He would quickly replace two important members, naming Brigadier General Hugh Gaffey as his new chief of staff and Colonel

Kent Lambert as his operations officer, or G-3. Patton found it almost comical that Fredendall planned to depart before dawn the next morning by car instead of flying to Constantine. "I think Fredendall is either a little nuts or badly scared," he wrote in his diary that evening.[2]

Following his meeting with Fredendall, Patton called in Major Generals Terry Allen, head of the First Infantry Division, and Pinky Ward, head of the First Armored Division, to learn of their next planned operations. In Allen, Patton saw a soldier he could be proud of. After he was wounded in the jaw during World War I, Allen's injuries caused his words to emanate with a hissing sound when he spoke with intensity. Correspondent Ernie Pyle said that "Terrible Terry" lived and breathed to fight, was the only general he knew that slept on the ground, and "hated Germans and Italians like vermin."[3]

Patton set to work on implementing discipline within II Corps. He started with the most basic rules, including how to salute and how to dress. He was appalled that no such orders had been enforced previously. "It is absurd to believe that soldiers who cannot be made to wear the proper uniform can be induced to move forward in battle," he wrote in his diary. Omar Bradley, who remained with Patton as a special observer for Eisenhower, felt that Patton wanted to impress upon his troops "that something new was taking place, and that they had a different commander."[4]

Patton had a long history of shaking things up. At Fort Benning in 1941, he had urged his personal driver to break the speed limit or "just stop and get the hell out and I'll drive myself." When a military policemen advised him his car could not drive the wrong way up a one-way street, he had shouted, "The hell I can't!" During desert training in 1942, his officers learned to always stand in the sun versus running the risk of Patton catching them taking shelter in the shade.[5]

At II Corps headquarters, he wasted no time setting his tone.

Patton took his breakfast at 0700 on March 7 and found only chief of staff Hugh Gaffey there. Learning that under Fredendall the II Corps staff had casually taken its breakfast around 0900, Patton immediately passed orders to the cooks that the mess hall would be closed at 0730 on this day and every day forward. "Tomorrow, people will be on time," he noted.[6]

Patton spent the next several days meeting with and instilling order in the 88,287 men under his II Corps command. He had at his disposal one armored division, a field artillery brigade, seven battalions of tank destroyers, and three American infantry divisions. The latter three were: the First Infantry Division, known as the Big Red One, commanded by Major General Allen and Brigadier General Ted Roosevelt Jr.; the Thirty-Fourth Infantry Division, under Major General Charles "Doc" Ryder; and Major General Manton Eddy's Ninth Infantry Division, which had been keeping watch on the border of Spanish Morocco. Patton began to immediately consolidate his widely scattered II Corps troops, making it the first time in the Tunisian campaign that the three American divisions had been brought together under an American commander. His desire to quickly change British impressions of the U.S. Army's fighting ability would be held on a short leash by his Allied boss, General Alexander of the British Eighteenth Army Group.[7]

Patton despised having Omar Bradley moving about just to inspect troops and make his own reports to General Eisenhower's Allied headquarters in Algiers. So he rang up Major General Beetle Smith and asked that Bradley be appointed as his deputy II Corps commander. Eisenhower was quick to phone back his approval, a move he had already been contemplating. Although Bradley was invited by Patton to move in with him to the mine manager's house at Djebel Kouif, he did not cease being Ike's legman.[8]

On March 8, Patton and Bradley inspected Brigadier General John A. Crane's Thirteenth Field Artillery Brigade and Doc Ryder's

Thirty-Fourth Infantry Division. Patton found their discipline, uniforms, and behavior to be poor, with anti-tank guns weakly placed on the crest of a hill "instead of on the reverse slope where they belong." Sergeant Hubert Edwards and the men of the Seventeenth Field Artillery had been busily drawing new howitzers from II Corps reserves to replace their losses in the Kasserine Pass battles. As word made the rounds of General Patton's strict new expectations for officers and men, Edwards was skeptical. "I didn't like him a bit in this world, but I had to respect him because he was a known fighter," he said.[9]

One of the officers attached to Edwards's First Battalion saw hope that Patton would whip the army into shape. First Lieutenant John Patterson, a "ninety-day wonder" who had recently graduated from officer candidate school, felt the Seventeenth Artillery would see real action sooner than later. "The Corps had less than two weeks to get ready for action again," said Patterson. "From then on, divisions were to live, train, and fight as divisions. There would be no more withdrawals. Discipline would be strict." Patterson wrote his family about his new assignment, predicting he would "kick hell out of the Huns." The young artillery lieutenant was not fond of Patton's new strict dress requirements, but did respect the II Corps leader's propensity to be on the battle lines. "He's the kind of son of a bitch who'd get you killed," said Patterson. "But he'd be there chewing on your rump when it happened."[10]

Patton further signified his intentions to kick the hell out of his enemy by ordering his key division and brigade commanders to Djebel Kouif for dinner on the evening of March 8. Present for this first formal staff briefing were: Deputy II Corps commander Bradley; Terry Allen, First Infantry Division; Pinky Ward, First Armored Division; Doc Ryder, Thirty-Fourth Infantry Division; Manton Eddy, Ninth Infantry Division; and John Crane, Thirteenth Field Artillery. The enemy situation and Allied plans were presented after dinner by two Patton staffers: his new G-3, Colonel Lambert, and the G-2 (intelligence officer) he retained from Fredendall's staff, Lieutenant Colonel Benjamin "Monk" Dickson. Patton was ready to move, and his infantry and artillery would be allocated accordingly. "My concern is for fear the enemy will attack us first," he noted in his diary that night.[11]

Bill Darby's Rangers saw little action during the first days of George Patton taking command of II Corps. After a week of guarding Dernaia Pass, his men were moved by truck into reserve on March 1 for rest and refitting at the village of Le Kouif. Second Lieutenant Les Kness found it to be once again a period of patrols with little contact as they operated from an oasis outside Gafsa.[12]

Heavy thunderstorms assaulted the wadi where the Rangers had set up camp. Lieutenant Colonel Darby was awakened during the night by water that quickly filled the dry wash where he had gone to sleep. "With the water swirling above my knees, I am sure I presented a spectacle as I shouted for help," he admitted. The foul weather and cool night air caused Darby to become sick, forcing him to turn acting command of his Ranger battalion over to his executive officer, Herman Dammer, for several days.[13]

PFC Tom Sullivan passed his downtime with reading from a fresh batch of magazines and books that arrived from home in a barracks bag. Having finished a Civil War novel called *Long Remember*, he sank into another mass-market paperback, *Hunger Fighters*, during one melancholy day. On Sunday, March 7, he attended mass held by Father Albert Basil, the British Army chaplain attached to the First Ranger Battalion who preached on the distinction between killing and murder in a church carved out of rocky red soil.[14]

Shortly after arriving near Le Kouif, Staff Sergeant Phil "Snapdragon" Stern made a trip to Algiers to deliver forty rolls of film for the wartime press. During his months of shooting Darby's Rangers in action, Stern had developed an eye for snapping only the images that best told a story. "I only take a picture when I think it's important or see a story about to happen," he noted in his journal. "The secret is knowing where to look and where to frame the shot. I like to think I do art, not photography."[15]

During Stern's absence, the Rangers were pushed through further conditioning hikes to build up their stamina. "Tunisia is plenty rough country!" Tom Sullivan noted in his diary following slow, hard climbs up steep hills. His guts burned "like rotten whiskey" after one such conditioning hike through the mountains. By the time Snapdragon returned from his film delivery, he found his First Ranger Battalion had mobilized and was moving toward the front lines for a "big push into Gafsa."[16]

While the Rangers prepared for their next assault, Major General Patton spent the same week continuing to position and inspect his troops. Omar Bradley noted that by the third day after the arrival of Old Blood and Guts in Tunisia "the II Corps was fighting mad—but at Patton, not at the German[s]." Patton made his point by punishing men for uniform violations. He informed Bradley that hitting the pocketbooks of his soldiers was a method to gain quick response. His task of visiting all of his divisions to restore discipline proved to be "the most difficult I have ever undertaken."[17]

Patton's new Allied boss, General Harold Alexander, arrived at Djebel Kouif on March 9 and Patton took Alexander and his entourage to inspect General Eddy's Ninth Infantry Division and its Sixtieth Combat Team. Patton was impressed with Eddy and found Alexander to be pleasantly snobbish in all sorts of topics, including genealogy. Better yet, Alexander "seemed to agree with most of my ideas."[18]

Eddy's Ninth Division was not immune to their new general's harsh directives. Lieutenant Red Phillips noted that his M Company commander, Captain Jim Johnston, was among the first of their division to be dressed down by Patton. Johnston's command vehicle, driving from Sbeitla to the rear to collect his company's payroll, was twice forced from the road by German aircraft. "This did not upset our leader half as much as the $25 fine imposed on him by a roadside summary courts martial," said Phillips. Johnston's lack of a necktie had not impressed the new II Corps commander in chief.[19]

The following day, March 10, Patton took Alexander and his British chief of staff, Major General Richard McCreery, to inspect the First Infantry Regiment and First Armored Headquarters, located in a little oasis in the desert. Patton and Alexander found Generals Allen and Roosevelt to be competent and the Big Red One to be in better discipline and appearance than other regiments of his II Corps. Still, Patton went out of his way to degrade Allen for having so many carefully dug slit trenches to protect his men from Luftwaffe attacks.[20]

Aide Bradley, witness to the event that followed, recalled that Patton—apparently considering the trenches to be cowardly retreats—called in his squeaky voice, "Terry, which one is yours?"[21]

When Allen pointed out his trench, Patton strode over, unzipped his fly, and urinated in the dugout. As he zipped up his fly, he sneered at Allen and said, "Now try to use it."

Bradley felt that this earthy GI gesture by Patton virtually labeled Allen as a coward in front of his own men. Standing as equally shocked as Allen, Bradley could only wonder if his army's new leader was truly displaying good leadership.

Patton routinely called out individuals who were not dressed according to his new orders. Lieutenant Lawrie Marcus, second-in-command of a platoon of the 601st Tank Destroyer Battalion, was standing with several other officers when the major general approached. A number of men had grizzled faces and wore wool knit caps instead of combat helmets. "Every man old enough will shave every day," Patton snapped. "Officers will wear ties into combat."

Having spoken these words, Patton advanced to within a foot of Marcus's face and snapped, "And anyone wearing a wool knit cap without a steel helmet will be shot."[22]

Another armored division officer, Captain Thomas Hawksworth, commander of A Company of the 899th Tank Destroyer Battalion, recalled of Patton's frontline visits, "He believed in seeing, and in being seen." Wearing a shining helmet and ivory-handled revolvers, the new II Corps commander was highly visible to any enemy. "He became a hazard to everyone around him," said Hawksworth. "No one was safe from one of his visits. At the same time, though, no one would refer to him as 'that SOB' without looking over his shoulder first."[23]

In addition to his desire to make a strong impression on his troops, George Patton was burning with a desire for vengeance. His son-in-law Lieutenant Colonel Johnny Waters had been missing in action since the Kasserine Pass battles weeks earlier. While visiting the troops, Patton spoke with members of the graves registration unit who had searched the Sidi Bou Zid battle area. They had found no evidence of a grave for Waters. They assured him that his son-in-law was still alive. His payback desire against the Germans was evident in a letter written to his wife, Bea: "I feel better about John. I will capture the place soon and have a look myself."[24]

General Alexander took his departure from II Corps headquarters on March 11, and Patton prepared himself for his first action. "It is a difficult thing to go into battle with troops one has not trained," he wrote. The only staff members he knew were the four officers he had brought with him to Tunisia, but he was pleased to find his II Corps G-2, Monk Dickson, and his new G-4 (logistics officer), Colonel Robert Wilson, to be "very sound."[25]

At 1100 on March 11, the II Corps G-3, Colonel Lambert, issued orders for the First Armored and First Infantry Divisions to lead an attack on Gafsa, while the Ninth Infantry and Thirty-Fourth Infantry Divisions would provide security to the northeast. The assault would include all or portions of the Big Red One's three regiments. A portion of the Eighteenth Infantry would protect the northeast flank of the division. The Sixteenth Infantry would clear Gafsa of enemy troops, and the Twenty-Sixth Infantry Regiment would serve as divisional reserve. In addition, Lieutenant Colonel Darby's First Ranger Battalion had orders to push active reconnaissance northeast and south of the town of El Guettar and to secure important terrain east of El Guettar.[26]

The wheels were in motion for II Corps to go on the offensive under its new commanding general.

As George Patton surveyed his U.S. troops, the Desert Fox, sick and physically exhausted, was in his final days of commanding German forces in North Africa. Adolf Hitler had ordered him to take sick leave, but Field Marshal Rommel had lingered on into early March, disgusted with the Italian Comando Supremo, which directed his every move now. "I wouldn't mind having another job," he wrote on March 7. "I'm dictated to by Rome in every single thing, yet the full responsibility is mine. That I find intolerable."[27]

The latest thrusts by Rommel's army against the southern end of the Mareth Line met strong resistance from British forces on March 6 and forced him to call off the operation after suffering heavy tank losses. A gloomy mood set in with the Desert Fox as he realized his inability to interfere with Montgomery's forces, and he returned to his headquarters the following day to say his good-byes to his troops.[28]

Colonel Hans von Luck, one of Rommel's trusted reconnaissance commanders, was shocked by his first sight of his leader, who seemed sick. Rommel appeared to Luck to be visibly weak, suffering from tropical disease, and completely worn out. Rommel was poring over campaign maps when the colonel came to bid him farewell for the time being. As the field marshal stood, he was emotional. "The tears of a great man, now cast down, moved me as much as anything I saw in the war."[29]

Heinz Schmidt of the Fifteenth Panzer Division—a longtime aide to Rommel—saw the field marshal's departure as the last hope for victory in North Africa to be fading. "It was a grievous blow to the Afrika Korps," he said.[30]

Rommel boarded a plane at Sfax on the morning of March 9 for the flight to Rome to meet with the Italian leadership and then with Hitler the following day. So secret was his departure that Allied command would not learn of his absence for more than a month. Handing over command left him a broken man, as Rommel confided to his son, "I've fallen from grace."[31]

In his place, his Afrika Korps would be led by General von Arnim. With the departure of Rommel, longtime personal driver Rudy Schneider and others of his *Kampfstaffel* would be pressed into regular service with the Panzer divisions. The elite bodyguard members, numbering 389 soldiers, would be used both as infantrymen and at times even drove captured Allied vehicles still bearing their original markings. For Schneider, the final meetings with Rommel's staff would be his last time seeing the veteran field marshal.

As the Desert Fox's star in North Africa was fading away, Major General Patton's rise to glory was just beginning. He had little sympathy for Lloyd Fredendall, the man whose shoes he now filled. "Fredendall just existed," Patton wrote in his diary on March 12. "He did not command, and with few exceptions, his staff was worthless due to youth and lack of leadership."[32]

Patton was confident in the abilities of Major General Bradley—freshly returned from a trip to Algiers to meet with General Eisenhower—as his deputy II Corps commander through the coming offensive. Once the first phase of battle was successfully completed, Patton felt he could hand over his command to Bradley while he returned to planning for Operation Husky. They were joined at lunch on March 12 at Djebel Kouif by Terry Allen, followed by an afternoon tour with Allen of the Big Red One's artillery and infantry battalions staged at Bou Chebka, Tunisia. "Terribly cold," Patton wrote. "Took a drink to get warm."[33]

Old Blood and Guts returned in the late afternoon to his II Corps headquarters, where he received some uplifting intelligence at 2100. Major General Eddy of the Ninth Infantry called to relate news he had picked up on the radio: Patton was being promoted to lieutenant general. In celebration, Captain Dick Jenson produced a three-star flag he had been carrying around for the past year and presented it to his commander. Patton was pleased, recalling how as a boy he used to carry a wooden sword and declare himself to be George S. Patton Jr., Lieutenant General. "At that time, I did not know there were full generals," Patton wrote in his diary. "Now I want, and will get, four stars."[34]

TEN

"TOTAL SURPRISE"

Patton's pride at becoming a three-star general was soon tempered. The British Eighteenth Army Group sent orders to postpone his first big offensive by two days, to March 17. Torrential rains had set in, turning some of the roads into a sea of mud that his armored divisions would struggle to traverse. "I fear Rommel will take initiative, but I shall not assume the defensive," Patton grumbled to his diary.[1]

Based on the best available intelligence, he assumed the Germans would maintain a hold on Gafsa while attempting to withdraw to the southeast. He believed they would take up a strong defensive position on higher ground, on the hills Djebel Orbata and Djebel el Ank, where they could defend the key Gafsa–Gabès road. The delay of his D-Day did not sit well with Patton, who was already stewing over a recent letter from General Eisenhower. In it Ike said that II Corps was "not sufficiently offensive" due to the fact that no enemy contacts had been made. Patton had responded to that poke by ordering all patrols out until they made contact. His men quickly responded by capturing eighty-nine enemy soldiers, two aviators, and one spy.[2]

While his patrols gathered small numbers of Axis prisoners to help please Ike, Patton cranked up his assault on II Corps troops who did not follow his strict uniform regulations. His methodology was simple. "Discipline consists in obeying orders," he wrote. "If men do not obey orders in small things, they are incapable of being led in battle. I will have discipline—to do otherwise is to commit murder."[3]

Patton went to work on March 13 with his discipline program. By day's end he had fined thirty-five officers fees of $25 each for being in improper uniform. Unfortunately for Bill Darby's Rangers, the new II Corps commander's spotlight caught them with a large number of the fines. Still hunkered down due to heavy rains the previous day, the Rangers were engaged in various work details when Darby received new orders. Since American strength was deemed insufficient, the Rangers would be deployed on night attacks against various enemy positions to give them a false idea of Allied strength.[4]

The Rangers were to prepare to raid a German artillery position that evening, according to what Lieutenant Les Kness heard. The sun had returned, warming the Tunisian desert to the point that following Patton's latest orders—officers wearing neckties at all times and every soldier wearing a steel helmet with the strap snapped—was downright uncomfortable. Executive officer Herman Dammer called a meeting of his officers and laid out the plan of attack.

One lieutenant asked, "Do we have to fight in these damn neckties?"

"No," said Dammer. "You can remove your ties."

Following the morning meeting, Kness returned to the area where his E Company was stationed. He took a seat in the shade by Captain Jack Street, who had arrived in January with the first hundred replacement Rangers to augment the battalion's strength.

Noting the new second lieutenant still wearing his tie, Street grumbled, "Are you going to remove that necktie, or do I have to take it off you?"[5]

Kness shucked the tie and thought nothing further of it. Shortly thereafter, Captain Street ordered him to take a detail of men into the town of Le Kef to store the Ranger battalion's barracks bags in an assigned building. Kness passed the word for volunteers and quickly assembled fourteen men, including Second Lieutenant James Larkin of B Company. Kness felt the assignment would help settle his men, who preferred to be busy during the downtime preceding an attack.

Kness, Larkin, and their enlisted Rangers trucked several miles to the railhead near Le Kef, dressed in work detail clothing and soft caps. During their absence, Lieutenant General Patton's command detail moved past the main assemblage of Darby's Rangers, where Patton was seen prominently atop his half-track. In his usual fashion, he wore a battle helmet, ivory-handled pistols at his side, and his stars prominently displayed on his uniform. For Ranger Don Frederick, it was his first glimpse of the new II Corps commander. "He was dressed like he was going to a ball," recalled Frederick. Fellow Ranger Carl Lehmann was less than impressed. "He lashed about with a will, shrilling at any soldier without a tie or with unfastened helmet strap, and being his usual pain-in-the-ass."[6]

Kness was driving a company truck toward the railcars to unload baggage when he passed Brigadier General Hugh Gaffey of Patton's staff. One of the men in the back of Kness's six-by-six rapped on the cab roof and yelled that there was a general shouting for them to stop. Kness stopped the truck and ran back approximately a city block to see the general.[7]

"Second Lieutenant Kness, First Ranger Battalion, reporting, sir," he said.

Holding the lieutenant's salute at full attention, Gaffey looked Kness up and down in a disapproving fashion.

"Are you an officer?" Gaffey demanded.

"Yes, sir!" Kness replied.

"My God, you sure as hell don't look like one!" barked Gaffey.

The dumbfounded new lieutenant had little defense. *I suppose I do look pretty bad,* Kness thought. He wore no formal officer's clothing and had simply replaced his previous first sergeant stripes on his wrinkled shirt with a gold bar loaned to him by a comrade. His leggings had been removed and he had cuffed his trousers above his ankles. Gaffey chastised Kness for a helmetless Ranger he spotted in the back of the truck.

Kness saluted, about-faced, and walked back to the truck. "All right, the man who had his helmet off, unload," he said. To his amusement, the other Rangers in his detail truck promptly removed their helmets and clambered down as Gaffey advanced. Kness's former BAR man, Les Cook, had been advanced in rank to sergeant and given command of an Easy Company squad following the Sened Station raid. Now Cook worried that his fresh promotion was in jeopardy. Before him stood a general "almost frothing at the mouth, screaming at Lieutenant Kness for not having his necktie on and at us men for not having our helmets on."[8]

Kness lined the Rangers up in two columns. They marched behind Gaffey up a little hill about a quarter of a mile to General Patton's headquarters. In his diary Patton noted later that he had "collected eight soldiers and two lieutenants for improper uniform. Had them fall in and follow me—quite a procession." Gaffey's command party quickly found itself struggling to stay ahead of the irritated, well-conditioned Rangers. Kness's men stretched out their pace, advancing fast enough to catch up with the general. Upon arriving at the headquarters building of Old Blood and Guts, Kness was told to hold the men outside until further notified.[9]

He put his Rangers at ease and allowed them to take a smoke break. A sergeant appeared five minutes later and summoned the lieutenant into Patton's office. Stepping in front of the II Corps' commander's desk, Kness saluted. Gaffey informed Patton that the Rangers were out of proper uniform and had showed him no respect. In a high-pitched, squeaky voice, Patton asked Kness, "Is this true?"[10]

Patton turned to an aide at a desk to his left and snapped, "Recommend that this man be sent back to the States and separated from service!"

At the moment, Kness could not have cared less. *He couldn't have said anything nicer to me,* he thought. He saluted and turned to depart the II Corps commander's office, only to be ordered back by Patton. The general hammered his fist on his desk, his face aflame and angry. The lieutenant tried to explain how he was newly commissioned and that no proper officer uniforms were available to him, but Patton berated him for not wearing his necktie.

"Sir, we are in the process of moving out this evening to attack an enemy artillery position," Kness said. "We had permission to remove our neckties for the fight."[11]

"No one can rescind one of my orders!" Patton yelled. "Do you understand?"

The general handed down orders that each Ranger was to be fined $25 and held in the stockade overnight. Lieutenant Larkin would never forget the berating he and the other soldiers received from Patton that day. Once Generals Patton and Gaffey had departed, Lieutenant Kness was called back into the office to settle his debt. In an irritated mood, Kness muttered "armchair commando" toward one of Patton's staffers seated behind the desk. "He raised up and, to my surprise, was a full bird colonel," Kness remembered. "I found out what a master at reaming was really like."[12]

Their introduction to their new commander in chief was one the men of this Ranger detail would never forget. Battalion photographer Snapdragon Stern was among those chastised by the new general. "Old Blood and Guts caught me without a helmet," wrote Stern.

"For my infraction, he fined me $25 and a night in the military slammer." Sergeant Cook was more than relieved when his fine was dismissed. "I was only getting twenty-one dollars pay per month," said Cook. "Luckily, that fine was later rescinded."[13]

Stern, Kness, and the other "guilty" Rangers were released back to the First Ranger Battalion the following day, March 14. Their ire would soon be replaced with a sense of urgency as Lieutenant Colonel Darby received orders from the First Infantry Division. Action appeared to be imminent.

———

By the morning of March 15, the heavy rain storms had turned dirt roads near Bou Chebka into rivers of mud. In some places the dry wadis had filled quickly overnight, forcing troops to scramble for cover. PFC Harley Reynolds and others from his First Battalion, Sixteenth Infantry Regiment, scurried up rocky banks that night as water rushed through their camp, carrying away some of their possessions.[14]

Reynolds was able to reequip his squad in short order, but the tanker crews suffered greatly during the morning hours. Armored vehicles became bogged down in the mire, forcing some crews to replace tracks while others swore and labored in the daytime heat to dig theirs out.[15]

While his troops battled the elements, Patton was informed that the Germans were on the move. Allied scouts reported a reconnaissance force of armored cars and light artillery east of Gafsa, a central Tunisian town of about 10,000 souls. That evening Arab sources also reported Italian soldiers operating near El Guettar, an important crossroads town southeast of Gafsa. American forces were already staging closer to these two areas, so Patton decided that Terry Allen's Big Red One should make a move to seize both Gafsa and El Guettar.

Major General Allen passed the El Guettar mission to Colonel Frank Greer's Eighteenth Infantry Regiment of his First Infantry Division. Both Allen and General Eisenhower arrived at Patton's II Corps command headquarters at Djebel Kouif around noon on March 16 to discuss strategy. Patton found that Allen had no plans to cover his left column with armor, so he ordered him to add a destroyer company from the 601st to help protect his Eighteenth Infantry. Allen left to take care of this detail while Patton and Ike spent the afternoon inspecting their forces near Feriana.[16]

They started with the Seventeenth Field Artillery, which was preparing for action with battalions of the Thirty-Sixth and Eighteenth Infantry Regiments. Sergeant Hubert Edwards of the Seventeenth knew the fight ahead would be important. For the time being, all his unit could do was haul their fieldpieces around as ordered and stay dug in during the interim. German aircraft were an occasional nuisance, forcing the artillerymen to take cover in proper foxholes. During one such bombing raid, Edwards was amused to see a soldier from the ammunition supply trucks digging feverishly.[17]

"Throw that shovel down and get in the hole," Edwards warned as German warplanes approached.

"No, sir, it's not deep enough," replied the ordnanceman.

"How deep do you have to dig it?" Edwards said.

"Till I can stand flat-footed and look a grasshopper in the eye!"

Another hazard for the soldiers was the land mines planted on and near the key roads in the El Guettar region. One afternoon, one of the trucks used to haul the howitzers to their fighting locations had the misfortune of striking a mine. Late that day Robert Keeler called on his friend Hubert Edwards to drive him out to the wreck to determine if it was salvageable. Edwards had become adept at spotting where mines were planted due to changes in the soil coloration. When he spotted a patch of dead grass, he simply drove around it.

The pair determined that the truck was salvageable, so Keeler returned the next morning with parts. Edwards remained behind, allowing another soldier to borrow his jeep. The driver, who was stockier than Edwards, followed the tracks from the previous day but contacted a mine as he approached the disabled truck. The explosion killed him and destroyed the jeep. Edwards, left to wonder how he had driven over the mine without setting it off the previous day, could only guess that the other soldier's substantial weight was just enough to make a fatal difference.

The stress of leading his first Tunisian offensive left Patton restless, and a cold sore developed on his lip. "The hardest thing a General has to do is to wait for the battle to start after all the orders are given," he wrote. But he felt confident and made sure that his visits with the troops radiated his confidence. He took the time that evening to write a full account of his son-in-law John Waters's last stand to his daughter Bea. Action with the Germans was now imminent, and Patton would have his big chance to avenge the loss of Waters.[18]

Allen's Big Red One used the cover of darkness that evening to move by truck into forward assembly areas for the attack on Gafsa. At 1000 on March 17, tightly following Patton's directives, the attack commenced. Allen's second-in-command, Teddy Roosevelt Jr., accompanied the forces sweeping into Gafsa. Combat Team 18, reinforced by a 601st Tank Destroyer battalion company, cut off the town from the east while the Third Battalion of the Sixteenth Infantry advanced from the northwest without contest. Roosevelt's forces entered the devastated town after midday and found that the Italian garrison had fled, leaving only mines and booby traps.[19]

The expected battle for Gafsa had simply not materialized. Patton watched the action on March 17 from an advanced observation post hill, where he was able to see troop movements and the bursting artillery shells. He was very pleased with Allen's First Division in seizing Gafsa with almost no losses. "So far as I know, we had about

20 casualties," Patton wrote in his diary. "The great and famous battle of Gafsa has been fought and won."[20]

The First Division had lost sight of its Axis enemy as it rolled forward, something that Terry Allen deemed unacceptable. Advance patrols were reporting nothing of the enemy on March 17, although intelligence believed more than 2,000 Axis troops occupied the El Guettar area. Exasperated, Allen issued orders to Darby's Rangers to find the enemy.

Allen believed German and Italian forces were well organized at El Guettar and well positioned at Djebel el Ank. "You will move your battalion after darkness tonight and advance on El Guettar, securing contact with the enemy in that area, develop [observe] his strength and dispositions, obtain identifications, and maintain yourself in that locality," he directed. Allen declared that Darby's mission was "vital," and he further advised the Ranger Battalion leader to act aggressively without committing his men to any action from which they could not extricate themselves.[21]

Darby was up for the challenge. He had recovered from the illness at Djebel Kouif that had required his executive officer, Major Dammer, to take acting command for several days. By March 17, treated with sulfa and feeling stronger, Darby was again in good spirits as his Rangers accepted their key mission. His soldiers shouldered their light packs and strode out past the First Division troops to the base of the mountain.[22]

Darby decided to assault El Guettar from the mountains, figuring that the Italians would be oriented on the road, facing west. Under orders to strike at night, he had his five hundred men hug the ridge that bordered the north side of town. In two hours they were approaching El Guettar from the mountain side. They saw no lights but they could hear enemy troops digging foxholes and the hum of truck tires on the nearby highway. Darby had been told that the enemy troops numbered about 2,000. Against such numbers, he considered his force to be puny.[23]

The Rangers eased warily forward, slipping to the edge of El Guettar during the early morning hours of March 18. His advance scouts did not even fire a shot, and they soon reported that the town had been abandoned by the Italians. Darby's men scoured the settlement, and by 1625 on March 18 he sent word to the First Infantry Division of his good fortune. El Guettar had fallen to the Rangers without a fight.

By evening, Allied intelligence knew that enemy forces were occupying the hills beyond El Guettar. The success of the past forty-eight hours was surprising to the Americans. The First Division spent much of March 19 consolidating and reorganizing forces around Gafsa and El Guettar. Lieutenant General Patton complimented his engineering groups for the work they were doing to improve the local roads during the day while he inspected the First Armored Division. Patton found Pinky Ward's tankers to be bogged down in a sea of mud from the constant rain. While Patton was en route to see Ward's command, his motorcade was fired on, a bullet passing close enough for them to hear. Lieutenant Alex Stiller stood and fired a clip at an Arab sniper seen fleeing into the rocky terrain but missed him.[24]

Patton found Colonel Paul Robinett, commander of Combat Command B, to be defensive and lacking in confidence, so he talked to him about the attack. Rain continued to fall as he reached the command post of Ward, who complained that the mud would inhibit his tank movements. "I told him to do it with infantry," Patton wrote. "I want to hit Rommel before he hits us, also to help Eighth Army, which attacks tomorrow night."[25]

When Patton returned to his II Corps headquarters that evening, he was met by Alexander's chief of staff, Major General Richard McCreery, who detailed the upcoming campaign plans. Alexander planned to hold Gafsa, to seize the heights east of Maknassy, and to hold II Corps' large forces at a line running from Gafsa to Maknassy to the Faid–Fondouk axis. Once the British Eighth Army advanced north of Maknassy, Patton was to turn over his Ninth Infantry Division to the British First Army to relieve its infantry on the extreme left flank. Patton's army could then attack Fondouk from the west and southwest to secure the heights in that area while his Thirty-Fourth Infantry Division was to side-slip to the north and attack along the axis of Maktar and Pichon.[26]

Patton was not pleased. "It is noteworthy that these instructions definitely prohibit an American advance to the sea," he wrote later. "In other words, we continue to threaten the enemy's right flank, but we do not participate in cutting him off. In brief, this is to pinch us out as to insure a British triumph."

As McCreery finished the briefing, Patton controlled his anger and agreed to the plan. Silently he fumed that Eisenhower was allowing the Brits to get the best of him. He hoped that his forces would not be completely shut out before his time came to be returned to the Sicily invasion planning. "The more I think about the plan of pinching us out, the madder I get," he logged in his diary on the evening of March 19. "But no one knows that except me."[27]

Patton added, "Oh, God, let us win in the morning!"

———

Bill Darby's Rangers, some of whom had recently been fined and chastised by George Patton, were not to be pinched out. Having cleared El Guettar, they had moved one mile east of that town on March 19 to occupy an observation post on Hill 276, a distinct knob the Rangers dubbed "the Pimple." Open plains lay below, so Darby sent out patrols to ascertain Italian strength dug into the nearby hills.

The task of probing the enemy's position fell to a pair of scout teams. They were led by two of Darby's Rangers who had received their commissions since reaching North Africa: Second Lieutenant Bing Evans, the first to be promoted in November, and Second Lieutenant Walt Wojcik, who had been promoted only a month earlier following the Sened Station raid. Their mission was to search Djebel Orbata for enemy dispositions and for possible approaches into the enemy area. East of the city of Gafsa, the mountain called Orbata rose sharply to a height of 3,800 feet and roughly paralleled the course of the road from Gafsa through El Guettar.

The two teams moved out on the night of March 19. Under cover of darkness, Evans allowed his men to poke at enemy resistance directly to create a diversionary action. Evans advanced his ten men close enough to draw fire from the Italian sentries before dodging back into the dark, only to creep in from a different angle. Evans continually advanced his patrol close enough to stir up enemy fire from multiple angles. He learned where they were strong, without alerting them to the true size of his party.[28]

In the meantime, Wojcik led his small force through mountain passes, crevices, and gullies to surprise the Axis force's rear guard. The tortuous terrain and the darkness provided plenty of challenges.

By daylight the two Ranger scout patrols had gathered sufficient intelligence on the Italian forces, and they retreated back to report to Darby on the morning of March 20. They had found a regiment of infantry, two battalions of artillery, and some anti-tank and antiaircraft weapons among the ridges.

The Evans patrol returned at dawn to the Pimple, the small hill at the junction of the roads one mile east of El Guettar. Walt Wojcik's patrol continued to observe Djebel Orbata during the day of March 20, above and behind the enemy's defensive installations. His men slipped away during late afternoon and returned to Darby at 1700 with one prisoner.[29]

George Patton was feeling confident. His spirits brightened even more shortly after midnight when Omar Bradley woke him to share the good news that Patton's son-in-law Johnny Waters was alive, a prisoner of war of the Germans. He passed orders for Allen's Big Red One and Darby's Rangers to take the high ground and the valley of El Guettar. At 1630, Patton handed Allen three objectives: to the north, Djebel el Ank; in the center, Djebel el Mcheltat; and to the south, Djebel Berda, a high hill mass south of the Gabès highway, nine miles to the southeast of El Guettar, on the south flank of the enemy's defensive position.

In these directives Patton was acting against the orders given him the previous day by his Allied boss, General Alexander. The British commander had directed him to take the heights of Maknassy, from which he could then stage an armored raid on the German air base at Mezzouna. Patton's orders did not include sending his II Corps forces beyond the line of Gafsa–Maknassy–Faid–Fondouk, yet he was ordering Ward and Allen forward through Gafsa and El Guettar in hopes of taking the key heights in that region before the Axis forces could react.[30]

Patton resigned himself to sitting at his command post near the phone on March 20—"a hell of a way to fight a war," he wrote. He decided to move forward with the First Division the next day to be closer to the action, when both his First Armored and First Division would strike. The British Army was attacking this night, and Patton believed the Germans would react the following day. "I feel that I will lick him so long as the Lord stays with me," he wrote.[31]

═══════

As darkness fell late in the evening of March 20, Darby's First Ranger Battalion of the First Infantry Division made ready for its next offensive. The probing actions by the teams under Walt Wojcik and Bing Evans had provided crucial intelligence.

Wojcik, having already traversed the rough terrain the previous night, was selected by Darby to lead the entire Ranger group across Djebel Orbata's ten miles of rocky terrain to be ready to make the assault after daylight on March 21. The Rangers had rifles, grenades, knives, and two 60mm M2 mortars per company, and the battalion had twelve .30-caliber M1919A4 machine guns. Allen added D Company of the First Engineer Battalion, which included towed 37mm antiaircraft guns and two 81mm mortars for the unit. They were led by D Company commander Captain Gordon Pope, whose mortarmen called themselves "hell squads."[32]

Captain Jack Street noted bleak, ragged ridges and arid valleys that supported only scrubby desert brush vegetation. Street thought the sharp ridges favored the defender at every turn. Cover and concealment in the area were either nonexistent in the open spaces or very effective in the knifelike, jagged ridges, boulder-strewn hills, and precipitous wadis. El Guettar and its road junction were covered on three sides by mountain passes that presented formidable obstacles to any forward movement.[33]

Five of the companies would attack by rolling down the slopes of the mountain like an avalanche, while C Company would be held in reserve. The signal for the attack to jump off would be a bugle call from the battalion commander's observation post near the line of departure.[34]

The Rangers started their trek at 2300 on March 20. The ground through the mountains was rugged and treacherous. Toggle ropes were often necessary to effect the passage of men and equipment up and down cliffs and over ravines. They stumbled and cursed silently, groping through difficult gorges, breathing hard as they helped to pull other men up steep draws. Lieutenant Les Kness of E Company was up for the challenge. He considered the rough climbing to be just the thing his unit had been training for.[35]

Easing forward silently in the moonlight, Darby likened his soldiers to Rogers' Rangers, each man relying upon speed and the element of surprise. As they entered a gorge area, the moon disappeared behind the mountains, although it would make its return in the next hour to highlight the craggy peaks ahead. By 0300 he received a report that Pope's mortarmen were falling behind. Kness, moving forward near his commanding officer and Captain Max Schneider, heard Darby radio for them to do the best they could, as he wanted their firepower.[36]

Around 0400 the trail disappeared into heavy shadow, where the Rangers reached a sharp drop. Each man climbed hand over hand down the cliff, silently passing equipment to one another. Kness led his E Company men around to the right of the bluff, where they were better able to make the ascent. Once the hurdle was cleared, Darby excitedly whispered to Dammer, "Do you realize what we have done? We've got five whole columns through!"[37]

Daylight was fast approaching on Djebel el Ank as Darby directed his companies toward their final assault positions. Kness's men were closest to the center of assault as they came up over the mountain rim to confront the enemy. His Second Platoon moved out to go over the rim toward the enemy positions. Sergeant Les Cook, leading a nine-man squad from Easy Company, was sweating from the exertion. For his tommy gun, Cook was carrying ten magazines with twenty rounds each, five mags on each side of his belt.[38]

By 0500 the five advance Ranger companies had moved rapidly into an extended skirmish line. All was in order. Darby's men had crept to the very rear of the defensive positions held by unsuspecting Italian infantrymen. Street heard the distant bugle call signaling attack, and his men swept forward. Surprise was complete.[39]

Darby could see the black dots of First Division forces advancing toward Djebel el Ank and their shells bursting on Axis positions farther east of the plain. German artillery opened up on his men, and the explosions rocked the plateau where they lay. The enemy fire was directed toward his infantry division's command post, silhouetted sharply against the rocks. The Ranger commander sent two squads forward to silence the artillery piece.[40]

Others came under fire from an Italian machine-gun nest. Peering through a telescopic scope mounted on his 1903 Springfield bolt-action rifle, Corporal Robert Bevan of Estherville, Iowa, spotted the enemy team 1,350 yards away. As a sniper, Bevan typically picked targets that were out of range for the riflemen. He went to work on the machine-gun nest, ranging in with tracers before placing two shots right into the position. The enemy gun went quiet for a couple minutes. Then an Italian soldier threw a dirty towel over the gun and the entire crew stepped forward and seated themselves on the ground.[41]

The black-faced Rangers surged forward, firing their guns and using bayonets on the Italian soldiers, many wearing long, dark overcoats. Second Lieutenant Chuck Shunstrom's C Company squad charged in with rifles, grenades, and tommy guns roaring, surprising a squad of ten Italians into quick surrender. His men killed several of them as a warning. Then Shunstrom sent the others down the hill to inform the remaining Italian defenders that they were completely surrounded and would be slaughtered if they refused to surrender.[42]

The ploy worked. White flags waved about. Kness spotted one Italian soldier racing down the hill, shouting at his comrades, until scores emerged from their positions without weapons. Jack Street estimated that within twenty minutes, more than two hundred prisoners had been taken. "We caught them in a total surprise," remembered Lieutenant Bing Evans. "It scared the living daylights out of them, and they gave up by the hundreds." Compared to the bloody combat he had endured in the Dieppe and Sened Station raids, Kness considered the surprise assault on Djebel el Ank to be "a cake walk."[43]

The next half hour deteriorated into a series of scattered assaults. Small pockets of resistance remained to be cleared, while other Italians gave up the fight in groups. Two hours after the assault commenced, Captain Pope's straggling mortar squad arrived and quickly knocked out another troublesome Italian machine-gun nest. By the time two battalions of the Twenty-Sixth Infantry reached the pass, the Rangers had the situation well in hand, their only organized resistance being other dug-in machine-gun positions south of the road.[44]

Father Albert Basil, fluent in Italian, was instrumental in convincing many of the Italians to surrender. Some even lifted the mines from in front of their positions, saving many American soldiers. The six Ranger companies fanned out over the slopes of Djebel Orbata and Djebel el Ank through the late morning hours, overtaking the last resistance groups. The Italians reported that the Germans had pulled out two days before.[45]

By 1220, Darby reported by radio that the inner portions of the pass had been cleared. He ordered two of his Ranger companies to attack and secure Bou Hamran, three miles northeast of the pass. Terry Allen's infantry pressed up Gumtree Road, and the total Axis prisoner haul soon exceeded 1,000 men. The other four Ranger companies began assembling the prisoners to march them toward El Guettar, severely congesting the road through the pass.[46]

Twelve Junkers Ju 88 twin-engine bombers appeared at this inopportune time, diving over Djebel Orbata to bomb and conduct low-level strafing of the massing Allied vehicles near the pass. Four hundred Ranger rifles firing at the aircraft could not prevent the loss of three men killed and five wounded, in addition to a small number of trucks, half-tracks, and howitzers that were hit by the bombers. Captain Street's principal difficulty following the raid was the successful recapturing of some 1,400 prisoners who had bolted into the nearby rock formations when the Luftwaffe appeared.[47]

At 1430, Darby's Rangers were ordered to return to El Guettar to reconstitute the division reserve. Photographer Snapdragon Stern had his cameras ready as the Axis prisoners were marched back toward town through twisting, mountainous goat trails. To calm his nerves, Stern began singing the popular Italian song "Funiculì, Funiculà." The Italian prisoners took his cue and joined in. En route, Stern was surprised to encounter Lieutenant Ralph Ingersoll, attached to the engineers and also a managing editor with Time-Life publications. Before the war Ingersoll had hired Stern in New York to be a staff photographer for his tabloid *PM*.[48]

The Rangers returned to their El Guettar bivouac area by late afternoon, turning over their prisoners for further handling. Darby's men had conquered Djebel el Ank with only six men wounded. The weary First Ranger Battalion was happy to accept hot stew, ladled into their helmets and canteen cups from kitchen truck cooks, while Allen's infantry regiments pushed southeast of El Guettar before digging in for the evening. Lieutenant General Patton could now boast that his troops had reclaimed more than 2,000 square miles of territory—capturing Gafsa, El Guettar, and Sened Station—in a mere five days.[49]

ELEVEN

PUSHING FORWARD

Proudly sporting his new three stars, George Patton went to the front lines to watch the show. Darby's Rangers were overrunning the Italians near El Guettar as he left his II Corps headquarters on the morning of March 21 to visit the First Infantry Division. Patton's first stop was the command post of Colonel Frank Greer's Eighteenth Infantry Regiment.

Greer's three battalions had advanced on foot overnight with heavy machine guns and jeep-hauled 81mm mortars. Their objective was to push forward from Lortess toward El Guettar and to seize and hold Djebel el Mcheltat and Djebel Berda to the southeast. By daybreak, Lieutenant Colonel Robert York's First Battalion was approaching the knob south of the Gafsa–Gabès highway. At 0550 an enemy gun opened fire on the battalion's eastern flank and Captain Herbert Scott-Smith of C Company ordered his men to attack. York ordered the rest of the battalion to follow as Scott-Smith's company assaulted and took command of Hill 336 from the small group of Italians.[1]

"By dawn, the show was on," wrote Major General Ted Roosevelt. "We caught the Italians unprepared." The combat lasted nearly ninety minutes, but the Italian artillery failed to kill or injure anyone from C Company. Greer's regiment captured more than four hundred of the enemy, most of them from the Seventh Bersaglieri Regiment of the Italian Centauro Division. Roosevelt and Patton observed the battle from the regimental command post and moved to a forward observation post after daybreak. Patton watched the Italian prisoners being marched in and noted that their wounded were treated by American medics with "equal care with our own soldiers."[2]

Patton's presence on the front lines during the fighting on March 21 was evident to many. Before noon his command group left the division post and headed east toward the front line to be closer. He found Greer's Eighteenth Infantry on the forward face of a hill and boldly advanced ahead of the company on the right flank. "The soldiers told me to get back, which, of course, prevented me from doing so," wrote Patton, who hoped to instill courage in his men.[3]

Captain Sam Carter's D Company, Eighteenth Infantry, was using an old French farmhouse as its command post when Patton arrived to greet Major General Terry Allen. In short order, Italian artillery found the mark on this area, landing a salvo of 150mm shells in the road immediately to their rear. Carter's infantrymen dived for their newly dug foxholes, and the captain suddenly found his dugout piled high with Patton's command staff on top of him. As soon as the sea of bodies was unscrambled, Carter heard Patton bark, "It's too damned hot. Let's get the hell out of here."[4]

Patton shifted several miles over to the First Armored Division, but the shelling again compelled his command team to move on. Twice during its movements, Patton's vehicles were strafed by

German planes, but they were not hit. Greer's infantry kept moving during the day and managed to establish an artillery gun line just behind El Keddab Ridge. His men also set up a forward observation post on Hill 336, where they had a good view down the valley to monitor enemy troop movements.

Around 1350, II Corps' G-2, Colonel Dickson, alerted the Big Red One that enemy air units were approaching. Ten Bf 109 fighters escorting twenty Ju 87 Stuka dive-bombers attacked the Eighteenth Infantry Regiment. The Stukas targeted the recently established artillery battery behind El Keddab Ridge, starting a number of fires and killing or wounding a dozen II Corps soldiers.[5]

Lieutenant Lawrie Marcus, the retail store man from Dallas, heard the wail of the air raid siren as the German air attack approached. He was ready for action. He had escaped German capture in Ousseltia Valley in January and was now the commander of A Company of the First Platoon of the 601st Tank Destroyer Battalion. His men were positioned along the southern edge of El Keddab Ridge.

Marcus's division had been held in reserve during the morning fighting, less than one mile away from the Thirty-Second Field Artillery's new position. From his vantage point he had seen the morning battles near El Guettar play out and had witnessed the Italian soldiers surrendering. The sound of the afternoon air raid on El Keddab Ridge sent many of the 601st tanker men scrambling to take cover in foxholes. Not Marcus.

Each of his half-tracks was mounted with a .50-caliber machine gun, less than ideal for effective use against German aircraft. Technician Fifth Grade Tom Morrison, gunner on one of Marcus's A Company M3s, found little comfort in the fact that his unit's only antiaircraft defenses amounted to jeep-mounted .30-calibers and .50-calibers mounted in the backs of three-quarter-ton weapons carriers. Morrison, being four feet above the group in his track, felt particularly vulnerable to flying shrapnel. He knew the armor in the back of his M3 was incapable of stopping it. He felt that anyone manning one of these weapons was likely to be hit.[6]

Now the lieutenant raced to his command half-track, leaped behind the .50-caliber machine gun, cocked it, and waited. Within minutes he could see thirteen planes coming over in formation from the east. They attacked the Thirty-Second Field Artillery and then passed almost overhead as they circled to make their return. Marcus opened fired with his Browning AN-M2 .50-caliber machine gun, which had a maximum range of about 1,800 meters (5,906 feet). As the Stuka dive-bombers approached at speeds near 200 miles per hour, he fired several rounds. Then his gun jammed. Marcus cleared it and fired until it jammed again. He cleared it once again and continued firing at the German planes.

The wail of the diving German bombers was unsettling to tanker Bill Harper, manning his half-track seventy-five yards away from that of Marcus. Harper could clearly see his lieutenant firing the .50-caliber as the planes roared in. As the Stukas flew past his half-track, Marcus switched the gun to his assistant—Staff Sergeant Kenneth Lynch—who continued to fire on the departing aircraft while Marcus began struggling to clear its feed tray.[7]

The platoon medic, PFC Henry Hunt Jr., climbed aboard the half-track and began firing the .30-caliber machine gun mounted on the back of the vehicle. The three men shot at the German planes as another Stuka swooped toward them.

Marcus looked up in time to see a large bomb separate from the plane. It came sailing straight toward him. He jumped from the half-track, but before he could hit the ground, the bomb exploded. Sergeant Lynch and PFC Hunt were killed. Red-hot bomb fragments ripped under the half-track and hit Marcus in his left arm, kidneys, and heart.[8]

Marcus lay facedown on the ground in shock. He rolled over and noticed that both of his hands were clenched into fists. He labored to open them and finally succeeded in spreading his right fingers. He used his right hand to open the fingers of his left and was relieved to find that his arm was still attached. Medics soon arrived to help him, but his action in the battle was over. Marcus would be medevaced back to the United States for surgery.

The German dive-bomber attack had knocked out two field artillery pieces, some jeeps, and Marcus's half-track. Tom Morrison, who had taken cover in the trenches, saw two other 601st tanker men crumple to the ground during the Stuka attack. One soldier would survive his injuries, but Technician Fourth Grade Austin Hritchkewitch was mortally wounded. First Lieutenant Frederick Miner of Seaford, Delaware, became acting commander of the First Platoon's A Company following the loss of Lawrie Marcus. Morrison considered Miner to be a natural leader and a fitting choice as his new CO.[9]

During the morning of March 21, Lieutenant General Patton moved to Sened Station to confer with his CCA leader, Brigadier General Mac McQuillin. Old Blood and Guts felt things were "going too slow" and wanted action. Reports were circulating about the Stuka attacks and possible Panzer sightings. From its "Wop Hill" (Hill 336) command post, the Eighteenth Infantry sent a patrol out across the plain to feel out the enemy. A Company scouts returned at dusk to report they had found fifteen German tanks and some infantry to the east.

By the next morning, things were still not moving fast enough for Patton. The previous day he had urged Major General Pinky Ward's First Armored Division to push forward more aggressively, so he sent his chief of staff, Brigadier General Gaffey, to supervise the advance this day. "I might scare him to death if I went," Patton reasoned.[10]

Ward's tankers advanced to seize the town of Maknassy. Patton hoped they would also continue on to snatch the high ground east of town. His First Infantry Division spent the day executing local attacks as it pushed along the Gafsa–Gabès road. Patton placed a call at 0930 to Colonel Frederick Gibb at the First Infantry Division's Lortess area forward command post, which had been dubbed "Danger Forward." He wanted to know if his men had pushed south across the plain to capture the hill called Djebel Berda. The reply was negative. "Well, goddamn it, get moving, and get there right away!" barked Patton.[11]

At 0955, Gibb called to Colonel Greer's Eighteenth Infantry command post. He let them know he had direct orders from "the big chief" to seize the hill and was on his way with one of his artillery commanders. Teddy Roosevelt arrived at Greer's headquarters at 0945 to size up the situation with the command staff. They knew the enemy was several kilometers to the southeast in the mountains and that one patrol remained on the high ground near Djebel Berda as observers. They decided that the Eighteenth Infantry needed to seize key terrain northeast of the Djebel Berda hill mass, overlooking the Gafsa–Gabès road, and opted to focus on a hill labeled Djebel el Kreroua.[12]

Lieutenant Colonel York's First Battalion was to move forward and occupy positions to the right flank of Lieutenant Colonel Ben Sternberg's Second Battalion. Their forward movement would be aided by an artillery fire mission to suppress enemy defenses. At 1300, York's battalion advanced with platoons of heavy machine guns attached. Captain Sam Carter's D Company of the Eighteenth Infantry Regiment trailed three rifle companies in the move. He noted enough of a gentle rise in the desert floor to hide the column as they marched over the plain without being spotted.[13]

Greer and Roosevelt watched as York's infantrymen closed in on Djebel el Kreroua and climbed toward Djebel Berda. As York's battalion crested the ridge, they were spotted by German and Italian gunners, who opened fire on them. Casualties quickly mounted, but York pushed forward while his mortar platoons worked to knock out Axis batteries. By dusk the Eighteenth Infantry had reached its objective, Djebel Berda, and taken up a defensive position. York was not impressed with the situation: his troops lay in a crescent overlooked by another mountain, labeled Hill 772. "This terrain could just swallow our whole battalion," he said to Carter.

"All this and heaven, too," Carter muttered.[14]

Hill 772 was practically sheer, rising a thousand feet over their heads. A phone line was quickly strung to the regimental commander, Colonel Greer. York explained to his boss that he had three patrols out to the north, northeast, and east to feel out the enemy positions. At 1750, Greer ordered Sternberg's Second Battalion forward to join York's First Battalion so their advance could continue toward the Gafsa–Gabès road.[15]

Terry Allen moved artillery forward to support the infantry. Sergeant Hubert Edwards and most of his Seventeenth Field Artillery Regiment were ordered to perform a general support role for the advance, aided by a battery from another field artillery battalion. Other artillery pieces were advanced one mile east of Djebel Bou Rhedja to more directly support the operations of the Eighteenth Infantry Regiment. Edwards spent the evening helping to harden gun emplacements and lay wire to observation posts and the fire direction center in preparation for a German attack. As one of his officers, First Lieutenant John Patterson, put it, "We knew they could come at us from any direction."[16]

While the Eighteenth Infantry prepared to advance on Hill 772, Major General Ward's First Armored Division pushed forward on March 22 to capture the town of Maknassy. Patton, who had sent chief of staff Gaffey forward to urge Ward into action, was not satisfied. He felt Ward should have pushed past the town to the key ridge

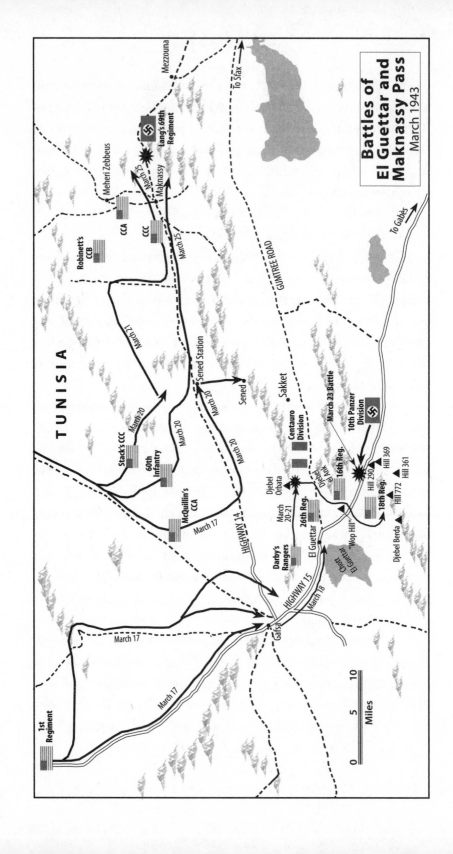

Battles of El Guettar and Maknassy Pass
March 1943

TUNISIA

To Sfax

Mezzouna

Lang's 69th Regiment

March 25

Meheri Zebbeus

Maknassy

CCA

CCC

Robinett's CCB

March 25

March 17

GUMTREE ROAD

To Gabes

Sened Station

Sened

Sakket

March 20

Stack's CCC

March 20

60th Infantry

March 20

March 20

Centauro Division

March 23 Battle

10th Panzer Division

McQuillin's CCA

March 17

Djebel Orbata

Djebel el Ank

16th Reg.

Hill 290

Hill 369

Hill 361

HIGHWAY 14

March 20-21

26th Reg.

18th Reg.

Hill 772

Djebel Berda

Darby's Rangers

"Wop Hill"

El Guettar

Chott El Guettar

HIGHWAY 15

March 18

Gafsa

HIGHWAY 15

March 17

March 17

1st Regiment

March 17

0 5 10

Miles

of Maknassy Heights as well. "If I had led the First Armored Division, we would have taken the heights," Patton wrote in his diary.[17]

Tom Morrison's tank destroyer battalion moved one step closer to combat during the late afternoon of March 22. For two days his M3 crew had observed the explosions and smoke of distant fighting near Djebel Berda and Hill 772 while sitting in reserve miles from the front. German Stukas had killed three of Morrison's comrades the previous afternoon and wounded several others, including Lieutenant Marcus.

Now under charge of Lieutenant Fred Miner, Morrison's A Company would no longer be held in reserve. Lieutenant Colonel Herschel Baker's 601st Tank Destroyer Battalion had been used to reconnoiter the eastern end of the El Guettar valley and the areas to the south and east of the Eighteenth Infantry's positions. By the evening of March 22, Major General Allen coached Colonel Frederick Gibb on where to place the tank destroyer platoons.

Baker positioned Captain Henry Mitchell's twelve destroyers of B Company and Captain Herbert Sundstrom's dozen M3s of C Company in front of the Thirty-Second Field Artillery's gun line. Lieutenant Miner's four destroyers of A Company were held in reserve behind C Company.[18]

"We were also to protect the division supply lines back to Gafsa from armored thrusts," reported Baker. Intelligence reports from Patton's G-2 indicated fifteen to twenty Panzers were located in this sector. During the overnight hours, Baker would use elements of his 601st to reconnoiter enemy positions while the balance of his crews dug in and prepared for a defensive action. His battalion's operational strength was thirty-one of its original thirty-six heavy destroyers (75mm on half-track) and six light 37mm destroyers.[19]

Shortly before midnight, Fred Miner called his chiefs of section from A Company together for a council of war. He made it clear:

their mission was to prevent any armored force from coming through the pass.[20]

Morrison's gun truck commander, Sergeant Fred Swartz, returned from Miner's briefing with details for his crew. "We are the only obstacle to the tanks and their overrunning the field artillery and cutting off the supply lines to other key combat units," Swartz relayed. "We ran from the Panzers at Ousseltia and Sbeitla, but this time we have to hold and fight back, no matter what the odds are!"[21]

Staff Sergeant Mike Stima, the platoon sergeant for Mitchell's B Company, found the pitch blackness difficult for effective positioning of his destroyers. Stima's First Platoon leader, Lieutenant John "Slim" Yowell, visited each dug-in gun, giving the commanders specific sectors to cover with their fire.[22]

The men sweated and cursed as they shoveled sand to position their half-tracks. Captain Sundstrom placed his First Platoon of C Company on the left side of the Gafsa–Gabès road with four guns extending left toward the mountains. He positioned his Third Platoon to the left of the First, stretching them out toward the mountains. Sundstrom was forced to send men back to the company headquarters to requisition extra shovels for the necessary digging.[23]

While his three main companies dug in, Lieutenant Colonel Baker ordered out two platoons of the 601st Recon Company to cover the movements of the others as they worked. By 0100 on March 23, the recon platoons had made contact with the Third Battalion, Eighteenth Infantry, to the north and with the Second Battalion, Eighteenth Infantry, to the south. By 0300, Baker's men were exhausted. Sergeant John Nowak, machine gunner for Lieutenant Yowell's half-track, had spent hours hacking at the earth with picks and shovels to entrench his M3. Nowak considered his half-track to be old-fashioned compared to the enemy's Panzer divisions.[24]

Finally positioned, all Nowak could think was that the 601st's Recon Company was closest to the German tanks reported to be nearby. "But it was still dark," he wrote in his diary. "It was hard to distinguish anything."

Old Man Baker had done his best to position his three dozen tank destroyer crews. Now all Nowak, Morrison, and their comrades could do was wait for dawn and the approach of the Germans.

Field Marshal Albert Kesselring, leading the German Army Command South, was concerned. His knowledge of all facets of the military was extensive: he had served as both an artilleryman and aviator long before Hitler gave him free control over the operations in Tunisia. Kesselring now feared that a possible U.S. counterattack might cut through his Axis lines and reach the Tunisian coast at Gabès. On March 21 he had flown to Tunis to meet with General Hans-Jürgen von Arnim, the commander of Army Group Africa. Although he was known as Smiling Albert for his ever-present optimism and toothy grin, Kesselring possessed less enthusiasm now.[25]

He came away from the conference with a lack of confidence. He noticed a neglect of the inside wings of the Fifth Panzer and First Italian Armies. Kesselring felt that the Centauro Division of the Italian Army had no hope of holding the position east of Gafsa and that the Imperiali Brigade west of Maknassy was similarly challenged with maintaining its position. Although Axis forces had reasonable intelligence on Allied strength and dispositions, Kesselring felt his Italian comrades "remained in a remarkable state of apathy."[26]

Kesselring directed Army Group Africa to block the American penetration by ordering the Tenth Panzer Division to move from theater reserve. Led by Generalmajor Fritz von Broich, the Tenth Panzer rolled out from Mahares, Tunisia, to conduct a frontal assault on the U.S. First Infantry Division, which had captured El Guettar and was pushing eastward along the Gafsa–Gabès highway. Assembling about nine miles east of El Guettar, Broich's force consisted of about 6,000 men. This included about fifty serviceable tanks, a company of tank destroyers, an assault gun battery, and infantrymen from Second Battalion, Sixty-Ninth Panzergrenadier Regiment, and Second Battalion, Eighty-Sixth Panzergrenadier Regiment.[27]

Under orders from the commander of the Deutsches Afrika Korps—Lieutenant General (Generalleutnant) Hans Cramer—Broich's force would strike the southern edge of the American penetration along the Gabès–Gafsa axis. Few German soldiers slept in the moonlight that bathed their Panzers, silently awaiting the battle orders that would come in a matter of hours. Broich ordered his division to muster at its assault position at 0300 on March 23.[28]

George Patton's troops had secured key ground in the past few days, but his men were about to face their greatest German offensive yet. As the Tenth Panzer Division rumbled to life long before dawn, its soldiers had every expectation that the weak American forces would be hammered as solidly as they had been at Faid and Kasserine Passes.

TWELVE

TANK DUEL IN "DEATH VALLEY"

Hubert Edwards was eager for redemption. Just weeks earlier, the Second Battalion of his Seventeenth Field Artillery Regiment had lost all of its howitzers and lost more than two hundred men killed or captured by the Germans. Now, in the early morning hours of March 23, Edwards and his unit's three batteries of 155mm howitzers were dug into the sand dunes two miles down the valley and 1,000 yards behind Herschel Baker's 601st Tank Destroyer Battalion's M3 gun motor carriages. Strategically placed to the left of the Gafsa–Gabès road west of Major General Ted Roosevelt's command post, the Seventeenth lay right at the anticipated advance point for the German Army.

First Infantry Division soldiers closer to the German lines would later report hearing motors rumbling long before daybreak. But Edwards heard nothing from his vantage point. "Fellows, I don't like what's going on," said Captain Paul Mulcahy, commander of B Battery. "It's awfully quiet."[1]

Mulcahy grabbed his binoculars and climbed toward the top of the highest sand dune. He sprawled out on his stomach, then slowly swept the horizon from side to side. When he finally returned to his field artillery batteries, the men were charged by his words. "Panzers," said Mulcahy. "I count about three dozen of them out there. They're lined up and ready to attack!"[2]

For Edwards, the moment of truth was at hand. Surveying the stacks of shells near his howitzer, he tried to steel his nerves and prepare for action.

─────────

Captain Sam Carter first heard the noise around 0400 when the roar of tank engines started reverberating through the still morning air. His D Company, Eighteenth Infantry Regiment, was standing by for the commencement of the assault on Hill 772. Some 1,000 feet of sheer mountain towered above their heads.[3]

It was still forty minutes before Lieutenant Colonel Robert York's First Battalion of the Eighteenth Infantry was scheduled to begin its assault on the El Guettar mountains ahead. The distant sound of engines was duly reported to Roosevelt, manning the Eighteenth Infantry's regimental headquarters some distance away on the small rise known as Wop Hill. Carter's men waited impatiently for the U.S. artillery barrage that would signal the beginning of action.

Farther away from the infantry, Technician Fifth Grade Tom Morrison was also awake and ready. His M3 half-track, commanded by Fred Swartz, a burly sergeant from New York, was in defilade—dug in defensively north of the blacktop Gafsa–Gabès road, which passed through the El Keddab Ridge. Lieutenant Fred Miner had carefully positioned the four gun trucks of his A Company. Swartz's M3 was closest to the road, in front of the sand dune. To the left were two other half-tracks, dug in atop the sand hill. To the south, on the right side of the road, was Miner's fourth M3, commanded by Sergeant Chester Karolewski. Morrison could see Miner to his left, dug into an observation post atop the dune slightly behind their tank destroyer. Miner stood ready with an assistant on the radio, ready to direct his men into action.[4]

Several thousand yards to the west of Miner's A Company position, the First Platoon of the 601st's Recon Company was the first to spot German movement. It was 0430. First Lieutenant Joseph Gioia could see the dark silhouettes of enemy foot soldiers on the move as the rumbling of engines commenced. A new distraction caught Gioia's attention. From out of the darkness the whining of a motorcycle engine announced the approach of a two-man German scout team. It was a motorcycle and sidecar barreling along the blacktop road right toward his recon platoon position.[5]

Gioia's crew opened fire. Technician Fifth Grade James Nelson let loose with a Thompson machine gun, disabling the motorcycle and seriously wounding one of its occupants. The uninjured German motorcyclist was subdued and sent back toward the U.S. command post. The 601st men knew these were enemy scouts, out looking for their opponents. "From the prisoner, we learned the Tenth Panzer Division was attacking at 0500," remembered Lieutenant Colonel Baker. "The entire situation had changed for the tank destroyer battalion. Whereas we had expected to repel small tank thrusts, we had taken positions primarily with the idea of defending the artillery against infantry infiltration. Now, with the Tenth Panzer having anywhere from 100 to 150 tanks, we knew our main action would be against heavy odds of enemy armor."[6]

Minutes later, at 0440, the El Guettar desert erupted in explosions. The II Corps artillery commenced its planned five-minute softening up of objectives in the Axis-occupied hills. Captain Sam Carter waited until this concentration ended with a round of white phosphorous from each gun, marking what he knew to be the signal for the attack. Then his Eighteenth Infantry pushed forward toward the hills, hoping to establish defensive positions before daylight. The desert valley beyond El Guettar was silent for a quarter hour following the initial artillery barrage, but the situation changed quickly just before 0500.[7]

Lieutenant John "Slim" Yowell's First Platoon of the 601st's B Company was positioned along the Gabès road. He had under his direction eight gun trucks: four from his own B Company, one from A Company, and three more from C Company. The radio in his half-track suddenly crackled to life: "An armored attack is coming down the road!" German Panzers had been spotted by II Corps scouts as they clanked west toward El Guettar. They were heading toward Yowell's platoon.[8]

Yowell shouted orders to Sergeant Willie Nesmith—whose M3 was dug in closest to the road—to keep a sharp eye out for the Germans. Within minutes Nesmith announced that by the light of a late moon he could see a Panzer rolling forward about 1,000 yards out from his position, with two companies of infantrymen interspersed between it and other trailing tanks.

Although it was still dark, Yowell yelled, "Fire when you see fit!"

Baker's 601st Recon Platoon, stationed closest to the approaching Panzers, was the first to open fire. German machine gunners quickly joined in the shooting, and their tracers lit up the landscape. Sergeant Mike Stima, standing over a machine gun on Yowell's half-track, felt the German gunners "were hunting for armor."[9]

Yowell's Third Platoon of B Company—located on the extreme right flank of the 601st battalion—was next to open up on the Germans. As soon as he could clearly see tanks and infantrymen silhouetted against the skyline, the Third Platoon commander, Lieutenant Francis Lambert from Hudson, New York, shouted, "Open fire!"[10]

Corporal Harry Ritchie's destroyer nailed a Mark IV tank with its first 75mm armor-piercing round, but the round clanged off the German's heavy armor. The second round stopped the tank, and Ritchie's crew fired three more rounds into it. From this same position, his M3 knocked out a second tank with four rounds. Ritchie's crew also lobbed ten rounds of high-explosive shells at the advancing *Panzergrenadiers*.[11]

Slim Yowell could see the distant fire from Lambert's Third Platoon. Panzers were approaching the dune occupied by his own First Platoon. Two of Yowell's destroyers, commanded by Sergeant Nesmith and Corporal Victor Hamel, could not lower their barrels enough to take the leading German tank under fire. Yowell shouted to them to back their half-tracks up a hundred yards or more to obtain a favorable firing position. As their M3s rumbled to life and moved back, the leftmost gun truck of Sergeant Adolph Raymond quickly maneuvered and was the first to open fire on one of the Mark IV tanks. His crew's first five rounds bounced off the thickly armored German tank, but their sixth shot slammed home with devastating effect and wrecked the Panzer.[12]

Raymond shifted his fire to a second Panzer and stopped it with his first shot. When he glanced back toward the point where the first German tanks had come into view, he could see even more Panzers emerging from the darkness. He was relieved to see four gun trucks from Captain Herbert Sundstrom's C Company—positioned to his left—commence firing on them.[13]

Sundstrom counted at least eighteen tanks moving toward his position. His M3s eagerly blazed away, but the enemy was still out of range. He radioed all platoons to hold their fire until the tanks were within range. The 601st Tank Destroyer Battalion command post advised him that units from B Company were maneuvering to assist against the German advance. Sundstrom conferred with his assistant, Lieutenant Charles Munn, and determined that the Panzers had gotten between the battalion's First and Third Platoons.[14]

Yowell's First Platoon began absorbing heavy damage. Sergeant Raymond's half-track had no sooner hit two Panzers than it took a German round that ricocheted off his armor plating. Sergeant

Nesmith, who had moved his gun truck to a more favorable position, immediately opened fire on the Panzer that had struck Raymond's vehicle. Although his shots punished the Mark IV, other German tanks zeroed in on Raymond's half-track. At least three direct hits completely destroyed his armored vehicle.[15]

Choking black smoke poured from the shattered engine of Raymond's M3, and he ordered his crew to abandon the gun truck. Platoon Sergeant Mike Stima, just yards from the blazing wreck, used a jeep-mounted .50-caliber machine gun to lay down covering fire as Raymond's crew sprinted for the safety of Corporal Hamel's M3. Yowell shouted for the tankless crew to make their way toward safety at the rear.

His remaining tank destroyers fired at will at the plethora of German targets. By the time dawn began to break, the lieutenant was in awe of the size of his opposing force. Enemy tanks were laying down smoke cover as more lines of Panzers advanced and enemy artillery exploded close by. He estimated the Germans to be pushing forward with at least four to five lines, with fifteen to twenty tanks in each line—what looked like more than a hundred Panzers.[16]

Within twenty minutes of the first firing, the various platoons of the 601st Tank Destroyer Battalion were embroiled in their own desperate fights. Captain Michael Paulick, commanding the battalion's Recon Company, was quickly in dire straits.

Both of his platoons opened fire with machine guns, 37mm weapons, and rounds of 75mm high-explosive and antipersonnel shells. He estimated this fire cut down at least fifty German infantrymen. By 0520 he found his Recon Company destroyers were poorly positioned to hit the Panzers. Paulick ordered them to withdraw to a fresh rallying point along the southern spear of El Keddab Ridge. In the course of shifting defensive positions, two Recon Company half-tracks were hit and disabled, injuring the Second Platoon leader in the process.[17]

The Panzer crews displayed effective firing techniques. The Germans carefully fired tracer bullets from a light machine gun mounted coaxially with their heavy-caliber gun. Then they followed with heavier-caliber shells once the machine guns had locked in the American position. Paulick's Recon Company platoons would spend the next half hour jockeying for a better position at El Keddab Ridge.

By 0545, Captain Henry Mitchell's B Company—positioned southeast of the ridge—was heavily engaged with German tanks and infantrymen. First Lieutenant Robert Luthi saw 75mm high-explosive shells from his guns taking a heavy toll on German infantrymen during the next half hour. Even under this withering fire, the German foot soldiers continued to advance, and some began sweeping around Luthi's left flank. He responded by ordering his Second Platoon of B Company destroyers to withdraw to a hill 1,000 yards behind their current position, where they joined Fred Miner's A Company.[18]

Lieutenant Lambert's Third Platoon of B Company engaged the approaching German tanks until the Second Platoon began falling back. Two of Lambert's own M3 crews followed suit, leaving the lieutenant with only two half-tracks completely exposed to fire from both the left and the right. He reluctantly ordered his two crews to also fall back, but en route Sergeant John Christian's vehicle struck at least two mines, leaving his track almost completely demolished, with several injured crewmen.

Upon reaching the rallying point hundreds of yards to the rear of his original position, Lambert was down to three guns of his Third Platoon. Corporal William Bailey's half-track had blown a tire on the way, forcing the lieutenant to order him to pull back and try to fix it. Minutes later Corporal Ritchie's half-track suffered a damaged latch on the breechblock of its 75mm gun, which the crew could not open. In less than an hour of combat, Lambert's platoon was down to one effective gun truck. Now rendezvoused with Lieutenant

Luthi's surviving Second Platoon tracks, Lambert continued to pour lead on the Germans while awaiting new orders.

Sergeant Stima could see numerous fires burning in the desert landscape around him. One of his First Platoon tank destroyers had been knocked out, but the remaining half-track crews were firing into draws to their front. Stima's M3, the command half-track of Lieutenant Yowell, was positioned near the Gabès road. Dug in to his right was the half-track of Corporal Hamel. To Stima's left was the M3 of Corporal Longin Meczywor, who was in contact with the nearby dug-in C Company. The only M3 plainly visible above the sand was the blazing wreck of Sergeant Raymond, whose shells continued to explode due to the heat. Behind it, in partial defilade, was the First Platoon's personnel carrier. Stima felt that his platoon's concealment led the Germans to believe that they had withdrawn. But, for the moment, the Panzers had halted, making it difficult for him to ascertain which ones had been hit.[19]

As broad daylight revealed the full scene before him, Stima could see numerous German infantrymen on the move near the distant tanks. Yowell's three tank destroyers, joined by C Company to their left, began pounding the ground troops with high-explosive shells. The Germans proceeded to lay down heavy smoke screens east and west along the southern ridge. By the time the smoke began to clear a half hour later, the area was filled with Panzers. There was enough light for Stima to make out the ridges, whose layouts he had become all too familiar with. *We are now really cut off!* he thought.

The half-tracks of Yowell, Hamel, and Corporal Meczywor opened up with a vengeance on the German tanks. Their fire was joined by that of nearby C Company as well as 105mm howitzers to their rear. During this firing, Stima noticed the distant platoons of Lieutenants Lambert and Luthi falling back to better defensive positions.

Yowell's platoon began scoring direct hits. For the moment, his

M3 crews were enjoying the benefit of confusion that Lambert's platoon had inflicted upon the Germans' exposed right flank. Corporal Vic Hamel saw Nesmith's crew fire at a Mark IV tank about eight hundred yards distant, landing a direct hit that knocked its turret sky-high. Hamel's gun truck succeeded in torching another German tank before Nesmith's M3 took a direct hit. German infantrymen were harassing the tank destroyers with machine-gun fire. But Hamel leaped from his mount and scrambled to help one of Nesmith's wounded gunners to the nearby personnel carrier.[20]

By this time the German Panzers had spotted Yowell's position near the top of the sand dune. They turned completely around and came back over the same route. Yowell figured that his enemy was returning both due to impassable terrain and also to put his four remaining guns out of action. As the Germans pinpointed Yowell's position, they fanned out and churned forward toward the hill held by the American tanks.[21]

"Here they come!" someone shouted.

Mike Stima fired his .50-caliber machine gun at German foot soldiers advancing with the charging tanks. He used tracers to point out key targets for his heavy gun crew. Hamel's nearby M3 crew disabled a second enemy tank by hitting it in its bogie wheel. Yowell quickly found it difficult to see anything well due to the density of smoke, gunpowder, and dust.

Corporal John Nowak, the Massachusetts gunner assigned to Yowell's half-track during the Kasserine Pass actions, assisted Stima in pouring more than 3,000 rounds of machine-gun fire into the approaching infantrymen. The German crews helped to further conceal their Panzer columns by firing smoke shells.[22]

Yowell was frustrated by the lack of visibility. He knew his thin-skinned half-tracks were no match for the advancing German tanks, so he prudently ordered Meczywor, Hamel, and Nesmith to move their vehicles to the next ridgeline. Yowell's command track followed the first three as a trio of C Company destroyers covered him. German tankers pounded away at the scrambling American M3s, and one of their 75mm shells slammed into Nesmith's gun truck, killing one man and wounding the others.

Nowak saw the survivors scrambling toward the protection of Hamel's track. Before they could reach it, Nesmith's track was permanently disabled by a second German shell that exploded in its rear section. Nowak and Yowell assisted the four wounded survivors of Nesmith's half-track while Stima covered them with machine-gun fire. The wounded tankermen had their lacerations coated with sulfanilamide powder and bandages. Yowell then ordered them onto a three-quarter-ton truck and raced back to an aid station. Other nonessential men were also sent to the rear in a First Platoon quarter-ton truck.

Yowell's platoon was knocking out targets. But with only fifty-nine rounds per M3, his men soon ran short of ammunition. Yowell and Nowak took the chance to retrieve desperately needed ammunition from Nesmith's wrecked M3. Yowell's mixed command maintained a steady fire against the German tanks maneuvering about in the valley around them. Despite their valiant efforts to fire and maneuver, his forces were slowly being whittled down.

The half-track of Corporal Meczywor was next to take a direct hit. Yowell ordered two uninjured soldiers, Privates First Class Carl Nerthling and Charles Grigiss, to remove the remaining high-explosive rounds from Meczywor's M3 and take the time to use delay fuses on their next targets. As the 601st gunners completed this process, some of the Panzer gunners found their mark on the stationary vehicle of PFC John Sauklis.

A German shell slammed into the engine block of Sauklis's M3, rendering it useless. The enemy's infantrymen and 88mm artillery shells began raining lead down on Yowell's destroyers. The lieutenant's gun truck, and those of Corporal Leo Cook and Sergeant

Woodrow Puckett, were tightly bunched within eight feet of one another. The 88s were coming so close, Cook could feel the breeze they created. His crew opened fire on a cluster of ten German trucks. Cook was certain his crew disposed of at least two enemy trucks and two tanks with their super-high-explosive shells. In between firing at these targets, Cook used his rifle to fire shots at a pesky German machine gunner whom Sergeant Stima was also firing on.[23]

Before Stima and Cook could knock out the German gunner, they were rocked by the concussion of a 77mm shell. It slammed into the front of Puckett's C Company vehicle. Hours into their duel, the surviving half-track crews were now in danger of being overrun. John Nowak shuddered with the realization that his platoon was one of the few left. Lieutenant Yowell sent two half-tracks that were depleted of ammunition back toward safety while moving his remaining M3s to the next ridge to dig in. By the time the First Platoon pulled out, B Company's original defensive line had been shattered and his destroyer crews were out of ammunition.[24]

One of the C Company gun trucks ordered back by Yowell was that of Sergeant Steve Futuluychuk. An enemy shot struck his M3's shield, destroying his machine-gun barrel. Withdrawing toward the last position of the Fifth Field Artillery, Futuluychuk's crew found the road impassable. He turned his vehicle around and headed toward the Thirty-Second Field Artillery position. But Futuluychuk flipped his half-track over while racing over the hill. In the chaos of battle, his crew had no choice but to abandon their M3 and clear the area on board another armored vehicle.[25]

Yowell's group quickly found their region swarming with German tanks and *Panzergrenadiers*. His men were under fire from enemy infantrymen. The U.S. artillery crews had blown up their guns and retreated over the nearest ridge a half hour prior. Another muzzle blast to his left, close enough that he could feel the concussion, was the deciding factor. Yowell ordered the survivors of his small force to follow his half-track. He was down to one A Company track commanded by PFC Carl Nerthling, one C Company track commanded by Staff Sergeant Hermann Bartling, his own B Company command destroyer, and his platoon's personnel carrier.[26]

The 601st Tank Destroyer men remaining with Slim Yowell opted to take to the hills to avoid any further German confrontations. Their fight through the remainder of March 23 would become one for survival.

———

The first two hours of fighting in the El Guettar valley had been equally punishing for II Corps artillery and infantry troops.

When the tank battle erupted at 0500, everything changed for Captain Sam Carter and his Eighteenth Infantry soldiers. He saw red, white, and blue tracers fired from the valley toward the noise. These were joined quickly by green, purple, yellow, and orange tracers. This kaleidoscope of color was followed by black puffs of smoke rising from heavier-caliber artillery guns. In the early darkness Carter could make out only the fiery sources of the gunfire that slowly moved westward toward him. Within half an hour, daylight started breaking, and before him in the valley was an entire Panzer division.[27]

The infantrymen dug in and prepared for a possible German counterattack. The early hours of the valley battle made quite the spectacle. To the east of Wop Hill, Carter witnessed the great fight between the Purple Heart boxes of the 601st Tank Destroyer Battalion and the Tenth Panzer Division. To him, the scene became "just a mass of guns shooting, shells bursting, armored vehicles burning, and tanks moving steadily westward."[28]

Within an hour after daylight, the German advance had become unsettling. Carter realized the Panzer division flanking Wop Hill might soon cut his troops completely off. The desperate situation of

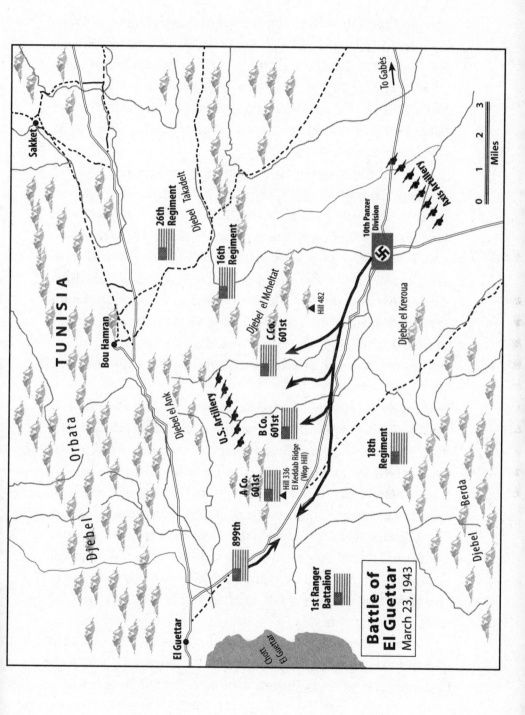

Battle of El Guettar
March 23, 1943

TUNISIA

Sakket

To Gabès

26th Regiment

Djebel Takadelt

16th Regiment

Djebel el Mcheltat

10th Panzer Division

C Co. 601st

Hill 482

Djebel el Kreroua

Axis Artillery

Bou Hamran

Djebel el Ank

U.S. Artillery

B Co. 601st

El Keddab Ridge (Wop Hill)

18th Regiment

Orbata

Djebel

A Co. 601st

Hill 336

899th

Djebel Berda

El Guettar

Chott El Guettar

1st Ranger Battalion

Miles
0 1 2 3

some of the forward forces played out dramatically over II Corps radio sets. Early in the action, Lieutenant Colonel Courtney Brown, manning the Eighteenth Infantry Regiment's Third Battalion command post near Djebel el Mcheltat (Hill 482), relayed to Colonel Frank Greer that he could hear what sounded like an entire German Panzer division moving up the valley toward Gafsa, although he could see only a few tanks.[29]

By 0630, Lieutenant Herbert Smith, the executive officer for M Company, Heavy Weapons, had enough light to see well out into the plain. He watched in awe as German Panzers advanced, counting at least seventy-five of them. The Germans in fact had only fifty Panzers, plus another nine Marder III tanks. Following behind them were infantrymen, some riding on Sonderkraftfahrzeug (Sd.Kfz.) 251 half-tracks as they proceeded up the valley. To the south, Smith spotted the main column of Mark III and Mark IV Panzers from the Seventh Panzer Regiment, plus a battalion of infantrymen, all appearing to be heading to seize Hill 336 and the 601st Tank Destroyer Battalion.[30]

As early as 0600, the Thirty-Second Field Artillery was under assault by German tanks. Their initial firing severed the wire between the gun line and the fire direction center, leaving the artillerymen without enemy coordinates for gun calculations. At the base of Djebel Bou Rhedja (Hill 483), Battery B of the Thirty-Second Field Artillery had four 105mm howitzers. The German thrust moved toward Batteries C and B and the Gabès highway in an attempt to turn the flank of the artillery battalion. The action came so close that men from the Thirty-Second were firing machine guns. By 0645, thirty German Panzers were four kilometers east of El Keddab Ridge (Hill 336).

From his command post at El Guettar, Colonel Greer dispatched two platoons from the Sixteenth Infantry Regiment to help the artillerymen. Colonel Fred Gibb, the division G-3 for the First Infantry, placed a call at 0652 requesting help from the artillery corps. "Get Long Toms on them," Gibb ordered. This was a call for the 155mm M1A1 howitzers, which had a maximum range of 23.2 kilometers. Supporting the First Infantry Division were two battalions of M1A1s, two battalions of 105mm howitzers, and one battalion of eight-inch howitzers.[31]

Brigadier General Roosevelt arrived at Greer's Wop Hill command post atop Hill 336 at 0700. Hobbling up the hill with his cane, he dropped into a chest-deep slit trench and roared encouragement to his men with his booming voice. "I could see it all," he wrote his wife two days later. "The plain became a smoky, dusty dream." Amidst the bursting shells, Roosevelt counted at least two dozen Panzers breaking toward the gap traced by Highway 15.[32]

Around 0730, German artillery and mortar strikes began raining down on the Third Battalion, Eighteenth Infantry Regiment, stationed at Hill 482. The battle was now on for these men as German tanks and infantry advanced on them. The Germans fired rifle grenades as the First Platoon was nearly overrun. One mortar team fired more than five hundred rounds of 81mm high explosive until they were in danger of being overrun. The rapid rate of fire of the mortars caused their barrels to turn a dull red color. German *Panzergrenadiers* started from an assembly area fifteen kilometers east of Hill 482 and worked up to within fifty yards of the Americans. Here it became a contest of grenade tossing at one point.[33]

Three batteries of the Thirty-Second Field Artillery Battalion had positioned themselves before dawn in wadis east of the base of Hill 483. By 0600, German *Panzergrenadiers* were moving in against C Battery and the Gabès highway to turn the flank of the artillery battalion. German tanks opened fire on the Americans while Thirty-Second Field Artillery men pounded back with 105mm howitzers and machine guns.

As the German foot soldiers closed in, Raymond Kociuba, a

member of A Battery's second gun crew, removed the greater part of his battery's powder charge. He lowered the barrel and fired at point-blank range. German soldiers continued to surge toward his position until the situation became untenable around 0820. Kociuba's captain soon ordered the artillery crews to abandon their guns and fall back along El Keddab Ridge to join the Third Battalion of the Eighteenth Infantry. Kociuba encountered a wounded comrade, who offered him his M1 Garand semiautomatic .30-06 rifle. Kociuba and his comrades scrambled to the top of the ridge and flopped down, facing the enemy. In little more than two hours, many members of the Thirty-Second had seen their armament reduced from 105mm howitzers to rifles.[34]

Roosevelt called Terry Allen on the phone around 0730, alerting him to the latest events. Three German units had infiltrated behind the Third Battalion of the Eighteenth Infantry Regiment and had overrun some of the fieldpieces of the Fifth and Thirty-Second Field Artillery Battalions. As the Americans' position became more challenged, Roosevelt ordered his division to send the 899th Tank Destroyer Battalion, attached to the Sixteenth Infantry, to help plug the gap, while he remained at Greer's Wop Hill command post.[35]

At Danger Forward, staff officers huddled around Allen. Some of them felt the enemy was too close, having pulled within four kilometers of their position. Roosevelt's report of the artillery being overrun unnerved them. One officer suggested to Allen that they pull their command post back to another location. "I will like hell pull out," Allen snapped. "And I'll shoot the first bastard that does."[36]

Some fifty yards from Danger Forward, British and American war correspondents were on hand to help document the action. Among them was thirty-eight-year-old journalist Abbott Joseph "A. J." Liebling, writing for the *New Yorker* magazine. Watching from a ridge, he noted the 601st Tank Destroyer Battalion "waddling into action like bull pups" to be knocked out by the German Panzers, "but only after they had wrecked thirty-one tanks." Shortly after the morning action commenced, Liebling could see four wrecked German tanks. "Their clumsy black bodies, belching dark smoke, remained on the field right below the command post."[37]

Danger Forward remained in place. By 0820, Allen was relieved to hear that some German tanks were beginning to withdraw. Requested air support soon arrived in the form of P-39 fighters, which began strafing German infantry forces along the Gabès road. This bright spot was replaced by new fears of being overrun as Allen's command post came under artillery fire ten minutes later. Despite mortars erupting in his vicinity, Colonel Greer sent out a morale-boosting message to his division. "General withdrawing of armor from sector," he phoned. "Our artillery is raising hell."[38]

Sergeant Hubert Edwards was among those artillerymen raising hell with the Germans. His Seventeenth Field Artillery batteries had laid down supporting fire for the tank destroyers that rushed forth. "We awoke to see the entire 10th Panzer Division looking down our throat," said First Lieutenant John Patterson, in charge of a thirty-man anti-tank platoon manning six 37mm defensive guns he dubbed "pop guns." Patterson's artillery was far inferior to the 155mm howitzers that Edwards was manning. "We got two guns in action, but it was ridiculous to shoot the things," he said later. "We were lucky they didn't pulverize us."[39]

Edwards's eight-man crew of B Company worked together as a well-oiled machine. Each 155mm shell, eight inches in diameter, weighed ninety-six pounds, quite a load for a rail-thin artilleryman like Edwards, who was also responsible for loading the correct powder charge based on the estimated range of the enemy. By the time Edwards was down to loading the number one charge, he knew his enemy was within one mile.[40]

The onrushing Germans left Edwards little time to be scared. For the moment he had but one thought: to keep loading the shells so his battery could help hold back the Afrika Korps armor.

———

Herschel Baker was frustrated. The lieutenant colonel was doing his best to help support the battle with the tank destroyers under his command. But the German tanks advanced so rapidly in such numbers that his destroyers were often forced to stand and fire as fast as they could load, exposing themselves for a considerable time to enemy tank and artillery fire.[41]

Baker's Recon Company, B Company, and C Company of the 601st Tank Destroyer Battalion—all being the most forward-deployed units—were heavily engaged during the early morning hours of March 23. Tom Morrison's A Company, being held in reserve on a sand hill along the Gabès road, could see the action unfolding. Morrison's company commander, First Lieutenant Fred Miner, waited until the leading German tank approached to within eight hundred yards of his position. Then he ordered his unit to ease its M3s up to the crest and open fire. Morrison watched the half-tracks prudently back down to the bottom of the sand dunes when the action got too hot, waiting until another worthwhile target presented itself. Miner helped direct the action from his observation post atop the sand hill, occasionally calling in artillery shots against targets.[42]

Morrison jumped on the back of his half-track and fired away at enemy soldiers marching forward. In order to slow their advance, his crew began lobbing delayed-action shells that hit the sand and bounced into the air before exploding with devastating results. Morrison was particularly pleased at one point when Miner was able to call in an artillery barrage against a Panzer that was seen to bog down in soft sand.[43]

The rising dust and smoke at times so obscured the valley battleground that Miner's A Company destroyers backed down the dune briefly to let the situation settle. By midmorning his company had inflicted its share of damage, turning back one German advance before it had gotten within 1,000 yards of his position. Morrison and his A Company comrades had slugged through the early hours without loss, but other companies of Herschel Baker's 601st Tank Destroyer Battalion had been less fortunate.

Captain Herbert Sundstrom's three platoons of C Company, dug in hull deep along the southern side of El Keddab Ridge, had been firing since sunrise. The 601st's B Company lay to his south. Staff Sergeant Bill Harper, an East Texan gunner of C Company, hoped for a better view of the scene. He crawled out of his M3 and counted seventy-five German tanks in the valley, moving toward him.[44]

His destroyer, positioned behind some of the sand hills, would roll forward to the top, fire, and then back down to reload. Harper watched another M3 crew take heavy enemy fire each time their destroyer neared the top of the dune. The vehicle had a twelve-foot antenna mounted on the windshield, which the Germans had learned to spot before the American tank destroyer topped the dune. Each time the M3 reached its elevated firing position, Harper could see the Germans had already zeroed in on its position.[45]

As the early fighting progressed, Baker—positioned at a forward command post along the southern side of El Keddab Ridge—learned that the Second and Third Platoons of B Company had pulled out of their positions without his authorization. He was furious. He immediately ordered his battalion's S-3, Captain Ben Fuller, to organize a counterattack to recapture these positions. Fuller opened up on the radio and ordered a platoon of B Company to accomplish this mission. Then he left his command post to hand-deliver the orders to First Lieutenant Kenneth Stark.

When Fuller arrived, Stark reported that he had only five operable trucks available for the counterattack. Within minutes a German shell struck the motor of the M3 commanded by Sergeant Mike

Dragon, forcing his crew to abandon it. Stark gathered his four remaining tank destroyers and placed them under the command of Lieutenant Francis Lambert, his Third Platoon leader.[46]

Lambert had withdrawn his platoon earlier in the morning—and drawn the ire of Herschel Baker in doing it. Now he was charged with leading four of his M3s onto a ridge to protect the Thirty-Second Field Artillery's howitzers. His charge included his own B Company command half-track, plus three destroyers borrowed from Lieutenant Luthi's command: those of Sergeant John Ritso, Staff Sergeant Joseph Kindall, and Corporal Clyde Holden.

En route to the ridge, Lambert's quartet was taken under extremely heavy German tank fire. Lambert's track was hit and disabled, forcing him and his men to abandon their blazing vehicle. He ordered the others to keep going at full speed in an attempt to get them in defilade behind a small ridge to the east.[47]

Sergeant Ritso surged forward with the three remaining gun trucks. Lieutenant Lambert and his M3 commander, Corporal Ernest Linkey, decided to leave the rest of their stranded crew and move forward on foot behind Ritso. Before they could reach Ritso's new position, the three American half-tracks commenced heavy firing. Positioned between their own artillery and the advancing Panzers, they began scoring hits.

The first shot from Ritso's half-track sailed over his target. Adjusting his range down, he scored a direct hit with an armor-piercing tracer. As the Germans abandoned their Panzer, Ritso slammed their vehicle again with a high-explosive round with a delayed fuse. As the Panzer burst into flames, Ritso's gunners landed another shell that wiped out the scrambling German tankers.[48]

Almost immediately, another Mark IV tank moved up behind the one Ritso had disabled. Two direct hits stopped it and set it afire. Using the last of his high-explosive shells, Ritso stopped a third approaching German tank but was unable to set it afire. Although disabled, the Mark IV continued firing at the three American de-stroyers. Ritso had his crew switch to armor-piercing shells to mow down advancing lines of enemy infantry coming over the ridge.

Rifle fire and machine-gun rounds bounced off the 601st tank de-stroyers as German tanks approached from three sides. With a large hill to their rear, Ritso found he was hopelessly pinned down. An-other of his half-tracks was hit, leaving only two effective M3s against the swarming enemy. Ritso reluctantly ordered his crews to destroy their remaining two guns to prevent the Germans from using them against the Americans. Shepherding their wounded, his men fled into the hills toward safety. They had failed to protect the Thirty-Second Artillery guns, but they left a number of German Panzers burning in their wake.

The retreat of Lambert and Ritso's team on foot was covered by the fire of Corporals Harry Ritchie and Bill Bailey's B Company de-stroyers, positioned on a ridge to the rear. Ritchie later estimated that his team destroyed four German tanks and hit at least two oth-ers before his own track was hit in the front. Ritchie's team took cover until the nearby U.S. artillery crews were forced to blow up their guns. His men then sabotaged their own half-track and re-treated on foot.[49]

Hundreds of yards north of this action, the tank destroyers of C Company's Second and Third Platoons were exchanging fire with the advancing Germans. Second Lieutenant Charles Munn, leading the Third Platoon, found his observation post under heavy fire from *Panzergrenadiers* sweeping their area with two machine guns. One of his NCOs, Sergeant Milford Langleis, used his .50-caliber ma-chine gun to rake one of the two German positions and kill the en-emy gunner.[50]

Munn's position soon came under more intense fire. A pair of German light tanks had reached a defiladed position where they could bracket the open-topped M3 tank destroyers with mortar fire.

One explosion ripped Corporal Kenneth Kalwite's half-track, wounding two of his crewmen. Munn turned command of his platoon over to a sergeant and hurried to join Lieutenant John Perry to fetch more ammunition for his besieged men. Their ammunition resupply half-track came under intense shell fire from a group of German tanks but succeeded in returning with a fresh supply of ammunition.

Munn soon found his platoon and the nearby B Battery of the Thirty-Second Artillery in danger of being overrun by swarming German infantrymen. Just south of his position, Captain Sundstrom's C Company of the 601st Tank Destroyer Battalion was forced to flee over the El Keddab Ridge. Sundstrom and Lieutenant Lester Matter Jr. escaped on foot, leaving Perry and Munn in command of the remaining tank destroyers in front of the Thirty-Second Field Artillery.

At 1100, Corporal Kalwite's damaged half-track took two direct hits that killed one man and injured the other crewmen. Kalwite was ordered to maneuver his crippled destroyer hundreds of meters to the rear, leaving only three half-tracks: Corporal Salvatore Migliaccio's from Second Platoon and two M3s of Lieutenant Perry's platoon.

Lieutenant Colonel Baker's 601st Tank Destroyer Battalion had fought valiantly throughout the morning but had suffered heavy losses. For the time being, Lieutenant Munn's remaining units took positions in the hills and soon became witnesses to a new charge of U.S. armored vehicles.

———

The arrival of the cavalry was a boost to Charles Munn's besieged destroyer men. The new force pulling onto the battlefield during the late morning was the reinforcements from the 899th Tank Destroyer Battalion. Lieutenant Colonel Max Tincher, a twenty-eight-year-old West Point graduate, led two companies of his 899th past the II Corps division artillery post at 0947. Operating under the direction of Lieutenant Colonel Baker, Tincher's tanks rolled forward to assist

Baker's 601st companies B and C in defending the exposed American artillery positions south of Hill 336 on the Gabès road.

The 899th men had the Army's latest weapon, the M10 tank destroyer, which carried a three-inch gun, larger in diameter than the M3's 75mm gun. Although the three-inch gun had higher armor penetration, Tincher's M10s were no match for the German Panzers. But his crews had made the most of their waiting period during the morning hours. Captain Clarence Heckethorn, commander of C Company, had ordered his crews to fill sandbags and pack the floors of their M10s and quarter-ton jeeps as protection against land mines.[51]

Captain Kirk Adams's B Company led the procession of the 899th Tank Destroyer Battalion down the Sidi Bou Zid road toward El Guettar. C Company was close behind. A Company brought up the rear. Heckethorn's half-track crews opened full throttles for the dash to meet the German Panzers. "My men were champing at the bit," said Captain Thomas Hawksworth, commander of the 899th's A company. Making nearly 45 miles per hour, the 899th armored vehicles sped down the two-lane road, which bisected the valley, and there met up with Lieutenant Colonel Tincher and his S-3 (battalion operations officer), Captain Joseph Morrison, along with Herschel Baker of the 601st.[52]

Lieutenant Gerald Coady, leading the First Platoon of B Company, charged through the mountain pass and immediately drew the fire of the Germans. One of his destroyers struck a mine, killing its commander and disabling the vehicle. The remainder of Coady's half-tracks moved to the north side of the road, took up hull defilade positions, and exchanged fire with the German tanks.

Captain Heckethorn's C Company fanned out on the mounds surrounding the area to support B Company, while A Company was held in reserve. Captain Hawksworth, having raced his M10s to the battleground, was furious. "To say my entire company was disgusted is an understatement," Hawksworth reported. "With our firepower and the field of fire, we would have had a field day."[53]

Lieutenant Coady's B Company was poorly positioned, and German tanks began making their shots count. The half-track of Captain Adams was soon disabled and the tank destroyer of Corporal Thomas Wilson took hits. Wilson's crew continued firing its three-inch gun on German machine-gun emplacements and artillery pieces until a third hit forced his wounded crew to abandon their M10. The 899th's casualties were hauled off the field on stretchers strapped to their armored vehicles, but Coady's unit remained in the fight for hours.[54]

Coady and other brave men from his company would later receive the Silver Star for their efforts in facing the German Panzers. The 899th Tank Destroyer Battalion claimed destruction of ten Mark IV tanks on March 23 but in return suffered four of its M10s knocked out, four men killed, and another fifteen tankers wounded.[55]

Ted Roosevelt spent the morning monitoring the victories of the artillery each time a German tank was hit. By midmorning the Americans were already referring to the battlefield gap as "Death Valley." German infantrymen added heavy doses of machine-gun fire, laid down so rapidly at times that Roosevelt felt it sounded like "tearing cloth." Roosevelt deemed the 899th battalion "gallant but green" as it sallied against the Panzers. But the two tank destroyer battalions had inflicted ample damage on the Germans, knocking out dozens of tanks. As the Panzer divisions retreated eastward to regroup, they managed to tow away some of their damaged tanks for repairs. The men with Roosevelt burst into cheers.[56]

At Danger Forward, Terry Allen felt enough confidence in the morning's victory to call a press conference for the dozens of American and British war correspondents, whose forward quarters were only fifty yards away from the First Division command post. To Liebling, Allen seemed to have the confidence of a football coach right after winning a big game, although he admitted that none of his First Armored Division tanks had taken part in the victory. The credit instead fell on the smaller tank destroyers, the artillery corps, the infantry, and the First Ranger Battalion. "Everybody in the division deserves credit," announced Allen. He even quoted lines from the First Division song that seemed appropriate: "We're a hell of a gang to tangle with; just stick with us and see. The First Division will lead the way from hell to victory."[57]

Lieutenant Colonel Bill Darby's Rangers had been called forward during the morning battle and were ordered to take a defensive position on the left flank of the Third Battalion, Eighteenth Infantry, as the German attack continued. Shortly after noon, Captain Jack Street watched U.S. artillery and tank destroyer units hold off German tank and infantry advances with heavy firepower. As the Rangers advanced, Les Kness was awed by the sight of First Division artillery pieces lined up nearly hub to hub for a half mile across the desert. He watched the gallant M3 crews dashing about in their half-tracks, laying down fire before pulling back to take cover again.[58]

March 23 proved to be the last day Rangers photographer Phil "Snapdragon" Stern would capture images of the battles near El Guettar. He volunteered to join a Headquarters Company party setting up an observation point where observers helped to direct artillery fire down on the German tanks. Marching alongside Tech 4 Harry Launer, Stern heard another Ranger yell out. They dived to either side of a rocky hillside to take cover, but incoming Axis rounds wounded the radio operator and Captain William Martin. Stern and Captain Frederic Saam took their positions to resume the task of directing II Corps artillery fire.[59]

Disregarding his own safety, Stern hoped he would capture some worthy action shots from this vantage point. He had just exposed a frame of several infantrymen advancing alongside a Sherman tank when a German 88mm shell exploded nearby. Stern was knocked unconscious by the explosion. Shrapnel ripped halfway through his right hand and into his neck and right arm. His left leg was shattered. Dazed and with his right hand hanging by tendons, Snapdragon ripped open a sulfanilamide pack with his teeth and left hand to pour antibiotics on his wounds.

First Ranger Battalion medics managed to stop the photographer's blood flow before hustling him to a nearby field hospital on a jeep. "When we arrived at the aid station, I remember being given the last rites from the Army chaplain," Stern wrote. "I told him I had to decline because I still had five more payments to make on my car."[60]

The popular Rangers photographer was out of action. He was hauled to an evacuation hospital in Tunisia, where he was given emergency surgery, then driven to the airport and flown to the General Hospital in Morocco. Working in his favor was the fact that this hospital was staffed by doctors from Massachusetts General, including a skilled hand surgeon who repaired the tendons in his shooting hand so well that Stern later felt it "worked better than before."[61]

Snapdragon Stern's time with the Rangers in Tunisia was cut short by the German shell explosion, but the unflappable photographer would recover in time to rejoin his beloved Rangers prior to deployment for the upcoming Operation Husky.

⸺

The German assault had started well enough on March 23. They had moved forward under cover of darkness toward the American positions and then split into attack formation at the foot of the hills. One group of tanks advanced toward Djebel el Ank with Panzergrenadier Regiment 69 while the bulk of the tanks attacked along the road toward Wadi el Keddab with Panzergrenadier Regiment 86.[62]

The soldiers of Panzergrenadier Regiment 69 moved swiftly at first over the ridges and washes. Nineteen-year-old machine gunner Ernst Breitenberger found that the ground quickly became too steep for the German half-tracks to proceed any farther. His company of

140 men was loaded with two dozen light and four heavy MG 34 machine guns, capable of firing more than eight hundred rounds per minute. Breitenberger's squad hopped from the half-tracks, formed up, and began their attack by moving due north.[63]

Panzergrenadier Regiment 69 pushed to the foot of Hill 482, where they were greeted by murderous fire. The U.S. Eighteenth Infantry Regiment soldiers were dug in behind walls of rocks. Breitenberger found the ground so hard that he and his comrades could dig in only a few inches. Amidst the small-arms fire, artillery barrages, and tank destroyer rounds, his company lobbed grenades toward the American positions, but snipers soon began to whittle down the German machine-gun crews.

Advancing east of Hill 336, the infantrymen were soon caught in another bad position. The German force was successful early on, breaking through American infantry units and overrunning some of the U.S. artillery positions. But stout resistance from the II Corps tank destroyers and other artillery units eventually halted the Eighty-Sixth Regiment's advance. Hauptmann Wilhelm Leyendecker, the commander of Panzergrenadier Regiment 86, exhorted his troops to get moving again through the furious barrage, but he was badly wounded and had to be hustled to the rear for treatment.[64]

Each of the German assaults had stalled out before noon on March 23, forcing the leading units to pull back slightly. Damaged tanks were towed away for repairs while German leaders regrouped their divisions. The morning battle had not gone according to plan, but the fight for El Guettar was far from over.

Major General Lloyd Fredendall, the U.S. Army II Corps commander in North Africa, who more often than not commanded his troops from a distant underground bunker. In the wake of II Corps losses at Faid and Kasserine Passes, Fredendall would be replaced.   *U.S. Army*

George Smith Patton Jr., wearing the two stars of a major general, is seen in November 1942 during Operation Torch, the Allied landings in North Africa. Patton is standing on the beach at Fedala, Morocco, with his trademark ivory-handled Colt revolvers on his hips and his general stars conspicuously visible to any potential sniper.
NARA, U.S. Army/
Real War Photos

ABOVE: Field Marshal Erwin Rommel, the Desert Fox, seen in North Africa in late 1941 with the Fifteenth Panzer Division.
NARA

RIGHT: Rudolf Schneider, one of Rommel's personal drivers, is seen in early 1943 in North Africa digging out a captured Willys jeep of the British Army's Long Range Desert Group recon unit.
Gavin Mortimer

Carrying a submachine gun, a U.S. infantryman advances on a blazing German tank near Medjez-el-Bab, Tunisia, on January 12, 1943.   *NARA, U.S. Army photo*

Captured German Mark IV medium tank equipped with a 75mm gun of higher velocity and range than U.S. Army tank guns.

U.S. Army

German Panzer "Tiger" tank with 88mm gun and turret able to traverse 360 degrees.

U.S. Army

ABOVE LEFT: General Hans-Jürgen von Arnim, seen after his capture in North Africa in May 1943. *NARA, U.S. Army photo*

ABOVE RIGHT: Captured Nazi leaders in North Africa, May 1943. Left, General Hans Cramer, commander of the German Afrika Korps, and General Friedrich von Broich. *NARA, U.S. Army photo*

LEFT: Rudolf Schneider is seen at right with a comrade with fresh antelope kills in North Africa. *Gavin Mortimer*

DJEBEL KSAIRA · TO SFAX · FAID · GARET HADID · TO SBEITLA

A 1943 view of Faid Pass looking westward toward Djebel Ksaira and Sidi Bou Zid.

NARA, U.S. Army photo

ABOVE: Lieutenant Colonel John Knight Waters, son-in-law of General George Patton.

U.S. Army photo

RIGHT: A gun crew loads a towed M2 105mm howitzer in action at Kasserine Pass in February.

NARA, U.S. Army photo

ABOVE: Reconnaissance party of the 894th Tank Destroyer Battalion advances through Kasserine Pass on the Kasserine–Thala road in late February 1943. The Germans made their approach up this road.
NARA, U.S. Army photo

LEFT: U.S. M4 medium tanks, known as Shermans, on the move toward Kasserine Pass on February 24, 1943.
NARA, U.S. Army/ Real War Photos

Soldiers of the Second Battalion, Sixteenth Infantry Regiment, march east through Kasserine Pass toward Feriana, Tunisia, on February 26, after Rommel's withdrawal.
NARA, U.S. Army/ Real War Photos

ABOVE LEFT: General Dwight Eisenhower pins George Patton with a third star to mark his promotion to lieutenant general on March 16, 1943.   *U.S. Army photo*

ABOVE RIGHT: Major General Orlando Ward, commander of the First Armored Division, received plenty of criticism from his new II Corps commander. Nicknamed "Pinky" for his once-reddish hair color, he received the Distinguished Service Cross for his valor in Tunisia.   *U.S. Army*

RIGHT: One of the more colorful leaders at El Guettar was Brigadier General Teddy Roosevelt Jr., the twenty-sixth president's son and second-in-command of the First Infantry Division. Roosevelt is seated before his "Rough Rider" jeep.
NARA, U.S. Army/Real War Photos

BELOW: An M4A1 Sherman medium tank from Company G, Third Battalion, First Armored Division, tows a disabled M3 half-track near Djebel Lessouda.
NARA, U.S. Army photo

ABOVE: U.S. soldiers examine a German Mark IV tank knocked out by American artillery fire near Kasserine Pass. One shot entered the tank and blew up its ammunition. *NARA, U.S. Army/Real War Photos*

RIGHT: Acting corporal Harley Alvin Reynolds, Sixteenth Infantry Regiment, First Infantry Division. *U.S. Army photo*

Second from right, facing forward, Patton is seen in his M3A1 scout car en route to Gabès, Tunisia, on March 14, 1943. *NARA, U.S. Army/Real War Photos*

U.S. Army Rangers on maneuver in the mountains near Arzew in late January 1943. The Rangers made a name for themselves with night raids through the mountains in North Africa in February and March.

NARA, U.S. Army Signal Corps photo/ Real War Photos

Ranger snipers. Corporals Robert Bevan (left) and Carl Drost seen on the morning of November 8, 1942. This photo was taken by Rangers photographer Phil Stern above the Algerian port town of Arzew. Bevan and Drost are firing at distant snipers using the open sights of their M1903 Springfield rifles.

NARA, U.S. Army Signal Corps photo/Real War Photos

ABOVE LEFT: Lieutenant Colonel William Darby, the original commander of the First Ranger Battalion. *U.S. Army photo*

ABOVE RIGHT: Lieutenant Lester Kness of C Company earned a battlefield commission while serving in the Rangers during the North Africa campaign. *Wade Kness*

Immediately following their night raid on Sened Station, Bill Darby's Rangers stand at attention for an award ceremony in February 1943. Major General Fredendall and his staff are pinning Silver Stars on Darby and thirteen other Rangers. Seen at far left are Rangers Chuck Shunstrom and Frederick Saam. Darby is to right, with the award group, with his arms behind his back.

U.S. Army Signal Corps, 241428

ABOVE: More than 2,000 captured Italian soldiers are marched back through British Eighth Army lines outside El Hamma, Tunisia, in March 1943.

Imperial War Museum

LEFT: Sergeant Lester Bernard Cook was twenty years old at the time of the El Guettar battle. At the time of Cook's passing in 2020, he was the last original member of Darby's Rangers. *U.S. Army photo*

ABOVE LEFT: Battery B of the Seventeenth Field Artillery in action with a Schneider model 155mm howitzer at El Guettar on March 23, 1943. *NARA, U.S. Army photo*

ABOVE RIGHT: Sergeant Hubert Edwards of the Seventeenth Field Artillery. *Hubert Edwards*

RIGHT: The author with one-hundred-year-old Hubert Edwards in 2019, holding a modern Army howitzer shell casing given to Hubert when he visited Fort Bragg to observe modern artillery firing. *Author's collection*

601st Tank Destroyer Battalion veterans:

LEFT: Staff Sergeant Michael Stima, seen at his 1945 wedding. *Mike Stima*

MIDDLE: Sergeant John Nowak, seen in February 1942. *Nowak family, courtesy of Victor Failmezger*

RIGHT: Tom Morrison, Technician Fifth Grade at El Guettar, who was wounded in action on March 23. *Catherine Morrison Friedman*

601st Tank Destroyer Battalion at El Guettar on March 23, 1943. The officers studying the map are Captain Michael Paulick and First Lieutenant Joseph Gioia, standing before their radio-equipped command half-track. Two jeeps and an M3 gun motor carriage mounted with a 75mm gun are in the background. *NARA, U.S. Army photo*

ELEMENTS OF THE 601 T.D. BN. FIGHT A REAR GUARD ACTION AT SBEITLA TUNISIA 2-17-43

Thomas E. Morrison

Tanker Tom Morrison made sketches of some noteworthy action he participated in during the North Africa campaign. This sketch depicts his unit, the 601st Tank Destroyer Battalion, in action near Sbeitla, Tunisia, on February 17.

Catherine Morrison Friedman

Tanks advancing toward the El Guettar battlefield on the morning of March 23, 1943. The fight this day would be carried out by smaller tank destroyers.
NARA, U.S. Army/ Real War Photos

During the North Africa battles, Patton often stood out in the open wearing his three-star helmet and rode in command vehicles adorned with his stars.
NARA, U.S. Army/Real War Photos

Italian gunners manning a light gun in a cactus patch during the Tunisian battles of March 1943.
NARA, U.S. Army/Real War Photos

Three M3 gun motor carriages of the 601st Tank Destroyer Battalion, seen wrecked after their fight against German Panzers on March 23, 1943.
NARA, U.S. Army/Real War Photos

Scripps-Howard newspaper correspondent Ernie Pyle (center), sitting with an Army tank crew in 1944, wrote extensively of the North Africa campaign. *NARA*

A half-track crew advances at the western end of Kasserine Pass early in the fighting. Note the T19 105mm howitzer mounted on the M3.

NARA, U.S. Army photo

Three of Darby's Rangers stand atop an Italian gun that had fired shells at the Thélepte airfield in Tunisia. The Italians blew up the gun and fled.

NARA, U.S. Army/Real War Photos

Three stars at El Guettar. Observing the action from a forward trench on March 30 are Brigadier General Teddy Roosevelt Jr., Major General Terry Allen, and Lieutenant General George Patton.

NARA, U.S. Army/ Real War Photos

ABOVE: A U.S. Sherman tank crosses an anti-tank ditch during the advance through the Gabès Gap in Tunisia around April 7, 1943.
NARA, U.S. Army/Real War Photos

RIGHT: Gunners of the Ninth Infantry Division in action during the Battle of El Guettar.
NARA, U.S. Army/Real War Photos

BELOW: Allied North Africa campaign leaders in 1944. Left to right, George Patton, Omar Bradley, and British general Bernard Law Montgomery.
Imperial War Museum

ABOVE: Lieutenant Henry G. "Red" Phillips of the Forty-Seventh Infantry Regiment, 9th Infantry Division, was wounded at El Guettar.
Kathryn Phillips

Major General Manton
S. Eddy (seated),
commander of the Ninth
Infantry Division, seen
in 1943. Lieutenant
General Patton called on
Eddy's division to assault
Hill 369 in late March.
NARA, U.S. Army photo

Company D, Eighteenth
Infantry Regiment, First
Infantry Division, digs
into the rocky soil at El
Guettar in March 1943.
NARA, U.S. Army photo

ABOVE: Djebel Tahent (Hill 609) in northern Tunisia was the site of heavy fighting that began on April 28, 1943. This hill was a natural fortress that blocked the approaches to the plains near Mateur. *NARA, U.S. Army photo*

BELOW: Hundreds of thousands of Axis forces surrendered to Allied forces by May 1943. This view of a Tunisian POW camp was taken in early June. *NARA, USAAF photo*

THIRTEEN

"IT WAS LIKE MOWING HAY"

Save for his coat and shoes, George Patton had gone to sleep fully dressed on March 22. He rose early at his II Corps headquarters in Feriana, anticipating action with the Germans by daybreak. His expectations were realized by 0630 when a call from Terry Allen alerted him that his First Infantry Regiment was engaged with a hundred tanks. "Actually, there were 50," Patton wrote later in his diary, taking his major general's assessment as an exaggeration. He believed Allen's troops were "not well disposed" to meet their enemy's advance. He soon learned the Germans had broken through the Eighteenth Infantry, seizing two batteries from the Thirty-Second and Seventh Field Artillery Battalions.[1]

Although his men claimed to have knocked out twenty Panzers, Patton figured that number to also be inflated. The only bright spot to him was the fact that the Axis advance had been halted after the noon hour once it came within two miles of the U.S. divisional headquarters. Further optimism was afforded him by the fact that Allied air support, absent during the early morning hours, had arrived in sufficient force to provide his troops a better chance of regrouping before the Germans could renew their advance this day.

For Sergeant Hubert Edwards, the withdrawal of the German Panzers during late morning offered his Seventeenth Field Artillery howitzer crew a much-need respite. He found that between the dozen 155mm guns of his First Battalion's four batteries, there were only a handful of shells remaining. He could only think: *Imagine what the Germans would have done to us if they knew that.*[2]

For Tom Morrison, the morning had been relentless for his 601st Tank Destroyer Battalion. Two companies had sustained heavy losses, although Morrison's A Company, under Lieutenant Fred Miner, was largely unscathed by the time the Germans fell back to regroup. During the late morning, Brigadier General Ted Roosevelt visited Miner's command post to supervise the replacement of a 37mm anti-tank gun knocked out in the early action. His staff tried to persuade Roosevelt to return to the comparative safety of the sand dunes. Instead, the general hobbled along the rocky road with his swagger stick as if he were strolling some quiet avenue.[3]

Lieutenant Colonel Herschel Baker was impressed with the morning's slugging match. He was proud that his tank destroyers had knocked out a considerable number of the superior German Panzers. Baker's men had displayed great courage. Captain Ben Fuller, the battalion operations officer, commandeered a jeep even after suffering a severe wound. He raced to where a German 75mm gun had taken the 601st under fire. Fuller found five *Panzergrenadiers* lying about the mangled weapon and captured two of its survivors.[4]

Radio reports gave Baker a better understanding of his battalion's challenges. Most of his M3s east of the El Guettar area hill mass were out of action. Many forward artillerymen had abandoned their guns. His enemy's intentions and capabilities were understood, and the Axis strength was great. Baker thus had no intention of committing more tank destroyer units to offensive action at this time. His only radio communication for the moment was with Lieutenant Charles Munn of C Company. Munn told him that he had only one service-able M3 gun motor carriage and at least nine enemy tanks within 1,100 yards of him in defiladed position. Baker told Munn to remain concealed until dark and not fire unless he had to. Munn was to use his own judgment as to whether he should abandon his gun and flee on foot to save valuable armored personnel.[5]

A short while later Baker established radio communication with Lieutenant John Yowell, who reported his own B Company had only two serviceable tank destroyer guns and seventy rounds of ammuni-tion. Baker ordered Yowell to move north and northeast after dark to contact friendly infantry.[6]

The only intact portion of the 601st Tank Destroyer Battalion was Miner's A Company. Morrison's tank commander, Sergeant Fred Swartz, used the lull in the action to drive his M3 over the sand dunes near the Gafsa road and park it in a safer position. Then he took a jeep back to the rear supply area for gasoline and ammo. Miner remained at his command post with a phone line strung to the nearest field artillery battalion, content to help hold the line as the German Panzer divisions pulled back to lick their wounds.[7]

Reports poured in. From his El Guettar headquarters of the First Infantry Division, Colonel Frank Greer radioed at 1245 that the Eighteenth Infantry was still in position and that German tanks ap-peared to be covering the retreat of German soldiers. Ted Roosevelt reported a hundred Germans from the 580th Reconnaissance Unit and some from the Seventh German Infantry had been captured. He radioed that the Eighteenth Infantry and the Seventeenth Field Ar-tillery were doing "a grand job," having knocked out some two dozen Panzers. The Germans had overrun at least six howitzers of the Fifth and Thirty-Second Field Artillery battalions during the morning, so Roosevelt ordered a counterattack to restore the lost positions. Two companies of Lieutenant Colonel Joseph Crawford's Second Battalion, Sixteenth Infantry, were sent forward, along with guns, trucks, and resupply ammunition.[8]

Lieutenant Colonel Bill Darby's First Ranger Battalion was ordered to advance to take over the position being vacated by Crawford's battalion. As the Sixteenth Infantry began reclaiming the overrun artillery positions, Darby radioed at 1300 that the Germans were in full withdrawal mode. "Our trucks are dragging three damaged TDs back from the front to our OP," he said. "Everything looks quiet now."[9]

—————

As the Germans withdrew, Patton's II Corps used the time to resupply and reposition forces. But the relative quiet that had descended upon the El Guettar battlefield was disrupted at 1450 by the roar of a dozen Ju 87 Stuka dive-bombers. The Luftwaffe raiders did little damage to Greer's First Infantry Division headquarters, but their bombs and bullets created havoc for some of the U.S. artillery forces in midafternoon. The planes kept artillerymen in foxholes long enough for German tanks to advance and unleash their firepower. The air raids were conducted by Me 109 and Focke-Wulf Fw 190 fighters and Ju 87 Stukas.[10]

Sergeant Hubert Edwards became irritated after an Me 109 passed close overhead, stitching bullets into the sand near their Battery B guns. As the plane roared past and banked to prepare for another run, Edwards jumped to his feet. He shouted to a New Jersey battery mate, Michael Naeman.[11]

"Come on, Mike!"

"Where are you going?" called Naeman.

"To my jeep," yelled Edwards. "When that guy comes back, I'm going to take care of him!"

His battalion jeep was just twenty yards away. It was mounted with a .50-caliber machine gun, which the sergeant quickly rigged for firing. Naeman hurried over to assist with the ammunition belts.

Edwards swung the gun over the dunes in the direction of the distant whining of the aircraft's engine.

"He's on his way again!" Edwards said as the approaching Me 109 roared in for a second strafing pass on the artillery pieces. His first round was a tracer to adjust his aim. Then he unleashed a burst of armor-piercing rounds. Naeman shouted, "Give him hell! Give him hell!"

Edwards was dead on the money. His rounds shredded through the Messerschmitt's engine at short range. Fire and black smoke erupted from the fighter, which banked off to the right and slammed into the desert a half mile away. While he was proud to be credited with an Me 109 shoot-down, Edwards hoped that his rounds had killed the pilot quickly to spare him the agony of burning up in his aircraft after it crashed.

More than a mile south of the artillery, Baker's tank destroyers were also plagued by marauding Luftwaffe bombers and German artillery pieces midway through the afternoon. Due to the battering that Companies B and C of his 601st Tank Destroyer Battalion had taken, Baker had ordered Lieutenant Fred Miner's A Company to withdraw their gun trucks behind the sand dunes to refuel and restock ammunition.

Half-track commander Sergeant Fred Swartz ordered gunner Tom Morrison to clean out the ammunition. Housed in slits in the floor of his gun truck, the ammo had become fouled with sand from all the artillery bursts. Morrison set to work, cleaning the sand-coated shells while also loading fresh ammo from a resupply truck that drove up.[12]

Once the ammunition was cleaned and restocked, Morrison refueled the A Company half-tracks from the resupply vehicles. Howitzer shells continued to explode in the vicinity, coupled with German dive-bombers working over U.S. positions, so Morrison then turned to digging a foxhole for protection.[13]

Swartz called, "Dig that big enough for me, too."[14]

By the time he had excavated a two-man slit trench around 1400, Morrison was exhausted. He took a break to prepare coffee and began by filling an empty C ration can half full of sand. He added several ounces of fuel, lit it, and placed a steel canteen cup on top of the small fire to heat water. A few minutes later, hot coffee in hand, Morrison plopped down beside his half-track to munch on some rations.

"Where did you get that coffee?" two of his fellow gunners asked.[15]

"Well, I've got a fire going," he said. "Hand me a canteen cup of water and I'll get it for you."

Morrison prepared coffee for his companions, then crawled back out of the trench to finish his own. He had just leaned against his half-track and taken a sip when he heard the distinctive whistle of an incoming German mortar. Instinctively he hunched down just as the shell exploded, hitting the right-side gas tank of his M3.

He was struck in the mouth by flying metal, and the concussion slammed him into his freshly dug foxhole. As the smoke cleared, he saw flames leaping from the M3 and heard someone yell, "Two guys are in that half-track!"

Morrison collected his senses and with Private Peter Borowy ran to the blazing vehicle. Two members of their crew—PFC Charles Hird and Technician Fifth Grade Theodore "Corky" Kordana—had been killed. The inside of the M3 was scorched like a blast furnace. Their comrades had burned to death almost instantly. Swartz, in a daze, cried out, "I couldn't get to them."[16]

With his vehicle destroyed and his crewmates either killed or injured, Morrison joined others ordered back to the 601st's rear headquarters. After a quick lunch, he crawled into a buddy's hammock and fell fast asleep, bloodied and exhausted from the day's action.

Lieutenant Colonel Baker continued to monitor the position of his strung-out tank destroyer companies during the lull in the German armored advance. Around 1520 he received word from the corps' G-2 that an enemy attack would be launched at 1600 hours. A short time later, another radio intercept moved the time of the Axis attack back forty minutes to 1640. Baker worried the message might be a German trick, a broadcast the Americans were intended to intercept, but he briefed his men for another battle.[17]

By 1630 the Deutsches Afrika Korps was preparing to move forward again. Preceding this advance, Luftwaffe planes had conducted more raids on II Corps artillery and advance infantry positions. Thanks to the radio intercepts, the U.S. forces at El Guettar were prepared as the Tenth Panzer Division once again advanced, supported by artillery and two *Panzergrenadier* battalions.

By 1640, advance tank destroyer crews began reporting Panzers approaching El Guettar from the east. From his 601st Tank Destroyer Battalion forward command post along the southern side of El Keddab Ridge, Herschel Baker grabbed his binoculars and swept the horizon. He found two battalions of German infantry formed some 4,000 yards away and watched as they began to move forward. This time the German tanks remained behind the infantry, moving about, creating dust and confusion as the foot soldiers advanced abreast of the Gabès road.[18]

The U.S. tank destroyers held their fire. The enemy soldiers made no attempt to disguise their approach. This boldness led Baker and other officers to consider the move to be similar to Major General George Pickett's Confederate charge at Gettysburg. On July 3, 1863, Brigadier General Henry J. Hunt ordered his Union artillery to cease fire after a lengthy Rebel bombardment along Cemetery Ridge. Pickett's Confederate infantry marched toward the Union lines, believing that had knocked out the Union cannons. When Hunt's artillery finally opened up, they wiped out hundreds of Confederate soldiers.[19]

From his vantage point, Darby also felt he was viewing a replay from the American Civil War as he watched scores of Germans advance toward a death trap. One of his lieutenants, Les Kness, watched wave after wave of gray soldiers pushing forward toward the U.S. lines. When the II Corps artillery finally opened up, shells exploded both in the air and at ground level, chewing up the *Panzergrenadiers*. Kness's squad waited until the Germans were 1,500 yards away before they began firing 60mm mortars.[20]

The day's fighting had left only small shot-up groups of half-tracks from Baker's battalion to defend against the late afternoon charge. Among them, commanding what was left of the battalion's recon company, was Captain Michael Paulick. The closest German tanks were about five miles from his position, advancing behind the *Panzergrenadiers*. Paulick's Third Platoon commander, First Lieutenant Otis Rogers, waited until the German infantrymen were within 1,500 yards before opening fire with a 75mm gun. His M3 crew, using heavy-caliber, high-explosive shells, killed or wounded an estimated one hundred Axis soldiers in the opening minutes.[21]

"It was like mowing hay," Baker remembered. His remaining M3 crews were equally effective in decimating the approaching infantry. The desert floor near El Guettar was quickly transformed into swirling clouds of sand and billowing plumes of black smoke. Divisional artillery crews added to the chaos with concentrations from 105mm and 155mm guns.[22]

Despite the carnage, the *Panzergrenadiers* somehow weathered the barrage. They pushed forward toward the gun line of the Thirty-Second Field Artillery and the Third Battalion, Eighteenth Infantry. Members of the Thirty-Second's B Battery were forced to spike their guns and withdraw west toward El Guettar as German infantrymen scrambled up the hill toward their guns.

Sergeant Edwards, manning one of a dozen howitzers of the First Battalion of the Seventeenth Field Artillery, worked feverishly. His crew fired their guns so many times that parts of the fieldpiece were close to melting. Every man contributed. Cooks unstrapped water cans from the side of the battalion's kitchen truck and relayed water up the hill to pour on the smoking howitzer gun barrels. Sergeant James Moran of Edwards's B Battery watched as his captain, positioned in front of the guns, barked orders for various barrels to change deflection or elevation. At other times the captain simply ordered gunners to fire at will as the Germans surged forward.[23]

When shells from the Seventeenth crews occasionally connected with a German tank, Moran saw some Panzers "burst into flames in an array of incendiary color, like fireworks on the 4th of July," and fall apart "like the petals from a rose." The battalion's fire was further directed by an observation post (OP) overlooking the El Guettar battlefield, manned by Lieutenant Paul Frank, Major Joseph Couch, and a Captain Hirens. At one point the post sent coordinates down to B Battery that did not jibe, forcing the howitzer commander to call back for verification. The return message was succinct: "Damn it, fire!" To Moran, this meant the enemy was so close that the artillery crew had no time to reposition. He thought, *The only alternative is to get those 155s belching and roaring.*[24]

The field artillery OP became a favorite target during the day for both Luftwaffe planes and German artillery. At one point the Germans even used a captured American half-track pulling a light howitzer to attempt an assault on the OP. Spotting the M3 pointing its howitzer in their direction, Hirens shouted to a nearby infantry platoon to put their mortars to work.

"Can you put one on that half-track?" he yelled.

"I believe I can," came the reply.

"Then do it!" said Hirens.

From the nearby ridgeline, the infantrymen sent several mortars whistling toward the half-track, disabling it and sending the survivors fleeing. Couch would later receive the Silver Star for his efforts in directing the artillery fire at El Guettar. The time-fire shells—designed with fuses that delayed explosions that allowed them to burst just over the heads of the advancing German infantry—were particularly effective and deadly. One officer compared the soldiers cut down to "wheat falling before a sickle."[25]

More than a mile south of the American artillery position, Colonel Gibb's First Infantry Division El Guettar command post buzzed with activity. Phone reports came in from the various American units facing the latest German advance. By 1710 the German main effort was approaching the Third Battalion on El Keddab Ridge. Patton put in a call to Terry Allen to ask how things were going.

"We got a lot of air punishment," Allen advised. "The 18th Infantry is isolated." Patton asked Allen why he had lost so many tank destroyers this day. Allen offered a number of reasons, including Luftwaffe attacks. Patton, unsatisfied, abruptly ended the call.[26]

The brunt of the German assault bore down on the four platoons of K Company, Third Battalion, Eighteenth Infantry Regiment, located at Djebel el Mcheltat. Each forty-plus-man platoon had three squads sporting one Browning automatic rifle per squad and an M1 rifle carried by each soldier. The 60mm mortarmen of K Company eventually exhausted all of their mortars, forcing the men to become riflemen to pick off the Germans advancing on Djebel el Mcheltat.

Along the southern edge of Captain Clifford Raymer's K Company position, gunners were forced to abandon their M1917 machine gun during the battle. Raymer called for men to return to the water-cooled machine gun. He found two volunteers in the form of PFC Raymond Villeneuve, a twenty-one-year-old New Yorker, and Private Joseph Burlazzi from New Jersey. The pair crawled forward under heavy fire and reached the gun, then used it to mow down German soldiers and two machine-gun crews. Villeneuve and Burlazzi moved their gun to a new position to keep pressure on the enemy. But an artillery shell struck nearby, killing Burlazzi and badly wounding Villeneuve, who survived. Major General Roosevelt would later praise the men of the Second Platoon, which suffered nine killed, twenty-one wounded, and thirty-two taken prisoners of war. K Company earned a Presidential Unit Citation in the process, and Raymer and Villeneuve each received a Distinguished Service Cross, the nation's second-highest military honor. Burlazzi's DSC was awarded posthumously.[27]

Other companies were hit hard in the German assault. Hubert Edwards and his Seventeenth Field Artillery howitzers were deadly, raining high-explosive and antipersonnel shells down on the enemy infantry. Edwards's captain, spotting for his men from atop a dune, relayed details of the grisly carnage their antipersonnel shells were creating among the advancing *Panzergrenadiers*. "Boys, that's the very picture of the artillery," he told them. Darby's First Ranger Battalion advanced to help an Eighteenth Infantry battalion from being overrun. As nearly every advancing enemy soldier was killed or fell wounded, the late afternoon battle was devastating for the Germans.[28]

Patton watched the evening battle from an observation post near the divisional headquarters on Hill 336 in company with his aide Captain Chester Hansen. They saw German infantrymen collapse as time-burst artillery shells shredded them with shrapnel. Patton was dumbfounded at his enemy's persistence. "They're murdering good infantry," he muttered. "What a helluva way to expend good infantry troops."[29]

As evening approached on March 23, Patton's II Corps stood their ground. By 1845—just over two hours since the start of the German assault—battlefield commanders relayed the news that the torrential artillery fire had checked the Axis advance. The *Panzergrenadiers* were falling back behind the ridge at the east end of the valley, toward Gabès, signaling their desire to end the ill-fated thrust. The morning battle had been a duel of tanks and artillery, but the afternoon event had simply been a slaughter. "When the smoke cleared away, we found that not a single American soldier had given any ground," Patton wrote in his diary. "The Lord helped a lot today."[30]

Herschel Baker was much relieved that his few remaining tank destroyer units had weathered the final storm. Twenty-one of his destroyers had been hit and disabled, but his crews were able to rapidly repair eight of them for further action. His men had fired 2,740 rounds of 75mm shells, 33,395 rounds of .50-caliber, 12,050 rounds of .30-caliber, and 3,690 rounds of .45-caliber submachine gun. Baker's battalion had outmaneuvered and outshot a superior foe. Fourteen of his men had been killed on March 23, but an estimated thirty German tanks had been knocked out.[31]

Les Kness was relieved that the *Panzergrenadiers* had never advanced to within rifle range. His Ranger squad had effectively contributed to the defense with their mortar rounds. As darkness overtook the El Guettar valley, Kness surveyed his surroundings. The flat terrain ahead of him was littered with broken vehicles and tanks. He could also see a considerable number of dead and wounded Germans lying on the desert floor.[32]

———

The evening battle afforded some survivors from the morning action a chance to escape. Lieutenant John Yowell's First Platoon of the 601st Tank Destroyer Battalion had spent the late afternoon concealed in the El Guettar valley hills north of Highway 15. His force had been whittled down to just three tank destroyers, each completely or nearly out of ammunition.

As the battle raged, Yowell decided it was time to fall back, resupply, and regroup with his battalion. He gave his men the option of walking back toward friendly lines or remaining with the trio of M3s. Many retreated on foot, considering the half-tracks to be a prime target for enemy tanks, artillery, and infantrymen. Only eleven men stayed with the lieutenant and his armored vehicles.[33]

Yowell's command track surged westward in company with those of Staff Sergeant Hermann Bartling and PFC Carl Nerthling. As they left their concealed positions, German machine-gun bullets swept the tank destroyers, forcing gunner John Nowak to hug the floor for protection. With only enough rations and water to survive for a couple of days, he'd decided to remain with his M3 as long as possible for the added protection it offered. They managed to move out of the enemy's firing range through the mountains, but the route proved nearly impassable. Yowell ordered Nowak and others to get out and push large boulders aside and fill in ditches where the terrain might cause their half-tracks to become stuck.

It was discouragingly hard work. At times Nowak and two others were forced to scout ahead on foot, reconnoitering possible routes for their tank destroyers. After dark, Yowell halted his retreat. He ordered his men to bed down until daybreak. With all radio gear destroyed in the day's action, the lieutenant was unable to communicate his platoon's position to Lieutenant Colonel Baker. Yowell scouted ahead alone in the darkness while Nowak and the other enlisted men rotated guard duty every half hour to prevent a surprise attack.[34]

After daybreak on March 24, Nowak and his B Company radio operator, PFC William Barnes, moved ahead of the three half-tracks to dig paths for forward progress. In one place, the route through the jagged hills was so tight, they had to chip away rocks just to allow the M3s to squeeze through. After scraping through four hundred yards of rock walls, Yowell's half-tracks emerged into a wadi that proved easier to traverse. Moving forward, they picked up John Sauklis, a fellow tanker suffering from chest wounds who was being carried on a stretcher by medics.[35]

Nowak's companions shared their meager rations, water, and cigarettes. As the 601st stragglers reached a large clearing, Yowell went forward on foot to contact some troops in the distance to prevent them from mistakenly firing on the approaching friendlies. It was nearly noon on March 24 when the survivors finally reached their company.

All that remained of the First Platoon of B Company were a dozen men and three battle-damaged half-tracks. One M3 had a flat tire. Another suffered from a broken steering wheel spring that prevented the vehicle from making right turns. The third tank destroyer was unable to maneuver in reverse. Exhausted mentally and physically, John Nowak found that some of his battalion comrades had long since written them off. Among the handshakes and backslapping, one tanker told him, "We never expected to see you guys alive again."[36]

FOURTEEN

"GET MORE OFFICERS KILLED"

Les Kness enjoyed no rest during the night of March 23. His E Company mortarmen of the First Ranger Battalion had spent the late afternoon helping to repel the German infantrymen and tanks. As darkness fell, the second lieutenant was tapped to lead a thirty-man demolition group onto the battlefield to blow up damaged enemy fieldpieces, tanks, and other vehicles.

The first wreckage encountered was that of an American antiaircraft unit positioned in front of the artillery and tank positions. Kness saw dead American crews crumpled around the jeeps and guns. One soldier's body was still in a semi-standing position atop his gun. The Rangers provided cover for the demo squad as it searched the darkened flats for German vehicles. Just as the group exploded its first abandoned enemy tank, it came under rifle fire from their left flank. The Rangers opened up on the enemy gun flashes, exchanging heavy fire for five minutes. Once things quieted down, Kness gathered the demolition men and headed out to find more vehicles.[1]

The special squad exploded several more German fieldpieces and tanks, drawing more enemy fire and a second rifle fight that continued for ten minutes from their right side. As the evening dragged on, Kness's company engaged in other brief firefights as the blasting team carried out its mission. In each skirmish, his men returned fire and advanced swiftly on their opponents while the demo men took cover. Despite the sharp encounters, Kness's squad suffered no injuries.[2]

Kness's greatest danger was the result of one of his own explosions. Each damaged German vehicle and artillery piece was first packed with TNT by the demo squad before they took cover. Kness and a demolition officer took turns pulling the detonator before sprinting for protection. As they packed explosives into one large-caliber fieldpiece mounted on a German half-track, advance Ranger scouts yelled, "There's a German patrol advancing quickly. One hundred yards out!"

Kness ordered his men back behind a rise in the sand dunes. He waited until he could hear and see the enemy soldiers approaching. Jerking the detonator cord, he sprinted for the ten-foot-high sand dune. The blast erupted just as he topped the dune, and a large piece of jagged steel smacked into the sand just ten feet away. Kness rolled back over the dune top, ready to open fire on any survivors. He was relieved to hear only screams and German voices shouting for help.[3]

By the early morning of March 24, the Rangers had helped the demo squad destroy more than a dozen Axis tanks and guns. Kness was surprised that his crew found neither enemy bodies nor wounded survivors during the night. Clearly, the Germans went to great lengths to retrieve casualties before attempting to recover damaged military hardware, just as the Rangers did.

———

British intelligence intercepts showed that the German Tenth Panzer Division had suffered heavily during the previous day. Only nine

Mark IVs and seventeen Mark IIIs remained serviceable, and one of the *Panzergrenadier* battalions was exhausted. The division had sustained more than three hundred casualties during the fighting on March 23, losing forty-five tanks and two self-propelled guns. Generalmajor Fritz von Broich nonetheless ordered his commanders to conduct spoiling attacks to keep the Americans off balance and secure key terrain along the ridges.[4]

Beginning around 0655 on March 24, German infantry moved into the El Guettar valley on the First Infantry Division's southern flank. An intense firefight erupted near Djebel Berda between Colonel Greer's Eighteenth Infantry and Axis forces. Artillery batteries from the opposing armies pounded away during the morning hours. From his command post, Major General Roosevelt called up Lieutenant Colonel Darby's Rangers shortly after 1100 to assist.

Having spent all of the previous evening helping to destroy German tanks and guns, Kness was exhausted. His patrol had returned to the Rangers' camp outside of Gafsa. They had only enough time to store their barracks bags before Roosevelt's orders arrived instructing them to help clear Germans from the Eighteenth Infantry's southern flank. Darby's special forces were trucked east toward the mountain range of Djebel Berda, whose promontory offered excellent observation for Axis artillery.

As the Rangers advanced, Generals Patton and Terry Allen arrived at Greer's Eighteenth Infantry command post around noon. En route, artillery shells rained down and shrapnel hit Patton's car. Upon arriving at El Keddab Ridge unscathed, Patton scanned the battlefield and noted the destroyed vehicles, most of which appeared to be American. "Fifteen German tanks were blown up by our engineers last night and sixteen others were removed by the Germans under cover of darkness," Patton wrote later. "The Germans showed great gallantry in the recovery of the tanks."[5]

Sergeant James Moran of the Seventeenth Field Artillery had a front-row view of the previous day's battlefield. He and his brother Thomas moved by jeep from their B Battery position to report in to the Seventeenth's field observation post. En route, they stopped to examine the burned-out American half-track used by the Germans on March 23 to attack the observation post. Moran noted that the M3 sported U.S. white stars on its door but had a German swastika on the inside. During the Moran brothers' return to B Battery's howitzers, they had to pull off the road to allow Patton's command procession to pass them on a hill.[6]

James Moran was close enough to see under Patton's three-star helmet. "I stared into those cold, ice-blue, unfriendly, frightening eyes," he recalled. His artillery comrades soon felt the heat from their fiery II Corps commander. Those not dressed to his orders were berated. Patton encountered one Seventeenth artilleryman sitting on his steel helmet. The general kicked his rear, growling, "Get off your ass, stand up, and put it on your head!"

Patton was frustrated that his armored division had taken unnecessary losses the previous day. He had warned the tank destroyer commanders to refrain from engaging with German tanks of superior armor and speed. He was annoyed to find on the El Guettar battlefield that his First Armored Division had lost twenty-four out of thirty-four M3 half-tracks that had engaged, and seven out of twelve M10 tank destroyers. "I told them what to do," Patton wrote, "but their faulty training crapped up in the heat of battle."[7]

While Patton fussed and fumed among his troops, Allen worked to direct offensive efforts from his Hill 336 command post. It consisted of little more than slit trenches hacked into the rocky ground. But he could see the movement of troops and trucks up and down the valley, including the two dozen trucks hauling in two units of Darby's Rangers. Shortly after noon, German artillery shells exploded close enough to the command post to cause a crowd of staff officers to duck. Allen directed in more units to engage the Germans, but the

Second Battalion of his Eighteenth Infantry Regiment would remain under fire throughout March 24.

═══════

Major General Pinky Ward had quickly become Patton's scapegoat. Disturbed by heavy losses of his M3s on March 23, Patton was even more displeased with the meager forward progress Ward's First Armored Division had made in the past two days near El Guettar. With 277 tanks and more than 20,000 troops of his own armored division and the Sixtieth Infantry Regiment, Ward should have achieved stronger results, in Patton's view. The friction between the two- and three-star generals had been visibly and audibly intense for days.

By March 22, Ward's force had pushed twenty miles east to Maknassy, which had been abandoned by Axis forces. Ward spent the day gathering his own forces before pushing into the hills beyond the town. Although the First Armored Division reported Djebels Dribica and Naemia to be "held in strength," German reports contradicted this claim. Colonel Rudolf Lang of the Tenth Panzer Division had only eighty German soldiers—men of Rommel's personal guard *Kampfstaffel* unit, including former Rommel driver Rudy Schneider—and the Italian Fiftieth Special Brigade to hold the well-fortified position in the heights.[8]

In his diary, Patton fumed that Ward "dawdled all day" on March 22 instead of pushing forward. For his part, Ward felt the Sixtieth Infantry soldiers assigned to him were sluggish, and he lacked trust in his Combat Command B commander, Brigadier General Paul Robinett—a martinet who had previously been critical of U.S. Army deficiencies. This mattered little to Patton, who felt Ward had "no drive," fueling a tirade in which he demanded his subordinate should "get up off his ass."[9]

Patton boiled over during an evening telephone call with Ward, who bragged of his good fortune in losing no officers in combat that day.

"Goddammit, Ward, that's not fortunate," said Patton. "That's bad for the morale of the enlisted men. I want you to get more officers killed."[10]

"Are you serious?" asked Ward.

"Yes, goddammit, I'm serious," said Patton. "I want you to get some officers out as observers well up front and keep them there until a couple get killed."

Patton ordered Ward to capture the Maknassy hills, just ahead, that night. At 2330, a half-hour bombardment from three dozen guns started the show. Two infantry battalions pushed from the orchards east of Maknassy and moved a half mile forward. By 0330 on Tuesday, March 23, the First Battalion of the Sixth Armored Infantry had seized its hilltop objective. The Third Battalion of the Sixtieth Infantry was stopped near the slopes of Djebel Naemia, a ridge overlooking Highway 14 in the throat of the pass. Ironically, they faced only Rudy Schneider's *Kampfstaffel* unit and the Italian Fiftieth Special Brigade.[11]

Although his Axis defenses were meager, Colonel Lang arrived on the scene and encouraged his scant troops to keep up the fight. Using harsh language, he implored them to use all means "to prevent even one single additional man or vehicle from moving on toward the east." Strong American artillery fire soon rained down. Lang and his adjutant dripped with perspiration as they sprinted from group to group. Turning to Schneider's *Begleit-Kompanie* (escort company) commander, Major Franz Medicus, Lang ordered Rommel's elite men to hold the line. He promised that two experienced battalions would arrive within the hour.[12]

Lang left to round up Italian stragglers, ordering them to the Maknassy front lines. He finally succeeded in bringing up reinforcements: eight Tiger tanks, 8.8cm long-range artillery pieces, and portions of two experienced *Panzergrenadier* regiments—the First Battalion, Eighty-Sixth Regiment, under Hauptmann (Captain) Hatt, and the First Battalion, Sixty-Ninth Regiment, under Major Friedrich-Wilhelm Buschhausen. Wishing to further bolster his defenses, Lang raced to the Italian command post at Mezzouna to request that more Italian troops be sent to Maknassy. "By the end of the day, five enemy attacks had been repelled successfully," Lang reported.[13]

Pinky Ward's initial assault had included only two of the six infantry battalions at his disposal. Four of his Sherman tanks had been rendered useless by mines on March 23. Colonel Lang's reinforced position continued to frustrate the First Armored Division commander. Ward's men had suffered heavy losses while enduring German shells, flares, and Luftwaffe raids through the night. At 0700 on March 24, Ward attacked again, this time with tanks and eight battalions of infantry. American scouts advanced along Highway 14 to within twenty yards of the German stronghold at the base of Djebel Naemia before they were cut down by grenades. Ward moved on foot through his troops, verbally urging them to quit taking cover and push forward. German artillery, mortars, and machine-gun fire prevented his men from gaining an inch of ground, and hundreds of American casualties piled up.[14]

Schneider and his comrades from Rommel's personal bodyguard section fought valiantly through the day. Colonel Lang was furious with the less aggressive Italian infantrymen at his disposal. "Those who did not run away as soon as the enemy attacked, surrendered," he remembered. He found only a small portion of his Italian allies to be "willing to go into action and ready to make sacrifices." Despite such command challenges, Lang's meager forces prevented Ward from making any progress in the Maknassy hills.[15]

By the evening of March 24, Lieutenant General Patton had returned from visiting Terry Allen to congratulate his Big Red One division on their victory the previous day against the Panzers at El Guettar. His dinner was interrupted by news from Lieutenant Colonel Russell Akers that Ward, fighting near Maknassy, had made no progress in two days. Patton picked up a field phone and demanded to have his First Armored Division commander respond to him.[16]

"Pink, you got that hill yet?" Patton asked. He listened for only a few seconds before erupting. "I don't want any goddamn excuses. I want you to get out there and get that hill. You lead the attack personally. Don't come back 'til you got it." He slammed down the receiver.[17]

"Now my conscience hurts me for fear I have ordered him to his death, but I feel that it was my duty," Patton wrote before going to sleep. "Vigorous leadership would have taken the hill the day before yesterday. I hope it comes out alright."[18]

Around 2000, Ward donned his helmet, grabbed his carbine, and prepared more than 2,000 men in three Sixth Infantry battalions to attack Djebel Naemia shortly after midnight. The fifty-one-year-old First Armored Division commander was shoulder to shoulder with his foot soldiers as they crossed two knolls and advanced on Djebel Naemia in the predawn darkness of March 25. Intense German fire soon greeted them, and in the hours that followed, Ward's men suffered heavy losses. A dispatch runner near him was hit in the leg, a machine-gun bullet burned a line across the back of the major general's jacket, and his face was bloodied by a shell fragment that clipped the bridge of his nose and the corner of his eye.[19]

The American advance stalled under German mortar fire. His men were forced to dig in 1,000 yards from the German strongpoints behind the ridge. Patton felt Ward had shown "good personal courage" in leading this assault, one that sent him back to Maknassy in an ambulance for treatment. At his Feriana headquarters, Patton read the latest dispatches from the front on the afternoon of March 25. In a letter to his wife, Bea, he said, "I think I have made a man of Ward."[20]

Ward would be pinned with the Silver Star at II Corps headquarters two days later, but Patton's opinions of him rose and fell like the tide during the El Guettar conflict. The fact that Ward's division was unable to flush the German forces from the Maknassy hills in the ensuing days continued to frustrate Patton. Although he deemed Ward's actions on March 25 to be worthy of a Distinguished Service Cross, he had him awarded only the Silver Star because it had been "necessary for me to order him to do it." Patton made it clear to Ward that if he failed in his next operation, he would be relieved of his command.[21]

"I have little confidence in Ward or in the First Armored Division. Ward lacks force. The Division has lost its nerve and is jumpy," Patton wrote. "I fear that all our troops want to fight without getting killed."[22]

———

Patton had other areas of conflict to command besides Pinky Ward's armored division stalemate in the Maknassy area. Near Djebel Berda, the Second Battalion of the Eighteenth Infantry had spent the daylight hours of March 24 under assault from German artillery and tanks.

Darby's Rangers reached the Eighteenth Infantry's command post tents early that afternoon. Pitched in the open about a mile from the Djebel Berda mountain range, the CP was perilously exposed to enemy artillery fire. *This is no place for a sane person to be,* thought Second Lieutenant Les Kness of E Company. He was much relieved that his Rangers spent only a few short minutes receiving updates there before they marched forward to the mountains.[23]

Kness's company had moved only a mile before German artillery shredded the command post tents. Darby's force silently made its way up the slopes of Hill 772 of the Djebel Berda chain in the late afternoon. The seizure was accomplished, and Djebel Berda was secured at 1730 hours following an arduous climb up the slopes and a brief skirmish at the top.[24]

Shortly after dark, Major Heinrich Drewes, the commander of

the Kradschützen-Battalion 10, ordered a night attack from his position north of the Gabès–El Guettar highway. Utilizing two motorcycle companies and more than three hundred men, Drewes pushed
forward toward Djebel Berda, where Lieutenant Frank Jakob's G
Company, Second Battalion, Eighteenth Infantry Regiment, was
resting after the day's combat. The serenity was shattered by a bright
flare erupting over the desert. It was followed by a quarter-hour barrage of German artillery that pounded the company's position.[25]

Explosions knocked out the last mortar and last machine gun
possessed by Jakob's men. Hundreds of black-uniformed German
soldiers charged their position, some wearing field caps and others
in battle helmets. The surging Germans fired machine guns, lobbed
grenades, and slaughtered American soldiers in their foxholes with
bayonets. Those not killed outright or captured were finally ordered
by Jakob to fall back toward a battalion headquarters a quarter mile
behind their position. Another Eighteenth Infantry leader whose
troops were positioned near the assault wrote: "Company G disintegrated under the impact."[26]

The news that G Company had been driven from the hill reached
Danger Forward, the Eighteenth Infantry's command post, at 2150.
Lieutenant Colonel Robert York's First Battalion, Eighteenth Infantry, and Lieutenant Colonel Ben Sternberg's Second Battalion were
under siege. Colonel Gibb ordered Darby's First Ranger Battalion to
be put under the immediate direction of Colonel Frank Greer's Eighteenth Infantry. With his Rangers in motion a half hour before midnight, Darby radioed back, "Darby coming to help Sternberg."[27]

Captain Jack Street's Ranger company was left atop Hill 772, with
his rifle and mortar squads positioned to provide fire down the
mountain. Unable to dig in due to the rocky formation of the hill,
his men rocked up individual firing positions in an all-around defense. Bill Darby led his other companies back down Hill 772, moving to assist the besieged Eighteenth Infantry. At one particularly

dangerous descent point, Kness had to position two men at the bottom of the bluff, ready to grab anyone who might slip to prevent them from tumbling over the larger cliff. Looking back at the sheer drop after daylight, Kness was amazed that his whole company had conquered the slope without loss in the darkness.[28]

While the Rangers descended Hill 772 in the predawn hours of March 25, reports were funneling in to Colonel Gibb that his Eighteenth Infantry had consolidated its forces. The action had quieted down, but he was fully aware that enemy forces were present. Only the return of sunlight would reveal what German resistance his infantry and the Rangers faced in the hours ahead.

FIFTEEN

THE FIGHT FOR HILL 772

At 0345, the shuffle of feet and the clink of machine-gun belts caught Jack Street's attention. They were the unmistakable sounds of a large group of advancing soldiers. The Ranger captain silently nudged and signaled his comrades to prepare for an enemy assault.

Positioned atop Hill 772 of the Djebel Berda chain, Street's small force had been left to hold the key position atop the steep bluffs. The balance of Lieutenant Colonel Darby's men were far below, providing cover for the Eighteenth Infantry. Rifles and machine guns were anxiously trained in the direction of the closing force. As the shadowy figures of infantrymen came into focus, Captain Street shouted a verbal challenge.

A startled American voice stammered an incorrect code word. Only the soldier's rapid explanations saved him from becoming a casualty. The approaching force was identified as E Company of the Second Battalion, Eighteenth Infantry. Once the situation was settled, the infantrymen took up defensive positions alongside Street's Rangers on Hill 772.[1]

Far below, Darby and Major Herman Dammer's force awaited daylight and the potential of a German attack. Second Lieutenant Les Kness, exhausted from being on duty for two straight nights, took the chance to get some sleep alongside a large rock.[2]

At 0630 the enemy assault opened like a thunderstorm. Heavy concentrations of German mortar and artillery fire slammed the peak of Djebel Berda. Five minutes later, intense machine-gun fire came from points down the northeastern slopes of the ridge. Within ten minutes Street's Rangers and the infantrymen of E Company could see German *Panzergrenadiers* advancing up the slopes, firing.[3]

At his lower position Kness was startled into consciousness as the first shells exploded. Forty feet from his position, the lieutenant saw a mortar shell slam into the rocks near the feet of First Sergeant Richard Honig. The round failed to explode, leaving Honig feeling secure enough to lie back in his position. "Lightning never strikes in the same place," he theorized to Kness as they rode out the enemy barrage.[4]

Street's company crouched behind rocks and fired into the advancing Germans. Spread over three knolls that formed Djebel Berda, his Rangers allowed the Eighteenth's infantrymen to withdraw down the northwest slopes. Mortar and timed artillery fire fell on the hill for the better part of an hour, during which time the German infantry began an envelopment along the slopes. By 0725, Darby radioed Street to have his Rangers withdraw from their delaying position and move toward the main battalion position at the southwestern base of Djebel Berda.[5]

Staff Sergeant Gino Mercuriali, the youngest of five boys from an Italian immigrant family raised in Sioux City, Iowa, commanded the last squad from Street's company to leave the rocky slopes. Actively engaged in firing back at the German troops, Mercuriali was surprised to survey the scene at one point only to find that his men were alone. The balance of his company, including all officers and even the company phone, were moving swiftly down the mountain.

Mercuriali scurried to round up his last two men—Sergeant Michael Yurko and Corporal Edgar Rote—who were manning a machine gun at the top of a steep slope. Private Larry Troxell assisted the squad's retreat by lobbing grenades at advancing German soldiers until the last bunch of Rangers had reunited with Street at the base of Djebel Berda. By that point Mercuriali was livid over being left behind, and he exchanged words with his company commander. To his surprise, Street congratulated him. "Darby thinks you need to be a hero, to be an officer," said Street. Still incensed, Gino replied that he had promised his mother he would return home from the war instead of dying as a hero.[6]

While Street's men rapidly descended near-vertical cliffs, Darby ordered out Lieutenant Chuck Shunstrom with a platoon of C Company to get around the German flank. The fight near the base of the mountain continued until 1040, when the Second Battalion, Eighteenth Regiment, was ordered to withdraw two miles to the rear. Darby's Rangers maintained defensive positions along the northwestern foot of the Djebel Berda hill mass, south of Highway 15. At 1400, Shunstrom's platoon came under attack, suffering five wounded and three killed in action.[7]

"The situation was still tight," remembered Darby. "We stayed out on this right flank, practically cut off for three days, but not giving an inch." It was not until the morning of March 26 that his Rangers were relieved of frontline duty by the Second Battalion, Thirty-Ninth Infantry Regiment, of the Ninth Division, and were able to move back toward El Guettar. Darby was thoroughly pleased with the performance of his battalion. He felt this battle had been the "payoff" for their training.[8]

———

Lieutenant General Patton monitored the losses piling up from the fighting near El Guettar. Colonel Frank Greer's Eighteenth Infantry alone had sustained more than 300 casualties between March 21 and

26, including 33 killed, 171 enlisted wounded, and 7 officers wounded. Another 113 were missing, the majority now prisoners of war of the Germans.[9]

At noon on March 25, General Harold Alexander issued orders to Patton to shift the weight of his attack to the south. He planned to use Manton Eddy's Ninth Infantry Division to join Terry Allen's First Infantry Division and punch a hole through Axis defenses southeast of El Guettar. He felt this would allow tanks from Pinky Ward's First Armored Division to strike down Highway 15 toward Gabès. Alexander hoped this harassment of German forces facing Field Marshal Bernard Montgomery would split the Axis armies and trap the Mareth defenders from behind.[10]

During the next two days the Germans occupied the highest ground on Djebel Berda, which included the key promontory labeled Hill 772. From these vantage points they were able to see almost every American movement. Following the decisive American victory on March 23, the Germans and Italians had taken losses, but the Tenth Panzer and Italian Centauro Divisions had regrouped. They had the advantage of fighting defensively in rough terrain full of sharp ridges and box canyons. One of their key defensive positions became Hill 369, which rose five hundred feet above the desert floor and stood two miles south of Highway 15. German engineers excavated five dugouts from solid rock on Hill 369. Machine-gun emplacements were positioned on three forty-foot knolls north of the hill, facing the road. German infantrymen dug into trenches near the machine guns. Ten 75mm anti-tank guns were placed around Hill 369, and three larger 100mm guns were spaced one hundred yards apart.[11]

The Tenth Panzer Division and its supporting elements held the eastern peaks of Djebel Berda and Djebel Kelbdib and the sandy hills of the Draa Saada el Hamra. A divisional intelligence officer's report indicated how taxing it was for the Germans to maintain these rocky hill positions. "The far superior enemy forces attacked without letup," he wrote. "The main weight of the attack was directed against the positions held by *Kradschützen-Bataillon* 10 and *Pz.Pi.Batl.* 49. Enemy pressure from Bou Hamran presented a threat to the division's northern sector. In addition to infantry attacks, the enemy's artillery grew stronger by the day."[12]

Oberleutnant Heinz Werner Schmidt, the former aide-de-camp for Field Marshal Rommel, had spent weeks in reserve, training his Special Group 288 battalion. Equipped with anti-tank guns, his men were ordered forward on March 26 to join the Tenth Panzer in the fighting through the hills and valleys of the El Guettar region. Schmidt formed an infantry line and moved his men swiftly forward to the right of the Gafsa road. During the next two days his men faced relentless artillery fire and shelling from advancing American Shermans. "We were truly in the heart of an inferno," he wrote. From his command post, guarded by a heavy machine gun, Schmidt worked to reinforce his position. After dark, one of his patrols crawled through the hills close enough to spot the glow of cigarettes from dug-in U.S. infantrymen. By the following day he realized it would be a long and bitter fight. "We scarcely distinguished one hour of tension and action from another," said Schmidt.[13]

These German forces would face three infantry regiments of Major General Eddy's Ninth Infantry Division: the Sixtieth, Thirty-Ninth, and Forty-Seventh. Eddy spent the day on March 27 regrouping his regiments, preparing for an assault on Hill 369. His II Corps boss, George Patton, became impatient, noting in his diary, "Things are going too quietly. The 9th Division will not be able to attack until the 28th." Terry Allen's First Division occupied a nine-mile front north of Highway 15, while Eddy's Ninth Division moved forward to take positions south of the highway.[14]

For the soldiers of the First and Ninth Divisions, March 27 was spent preparing for the offensive.

What a shitty way to spend an anniversary, thought Second

Lieutenant Charlie Scheffel Jr. as he stared at a photo of his wife, Ruth. It was one year to the day since he had married his sweetheart, Hetty Ruth Carnell, back in Enid, Oklahoma, during a happier point in his young life. He had been a twenty-two-year-old in the Reserve Officer Training Corps (ROTC), finishing his degree in banking and finance at Oklahoma A&M in Stillwater. Standing six-foot-two and weighing 175 pounds, Charlie had been a star athlete on a basketball scholarship who had even played a summer of professional baseball. Within months he had been commissioned as a second lieutenant in the U.S. Army's infantry, forced to part with Ruth when his regiment was shipped to England in preparation for the North Africa campaign.[15]

Following the landings in Algiers in November 1942, Scheffel received his baptism of fire as his unit advanced through the ancient town. During the ensuing weeks, half of his company was pulled into the First Infantry Division, but Charlie remained with the Thirty-Ninth Infantry in Algiers until his regiment was trucked into southern Tunisia in February 1943. The rugged desert, filled with tangled canyons, meandering wadis, and rugged hills, did little to impress the former Oklahoma farm boy. "With my second lieutenant's pay of $150 a month, I could buy this entire wasteland if I could find the owner," wrote Scheffel. "Then I would tell everyone to get the hell off my land."[16]

Charlie's first anniversary on March 27 proved to be a cold day of marching toward El Guettar. Wrapped in heavy overcoats, his platoon—part of Company B, First Battalion, of the Thirty-Ninth Infantry Regiment—was leading their battalion across the Tunisian desert. By noon, as they marched south of Highway 15, the temperature had risen 60 degrees to reach nearly 100 degrees. Scheffel halted his men to eat rations. They itched and sweated in their wool uniforms and long johns as they trudged toward higher ground. "The men bitched about everything all afternoon," wrote Scheffel.[17]

It was evening when Scheffel's men reached their objective, the heavily German-fortified Hill 369 near Highway 15. To the south, Scheffel saw a broad, desolate valley at whose south end a mountain range rose a couple of thousand feet. He assumed the hills were loaded with Germans and Italians as his platoon dug in for the night. The men huddled in two-man foxholes as the temperature dropped after dark. To keep his men warm, Scheffel had them climb out of their foxholes every hour during the night and continue digging more protective trenches. By daylight, the area reminded him of an Oklahoma prairie dog town. Scheffel counted at least five holes he had dug himself.[18]

North of Highway 15, Allen's First Division prepared for its part in the assault. For PFC Harley Reynolds, the new offensive would be a chance to avenge the loss of his cousin, taken prisoner by the Germans at Faid Pass weeks earlier. His B Company of the Sixteenth Infantry's First Battalion was loaded onto trucks to reach the staging area near Highway 15. Upon arrival, his squad scurried to set up their positions armed with nothing heavier than .30-caliber machine guns. From the volume of arriving troops, he knew something big was in the making. As each new outfit arrived, Reynolds's gunners shifted over to make room.[19]

First Lieutenant Henry "Red" Phillips and his Forty-Seventh Infantry Regiment were also preparing for battle on the evening of March 27. His Ninth Division had been trucked to its forward assembly area on the north side of Djebel Berda under cover of darkness. The quartermaster trucks entered the valley and drove toward the mountain, boiling up the dust until it hung over the wadis like a fogbank. An air of eager anticipation prevailed. Phillips found morale amongst his Forty-Seventh comrades to be at a high level.[20]

Near Djebel Berda, Phillips and other Forty-Seventh battalion leaders were given a briefing that evening by Colonel Edwin H. Randle. The decorated former World War I rifle company commander had been with the Forty-Seventh since its activation. Sporting a tightly clipped British-style mustache, Randle's trademark grouchy countenance had led some of his men to refer to him as the "Bear." His regiment had distinguished itself in battle during the Moroccan invasion in November. Since that time he had ruled his regiment with both strict discipline and a fatherly leniency to give some of his less experienced leaders a second chance. Phillips believed the colonel's leniency stemmed from his desire to get the most out of the hand he had been dealt in terms of personnel.[21]

Randle had once complimented Red Phillips on his dedication to training his machine-gun platoon. The only counsel the colonel had given to Red was issued in the Tunisian desert. Randle was notified by military censors that Phillips had included unflattering details in a letter to his wife, Lee, of another platoon leader whose unit had been shot up during the landings at Safi. "One should not be so quick to judge others," Randle told him before dismissing the lieutenant without further discipline.[22]

Now, on the eve of his first full-scale battle in the Tunisian desert, Colonel Randle offered advice to his officers. He directed their three battalions to advance from two large wadis extending into the valley from Djebel Berda's northern face. Captain Jim Johnston met Red Phillips and other M Company lieutenants, imparting additional instructions before their soldiers retired for the night in newly dug foxholes on the desert floor.

Back with his men, Red absorbed their mental state as they prepared for combat. Some chatted excitedly while heating C rations over their little stoves, while others enjoyed a few hours of sleep "after re-reading by candlelight for the hundredth time a crumpled and smudged letter from home."[23]

For Charlie Scheffel, Harley Reynolds, Red Phillips, and thousands of other II Corps troops, their first action in the desert near El Guettar was only hours away.

SIXTEEN

"ALL HELL BROKE LOOSE"

From a gardener's point of view, this is heaven, thought First Lieutenant William Butler. A cool but calm air prevailed during the
overnight hours of Sunday, March 28, long before the sun would
peek over the horizon to begin illuminating the El Guettar desert.
Huddled next to a rock alongside the Gafsa road, Butler—a medical
officer attached to Colonel Randle's Forty-Seventh Infantry—was
inspired by the peaceful desert landscape. [1]

Prior to darkness the previous evening, Butler had examined the
arid terrain. Scattered in clumps among the rocks and sand were
small desert poppies with two-inch flowers in shades of blue, yellow,
lavender, purple, red, pink, and white. With the blossoms now
masked by shadows, Butler and thousands of other soldiers from the
First and Ninth divisions awaited orders to march prior to sunrise.

A short distance from him, First Lieutenant Red Phillips of the
Forty-Seventh's M Company stood ready when the order to move
came at 0300. His division began uncoiling like a snake from where it

had lain at rest among the wadis. Phillips's men moved with quiet precision. Each soldier muffled his grunts as heavy loads of weapons and ammunition were shifted about. There was just enough light to see the fuzzy shadows of adjacent comrades. A sky full of stars and a partial moon were obscured only briefly by passing clouds as II Corps infantrymen slipped forward through the cold predawn air. Ahead lay the ominous, looming hulk of Djebel Berda.[2]

The darkness caused confusion. The available French maps of Tunisia were never intended for tactical purposes. Phillips found that one inch on the map covered more than three miles on the ground, so smaller details on the lay of the land simply were not charted. Neglecting all instructions and posted guides, the Forty-Seventh Regiment's L Company departed from its wadi, heading north rather than east. Phillips's own M Company followed L along the incorrect route, struggling through fields of huge boulders and sprawling wadis. Despite the cold air, Phillips was already beginning to sweat when German aircraft passed over the valley and dropped parachute flares. He found them too distant to affect his pace but near enough to keep his adrenaline flowing.[3]

By 0530 the eastern sky was beginning to lighten as the II Corps infantrymen eased forward. Butler captured the scene in his diary entry for March 28: "Dawn finally came with brilliant golden rays of light angling over the mountains of the valley and lighting up the opposite mountain range in gold and purple and black with a brilliant blue sky. For a time, the valley and myself were still covered in darkness and the scene reminded me of a recent Walt Disney movie *Fantasia*."[4]

As the bulky silhouette of Djebel Berda emerged starkly from its backdrop of blue sky, platoon leader Phillips suddenly realized that he and his fellow riflemen of M Company were not following their assigned course. First Lieutenant David Atkinson was sent racing ahead to alert the L Company commander that his men were leading two companies of the Forty-Seventh Regiment in the wrong direction.[5]

Far off to the right, Phillips suddenly saw pistol flares arching into the sky. They were followed by streams of yellow tracers. The Second Battalion of the Forty-Seventh Infantry had unwittingly wandered right into a German machine-gun ambush from the ridges of Djebels el Kheroua and Lettouchi. Captain Ben Humphrey's E Company was at the head of the Second Battalion's column when torrents of machine-gun fire, potato-masher grenades, and mortars erupted.

Humphrey was badly wounded and First Lieutenant David Conroy was killed. Those who survived the first ten minutes of slaughter took cover in the bottom of a draw. Many men of the Forty-Seventh were wounded, and some soon began to wave white flags of surrender. Those who did not surrender were quickly boxed in. Lieutenant Colonel Louis Gershenow's battalion command group was trapped. With Gershenow was First Lieutenant Craig Campbell, a junior aide of General Eisenhower's who had been sent to the front to learn about combat.[6]

As mortars and artillery rained down, Private Warren Evans and his comrades of the Forty-Seventh's A Company raced to high ground to dig in, "one big mass of officers and men." Gershenow's Second Battalion force lasted barely an hour before the Germans had them surrounded. Second Lieutenant Sidney Thal could hear the wounded crying as well as the voices of German soldiers calling out to the Americans to come forward with their hands held high. Once it became obvious he could not control the situation, Gershenow realized his men must either surrender or die.[7]

Eisenhower's aide Lieutenant Campbell helped fire mortars during the opening minutes of the battle. Dead and dying were all around him. One Forty-Seventh Regiment infantryman lay near Campbell, attempting to hold in his own intestines. The survivors were soon forced to surrender. Campbell was among the 10 officers and 242 enlisted men of the Second Battalion, Forty-Seventh Infantry, taken prisoner by the Germans on March 28.[8]

Lieutenant Ira Rosenfeld, leading his mortar platoon forward with the Second Battalion's E Company, found his five-man team pinned down by the heavy mortar rounds and machine-gun fire. His battalion commander finally concluded that the only option was to surrender, but Rosenfeld felt otherwise. "We were like sitting ducks," said one of his men, Joseph Farrell. Rosenfeld studied the enemy's firing pattern and turned to mortarman Julian Kadis. "After the next barrage," he announced, "we're going to make a run for it."[9]

When Rosenfeld stood to run, only Kadis followed, running like hell across the plain. Sprinting up the ridge toward his company, Kadis felt the rush of Axis shells all around him. Farrell and two others from Rosenfeld's mortar team who remained behind were overrun and taken prisoner. Colonel Randle held out hope throughout the day that many of his missing soldiers had scattered during the ambush and could be recovered. But the Forty-Seventh Infantry had been hit hard.

Still, his men regrouped and fought back. Red Phillips found that it took some time to restore order after the shooting started. His M Company under Captain Johnston had followed L Company in the wrong direction before dawn. Flat trajectory fire from German gunners had forced their men to take cover in eroded wadis and hillocks just east of Draa Saada el Hamra ridge. Once Captain Thomas Wilson found each of his platoon leaders and reestablished control, he noticed a larger, isolated hill dead ahead that appeared to offer superior observation.[10]

Wilson's L Company, supported by a platoon of machine guns from M Company, surged forward to gain control of the hill. Phillips was in awe of the heavy German antiaircraft guns being used against the advancing American infantry. "The 88mm was especially unnerving because its noise made it seem you were in the sights of a man with a very large hunting rifle," said Phillips. He heard the first report of each high-velocity gun as a distant boom from where the weapon was fired. This was followed almost immediately by a nearby shell explosion. The additional howitzers and mortar fire only added to the tension. Colonel Randle's reserve Third Battalion joined the fight for Hill 290, a lesser eminence a mile closer to the highway and not shown on the map. They mistook it for Hill 369 and soon found themselves pinned down through the day by German artillery fire.[11]

Phillips's machine-gun platoon spent the afternoon supporting another company's successful advance on a nearby ridge. But every time his gunners opened fire, they drew German mortar attacks. One of Red's section leaders, Sergeant Harold Havlik, stood to direct one of his squads and was killed by a mortar round that struck his chest.[12]

By day's end on March 28, Colonel Randle had two widely separated actions on his hands. Some of his Forty-Seventh Infantry Regiment had met strong enemy resistance on the north end of Draa Saada el Hamra ridge. Another strong German force had pinned down more of his men a mile and a half away to the south. Randle, ever puffing on his pipe, observed the artillery shelling from an exposed ridge while directing his troops.[13]

His presence was inspiring, but the losses his men were enduring at El Guettar were almost more than Randle could stand. Pacing about his command post, he muttered, "You sons of bitches. You sons of bitches."[14]

―――――

The morning assault on Djebel Berda was equally costly for the other battalions of Manton Eddy's Ninth Division and Terry Allen's First Division.

Second Lieutenant Charlie Scheffel's A Company, First Battalion, Thirty-Ninth Regiment, had spent the early morning hours advancing south of Highway 15 toward Hill 369. His two platoons were at the front of the advance, easing through a sloping wadi toward the distant ridge in broad daylight. Scheffel's men were so far ahead of the reserve troops, he wondered if his guys were the only ones fighting the war. He felt an almost uncontrollable urge to run.[15]

Three hundred yards short of the mountaintop, his platoon came under fire from a German machine gun. Bullets pierced the sand all around the soldiers, and Scheffel pressed himself into a slight fold in the ground. It was not quite deep enough to protect his head and butt. Scheffel yelled at his men to stay down as the machine gun swept their area, eliciting occasional screams and moans as bullets hit home. Scheffel had no entrenching tool, so he took his pocketknife to loosen the ground and begin shifting dirt and rocks to his sides. After an hour of that, he'd dug himself into a slit trench deep enough to get his behind below the surface.[16]

Once his men were sufficiently dug in, the German machine-gun fire died down. A soldier near him called out that the enemy was gone, but Scheffel ordered the private to keep his rear down and wait. Hours passed, forcing him to finally urinate in his pants to avoid rising up and inviting fire. Artillery shells shrieked overhead and exploded beyond. He cautiously peeked around to check on his men. At one point he looked to his right toward the nervous young soldier he had ordered to lie down. The boy suddenly stood up. Before Scheffel could yell a warning, the young man fell without even a whimper as a German sniper bullet found its mark.[17]

The cloak of darkness finally allowed sufficient cover for Scheffel and his men to begin falling back. They moved quickly back down the slope to their original point of departure and were the last platoon to return. They had lost seven men. Scheffel was unable to locate his company commander and found his battalion to be in a state of chaos. More than thirty men had been killed or wounded. The remnants of three rifle companies lay mixed together in a ravine cluttered with empty ration cartons, ammo boxes, five-gallon water cans, and a twisted mess of communication wire.[18]

———

PFC Harley Reynolds considered the battle erupting before him at daybreak on March 28 to be nothing short of "wild havoc." Positioned a little more than two miles north and slightly east of General Eddy's Ninth Division, forces of Terry Allen's Big Red One division were simultaneously advancing on another key ridge, Djebel Mcheltat. Reynolds and his rifle squad—part of B Company, First Battalion, from Allen's Sixteenth Infantry Regiment—had crossed the line of departure at 0550.[19]

Reynolds and the Sixteenth were positioned to the right of the advancing American forces, whose task was to smash through the Axis defenses blocking Highway 15 and Gumtree Road II. The grounds ahead were heavily fortified by German infantrymen, units of the Tenth Panzer Division, and Italian soldiers of the Centauro Division. Almost immediately, Reynolds's First Battalion ran into trouble at a large wadi southwest of Djebel Mcheltat. German flares began bursting in the air over his head. As the sky became brightly illuminated, enemy machine guns opened up from countless positions. Rifles, mortars, and artillery fire quickly added to the confusion.[20]

Captain Albert Smith Jr. ordered his First Battalion to advance. The B Company squad Reynolds was attached to was commanded by twenty-two-year-old Sergeant Clarence "Cots" Keilman from Portage, Pennsylvania. Their platoon, boasting two machine guns and three mortars, began moving forward. Cots Keilman and his twenty-four-year-old elder brother Bill had worked with their father in the Pennsylvania coal mines before joining the Army.

Bill Keilman, a powerfully built six-footer, dutifully followed his brother's lead as the Sixteenth Infantry advanced. "We were playing leapfrog," remembered Keilman. One company crawled forward and took position. Then the next company filtered through their position and crawled to the next forward position. The first company then repeated the process as the units steadily crept forward.[21]

Cots Keilman led his machine gunners to the base of a small sand hill in the opening minutes of the action. Captain Smith ordered his company to advance over the top. As Bill Keilman crested the hill, bullets stitched the sand all around him. The mortarmen advanced into a small wadi ahead, but there was insufficient cover for his machine-gun crews. German gunners and artillery fire made it a living hell for the Sixteenth Infantry.

Harley Reynolds heard numerous cries of "Medic!" Other men screamed as bullets and shrapnel found them. He heard orders being shouted, but in the din of battle none really made any sense to him. Lieutenant Colonel Charles Denholm, commanding the First Battalion, was wounded, along with Captain Smith. As senior officers were hauled toward distant aid stations, squad leaders stepped up to assume command of their remaining men.[22]

During the early advances, the Second Battalion of the Twenty-Sixth Infantry captured its initial objective, Hill 536, by 0635. Major General Ted Roosevelt joined Combat Team 16 (CT 16) and moved forward with them across the open ground under enemy fire. His forward position allowed him to send firsthand information to Major General Allen. Roosevelt quickly reported that the Sixteenth Infantry was getting pounded and was taking heavy casualties.[23]

Sergeant Keilman ordered his squad to dig in. Reynolds and his assistant machine gunner, Corporal Ivy Bradshaw, did not need to be told twice. The pair was already half dug in when the order was passed. Instead of the typical slit trench, they simply excavated the rocky soil straight down. Reynolds felt some relief once their hole was deep enough for both him and Bradshaw to drop down into it with their machine gun. Anytime Harley lifted his head above the hole, German gunners opened fire.[24]

Panzer shells further kept the Sixteenth infantrymen pinned down through the morning. At one point Reynolds felt nature's call and was forced to dig even deeper to allow himself room to lower his pants. Each time he threw out a shovel of sand, it drew a burst of enemy fire. In due time he managed to excavate one side of his foxhole deep enough to take care of his bodily functions and to cover it up by digging more dirt from the sides. Momentarily relieved of one pressure, Reynolds and his assistant gunner remained trapped in the open by widespread firing.[25]

Around 1030, Cots Keilman received orders to fall back over the crest of the hill they had advanced past. His older brother Bill passed the word to his squad, and they began rolling back. As they did, a German tank opened fire. Reynolds saw one of its shells explode among the retreating Americans, knocking down squad leader Keilman and a close friend, Wiley Gibson. Reynolds and Gibson had been nearly inseparable since joining the army together. Now he could only offer supporting fire for a medic who advanced to offer first aid to Gibson.

Bill Keilman rolled to the back side of the little hill and made a quick inventory of personnel. His thoughts immediately turned to his younger brother. He checked the guys he could see, but his sibling was nowhere to be found. Another soldier who crawled over the hill announced that Cots was still on the other side, badly wounded. Bill wriggled to the top to look for his brother. He found Cots yards away on his stomach, inching forward like a snake.[26]

"How bad are you hurt, kid?" Bill called.

"Pretty bad," Cots groaned. "Get me the hell out of here!"

A quick glance showed Bill that his brother's legs were mashed by shrapnel, with bones exposed. One of his hands was also shredded. The elder Keilman administered sulfanilamide pills to help him with the pain.

"Well, let's get going," Bill said. He struggled to scoop up his brother, a large man of 180 pounds and six feet in height. Unsure that he could handle the load, Bill realized there was no one else around to help. He spread out on the ground, allowed his brother to crawl across his shoulders, and then struggled to his feet for the laborious return trip.[27]

Behind the hill, Keilman stumbled across a long plain that sloped gently downward. Small rocks shifted under his boots as he staggered around large boulders with his brother's body. German mortar shells rained down, blasting them along the way with dirt and debris. Although severely wounded, Sergeant Keilman still had his sense of humor: he kidded his older brother Bill about making a lousy pack mule. Hundreds of yards to the rear of the main action, the Keilman brothers finally reached an aid station established for the Sixteenth Regiment's casualties.

Bill Keilman left his brother in the care of medics and returned to the front lines. His B Company spent the remainder of March 28 pinned down by heavy fire as their casualties continued to mount. Harley Reynolds and assistant gunner Bradshaw remained in their foxhole, hoping to escape injury until nightfall. Both were convinced they would be cut down if they tried to make a run for it. For the time being, Reynolds felt they would remain safe until darkness.[28]

Hundreds of Sixteenth Infantry soldiers remained pinned down by German artillery through the day. Lieutenant Ted Antonelli, a twenty-three-year-old from Connecticut with the Third Battalion, had one shell fragment pass within inches of his head. At one point his men could not determine if they were under fire from enemy or friendly pieces, necessitating a brief cease-fire from American artillery positions to sort out the confusion. After dusk, casualties were hauled to the rear, and officers were in short supply. Antonelli's captain had had his leg shattered by an artillery burst, and Antonelli was forced to step into acting command of his company.[29]

The German offensive tapered off after sunset, allowing Reynolds and Bradshaw to retreat to the safety of B Company's first aid station. There, Reynolds found his squad leader, Cots Keilman, bandaged and in pain from his shrapnel wounds but still able enough to bum cigarettes from Captain Smith, his wounded company commander.

Private Gibson, who had lain on the battlefield bleeding throughout the afternoon, was hauled into the aid station by a medic after dark. Reynolds was deeply pained to see that there was nothing the medics could do for his mortal wounds. "Wiley died alongside Sergeant Keilman, boasting of the party he was going to have when we got back to Fort Devens after this GD war was over," Reynolds wrote later. "He was one of the toughest little men I have ever known."

The March 28 assault on Djebel Mcheltat had taken a heavy toll on B Company. Bill Keilman's company had more than 180 able men at daybreak. Only thirty-four had returned that evening. The casualty rate was so severe that healthy men who had performed admirably under fire were given spot promotions. Squad leaders were normally corporals, but that evening PFC Reynolds was appointed as a new leader due to the lack of available replacements. He would remain a machine gunner but now had the added responsibility of leading other men. The El Guettar action would be a distant memory by the time Reynolds finally received his corporal's stripes.[30]

He and his fellow survivors of the Sixteenth Regiment's B Company used the evening hours wisely to regroup and replenish ammunition. Further enemy action was expected after sunrise.

———

Unlike his predecessor, Patton was conspicuous to his troops during the battles near Djebel Berda. Starting out with some of his staff from Feriana at 0750 on March 28, he drove first to the command post for Terry Allen's First Division. "Situation was O.K. but enemy resistance serious, due to excessively rugged nature of ground," he wrote in his diary. He noted that the Tenth Panzer Division and the

Italian Centauro Division were well dug in, having blasted out forti-fications in the solid rock base of the mountain.[31]

Patton continued his inspection of the front lines by moving on to visit the Ninth Division. He found Major General Eddy at the front with his Forty-Seventh Infantry combat team. En route, his command jeep, prominently displaying three stars, had to traverse four miles over open fields and was subjected to shelling. "Felt very conspicuous, but nothing happened," Patton wrote. "Fighting nasty in high, rugged hills, too steep to handle mortars in. We could use a pack train to good advantage."[32]

The arrival of the II Corps commander inspired many soldiers. Private Charles Hoffman of B Company, Fifteenth Engineers, stud-ied the lieutenant general as he strolled through the ranks, binocu-lars dangling from his neck and his pair of trademark ivory-handled Colt pistols strapped to his sides. Patton received an update from Hoffman's lieutenant while he stared at the hills ahead, which were occupied by the Third Battalion of the Forty-Seventh. "We'll beat the sons of bitches," Patton remarked. As Patton moved on, Hoff-man caught the eyes of his lieutenant. Neither could suppress their smiles of confidence.[33]

But Patton was far less confident in the progress he had seen thus far on March 28 by Eddy's division. He marched into the Ninth Divi-sion command tent, where he found Eddy poring over the regiment's situation map. Patton declined an offered cup of coffee, opting in-stead to pull his subordinate aside for a severe dressing-down for not being on the front lines with his soldiers. "In all my career, I've never been talked to as Patton talked to me this morning," Eddy confided to his Forty-Seventh Regiment commander, Colonel Edwin Randle, later that day. "I may be relieved of my command."[34]

His point made, Patton remained at Eddy's command post to ob-serve some of the battle playing out in the El Guettar desert. Officers dutifully pointed out key German positions on the next hill. Unfazed by artillery barrages, Patton walked to the highest point on Eddy's post, unfolded a map, and studied the terrain—a prime target, with stars showing on his shoulders, collar, and helmet.[35]

Axis shelling persisted during Patton's visit. His ire at the lack of progress being made by Eddy's division was unleashed against some he perceived to be underachieving. "Found a chaplain who was poking around the command post, while wounded were being put into ambulances close by, and gave him hell," Patton wrote that night. As artillery exploded uncomfortably close, the infantrymen were ordered into the trenches. Patton and his aide Colonel Hobart Gay were forced to move down off the crest and join the dogfaces in the foxholes until the bombardment ceased.[36]

When the dust settled, Patton headed for his jeep. He called to his chief of staff in his squeaky voice, "Well, come on, Hobart. No more war around here."[37]

Manton Eddy's Ninth Division—including the Thirty-Ninth, Forty-Seventh, and Sixtieth Infantry Regiments—took a beating on March 28. But the chastisement he received from Patton prompted him to renew the assault against Hill 369 the following morning. After darkness had cloaked the battlegrounds near Djebel Berda, Eddy met with his reserve commander, Colonel J. Trimble Brown, about the plan. Brown's regimental operations officer (S-3), Major Price Tucker, was present. Eddy said, "The key to the operation's success is speed." All signs indicated that the Forty-Seventh Regiment had occupied Hill 290, leaving a single battalion with only road mines and some Italian stragglers to contend with. Brown argued that his battalion should not be committed piecemeal without better enemy intelligence. Eddy, however, was adamant.[38]

The unnerving assignment fell to thirty-nine-year-old Lieutenant Colonel Walter Oakes, commander of the Thirty-Ninth Infantry's Second Battalion. As daylight of March 29 approached, Oakes sent his troops forward in trucks. They disembarked about two hundred yards west of a hill they took to be Hill 369. Once again, darkness played tricks on the troops as they mistakenly advanced on the unmapped Hill 290.[39]

The confusion over hills was understandable under the circumstances. "Our orders were extremely vague," remembered Second Lieutenant William Maloney Jr., a platoon leader of F Company. "No description or hill numbers, no formation, and no directions." Mahoney's men had dismounted the trucks and were grumbling as they moved forward. German flares, rifle fire, and machine guns suddenly opened up on them. Complete panic ensued as the battalion broke into scattered groups to evade the sudden hailstorm of fire.[40]

Those not killed or wounded in the initial ambush spent the rest of the day crouching in hastily dug foxholes under a broiling sun and merciless Axis artillery fire. Many of the Thirty-Ninth Infantry soldiers surrendered, while others escaped under cover of darkness that evening toward the rear. Colonel Oakes was among those taken prisoner.

Terry Allen's three First Division infantry regiments—the Sixteenth, Eighteenth, and Twenty-Sixth—fared little better on March 29. After advancing only a few miles down Gumtree Road, they came under heavy German assault as the opposing artillery slugged it out through the day. Two battalions of the Sixteenth Infantry were sent into action during the afternoon. Harley Reynolds, now acting corporal for his machine-gun squad in B Company, First Battalion, advanced with the remnants of his company. Sergeant Bill Keilman, who had carried his badly wounded brother to safety the previous day, was in command of Reynolds's unit. His men advanced through a small pass between two hills. En route, they caught hell from both mortars and 88mm artillery fire. Keilman's small force moved only about three hundred yards before they were pinned down.[41]

Axis shells shattered the terrain within thirty yards on either side of the Sixteenth soldiers. The man to Reynolds's immediate left was struck by a machine-gun bullet that passed through his mouth from one side to the other without striking any teeth. Although the man was not severely wounded, he struggled to prevent blood from seeping down his throat and impeding his breathing.[42]

Keilman took cover as enemy shells began raining down. He heard a whistle that almost instantly increased to a scream. "It was a big one coming, and it had my name on it," he said later. Knocked unconscious, Keilman lay seriously wounded on the battlefield until comrades could move him to safety after sunset.[43]

In a mere ten minutes, Reynolds and his Sixteenth Infantry comrades suffered 105 casualties. Many severely wounded men bled out in the desert during the day, as enemy fire was too intense to risk movement. The lucky ones were hauled out under cover of darkness. The situation thoroughly frustrated Major General Allen, who developed a nervous stutter and resorted to chain-smoking cigarettes through the afternoon.[44]

Lieutenant Ted Antonelli had assumed acting command of K Company, Third Battalion, after his captain was seriously wounded the previous day. He led his men forward as daybreak approached. "On my signal, we were going to yell and scream," he recalled. As they surged up a hill, the men were forced to take cover as casualties mounted. Antonelli became concerned that men would be lost needlessly in their trapped state. Waving his .45, the company's lone officer valiantly charged up the hill with his men running behind him. "Antonelli paid for his bravery," wrote correspondent Ernie Pyle. "A hand-thrown German grenade scattered fragments over his chest and he fell." Antonelli's men succeeded in capturing the Germans atop the hill, but he was hauled back to a field hospital for surgery.[45]

K Company was devoid of officers when Antonelli fell, but his position of acting commander was assumed by Sergeant Arthur Godwin, a former orchard farm truck driver from Alabama. He led his men in a bayonet charge that caused the Germans before them to flee. Hours later, Godwin was given a battlefield commission to second lieutenant for his valor.[46]

The situation became elevated enough late on March 29 that British general Harold Alexander sent new orders to Patton. He directed that an armored spearhead drawn from the First Armored Division was to smash through the Axis defenses down Highway 15. His orders, sent with his operations officer, Brigadier General L. C. Holmes, included precise instructions on how to deploy the American defenses. Frustrated, Patton explained that the splintering of his tank forces would leave him little to deploy when needed, and that all of his infantry regiments were currently in action and unable to be deployed as the British desired.[47]

Holmes called his superior, asking for approval to revise Alexander's orders based upon the input from Patton. In his diary that night, Patton grumbled that he must make a point to tell Alexander "that in the United States Army we tell officers what to do, not how to do it, that to do otherwise suggests lack of confidence in the officer and reduces him to the status of an adjutant general." He further doubted whether General Alexander himself had even issued the order. "For the honor and prestige of the U.S Army, I must protest."[48]

Patton planned for a renewed assault the following morning, but for yet another night his II Corps infantrymen would remain largely pinned down near Highway 15. Little ground had been given up to the Germans, and some valiant efforts had been made to probe the enemy's fortifications. One such mission was assigned to Second Lieutenant Charlie Scheffel.

Many of his men were becoming demoralized. Seven from his platoon had been lost on March 28, and days spent hunkered down in foxholes had done little to improve attitudes. After being in the field for weeks without a shower, Scheffel's soldiers stank horribly. Enemy fire prevented the digging of proper latrines and garbage disposal pits. Rats and lizards rattling through empty ration cans at night only added to the men's hygiene challenges.[49]

Scheffel was called that night to the battalion's command post, which was little more than a hole dug behind a large boulder. Lieutenant Colonel Charles Cheatham's intelligence officer spread out a map that they studied by flashlight. Tired and irritable from the incessant shelling, Scheffel grumbled, "This fucking map is not the right scale."[50]

He was nonetheless ordered to take a patrol out toward Hill 772, where intelligence indicated a group of Italian soldiers held high ground that could offer a key position for the Allies. After studying the maps to figure his route, Scheffel handpicked a dozen infantrymen from the First Battalion—including a corporal named Fiatto who spoke fluent Italian—to go with him.[51]

Scheffel's group pushed forward after midnight into the valley, headed southwest in a flanking movement around Hill 772. Artillery rumbled in the distance. Occasional flashes of explosions lit up the horizon. His team followed an old goat trail single file up the back side of the hill. Scheffel's men finally reached a steep slope that rose about seventy-five feet straight up. Each man struggled to pull himself up, grabbing handfuls of tough desert vegetation or whatever handhold he could find in the rocks.[52]

At the top of the steep bluff, Scheffel's patrol crawled forward over more level terrain. In the pale moonlight, he suddenly spotted a sandbagged enemy fortification on a ridgeline about fifty feet above. Assuming it to be an Italian position, Scheffel spread his men to either side and sent his Italian-speaking scout forward to order them to surrender.

Corporal Fiatto shouted in Italian up toward the enemy emplacement: "You are surrounded! Put down your weapons, and come out with your hands up." Scheffel was badly startled to suddenly see a soldier stand up just thirty feet in front of him from a position below the crest he had not noticed.

"*Ja?*" called the gray-clad infantryman.[53]

Scheffel realized his patrol had crept up on a German fortification.

His squad had only enough time to press their bodies as low into the rocks as possible before rifles and machine guns opened up. Bullets zipped over their heads, sending greenish-white tracers arcing down the slope behind the Americans. The Germans began tossing potato-mashers—handled grenades that came flying over their sandbags. Scheffel told his men to hold their fire, but he quickly began hearing cries and groans from some who had been hit.[54]

By the time the shooting died down, he knew he had wounded to contend with. The element of surprise had been lost. One of his men flung a grenade up the hill, provoking the German machine-gun crews to open up on the Americans again. Scheffel had only a split second to react before a German grenade thumped into the rocks near him. He instinctively covered his face with both arms and pressed his helmet down tight. The explosion sliced through the air above him, causing his ears to ring. His right hand stung from fragments that ripped the fingernail off his index finger and severed the strap from his rifle.[55]

Shaken but alive, Scheffel ordered his men to remain pressed down low until the firing eased again. As his head cleared from the ringing, he spotted the figure of a German infantryman climbing from his trench, heading down the slope toward him. With a finger on his trigger, Charlie took aim and waited silently as the German surveyed the American position. The enemy soldier stopped three yards from him, scanning the slope. After several seconds the German climbed back up into his defensive position. "He never knew how close we both came to dying," recalled Scheffel.[56]

With daylight approaching, Scheffel used the advantage of a strong wind blowing off the crest to quietly call for his men to prepare to evacuate the area. Several men crawled over to him, all wounded. Scheffel helped wrap a bandage around one comrade whose jaw was half shot away. His job now was to save what was left of the patrol. Moving in single file, he led his survivors in a slow crawl down the slope, their bodies occasionally exposed by an enemy flare. Each time, they froze until the flare burned away, then resumed their fast extraction from the area of German fortification. Upon reaching the base of the steep cliff they had climbed, Scheffel felt his way to the right for a less severe slope to descend. The movement of his men soon drew gunfire from another American company's defensive line, forcing the patrol to wait out the rest of the cold night, shivering and bleeding in the rocks.

Hours later, in full daylight, Charlie Scheffel was able to maneuver his tattered group down the rest of the mountain under the covering fire of other II Corps advance troops. He felt lucky to be alive as his men dropped into a ravine to patch wounds and mourn their eight comrades who had perished on the hill.

Someone else will have to clear the Germans off Hill 772, thought Scheffel.[57]

SEVENTEEN

"STUCK EVERYWHERE"

Harley Reynolds could feel his spirits draining. Nearly a week had passed since Lieutenant General Patton's first armored victory on March 23. But now, on the March 30, his Sixteenth Infantry Regiment was largely pinned down in various positions along Highway 15 in the desert north of El Guettar near Hill 369.

Axis mortars and artillery fire had been a regular event for days. At one point Reynolds noticed another rifleman yards away from him lose his cool when a heavy shell explosion dropped a severed leg on the edge of their trench. It took some effort to finally quiet the screaming soldier, who thought in his state of shock that the appendage was his own.[1]

During another period of heavy enemy shelling, Reynolds lay in his trench transfixed by an ant crawling over his body. He watched the tiny creature move up his side, across his stomach, and down his right side. He could have simply crushed it at any instant. But Reynolds was so mesmerized by the ant's movements that his mind became removed from the deadly explosions. "I felt a little too close to our Maker at that time to harm a creature that He had placed on this earth," he recalled.[2]

Boredom and stress under fire caused many infantrymen to resort to tobacco to help soothe their frazzled nerves. But smoking was a sure way to draw sniper fire, so many had turned to chewing tobacco. "We all did up there," said Private John "Red" Haney. "You couldn't smoke."[3]

During one stretch of close shelling, Reynolds saw his platoon sergeant, Edward "Patty" Pastuszynski, slide into an adjacent trench with the assistant platoon sergeant, Richard Swanger from Mansfield, Ohio. After one close explosion caught the attention of Reynolds and his nearby platoon sergeants, Pastuszynski seemed unfazed as he packed his lower jaw with another wad of tobacco. "Does that help, Patty?" asked Swanger. The platoon sergeant passed his box of snuff to Swanger, who was rarely thereafter seen without a lower lip packed full of tobacco—and became known as "Snuffy." Swanger kept one wad of tobacco in his mouth for nearly two straight days before changing it out.

Haney's days on the front lines were numbered. As his squad moved up into advanced detail one afternoon, the wadi he was crawling through came under intense German shellfire. He took cover in a foxhole as 88mm shells bracketed the area near the roadway. A runner sprinting across the opening to caution others to stay down was literally disintegrated. The concussion of the next shell drove Haney's face into the rocky terrain, removed his helmet, and left him blinded for days.[4]

In addition to enemy artillery fire, Swanger's machine-gun squad was under constant fire from German machine gunners. At one point Private Joseph Manak stood up just ten feet from his section leader to point out an enemy machine-gun nest he had spotted.

Before Swanger could react, he saw Manak crumple from a burst of machine-gun fire that riddled his chest and head.[5]

Harley Reynolds somehow escaped serious injury. Water was rationed to just two canteens per man per day, as supplies could be safely moved forward only after dark. German air superiority in the region meant open field resupplies in broad daylight could result in heavy casualties. As another night in his trench slowly passed, Reynolds wondered how long his men could hold out.[6]

———

Patton cursed the lack of forward movement made by his II Corps forces near Djebel Berda on March 29. But he was unaware of just how effectively his infantrymen were wearing down the Tenth Panzer Division.

The Sixth Company of the Second Battalion of Panzergrenadier Regiment 69 had taken Hill 536, only to lose it to the Americans on March 29. Once the German company finally expended its ammunition, the surviving members were forced to surrender. A Tenth Panzer Division report noted that Allied forces were massing against several key German-Italian positions: "His efforts to outflank the northern flank through the depression between Bou Hamran and Rass el Derka made further progress. There is heavy fighting going on for Hill 772 and the Italian strongpoints at the Draa Saada el Hamra to Bir Mrabott. The latter changed hands several times during the day."[7]

Machine gunner Ernst Breitenberger was among the Second Battalion members forced to surrender as Hill 536 succumbed to the Americans. As the *Panzergrenadiers* were marched past the vast American supply depots at Tébessa toward an Allied prisoner-of-war camp, Breitenberger realized the hopelessness of the situation his German Army was facing. In contrast to the scant rations and supplies his fellow *Panzergrenadiers* had subsisted on, he marveled at the enormous American hoard of food, tanks, ammunition, gasoline, and artillery pieces.[8]

German forces were furthered challenged by a strong advance made on March 30 by the U.S. Army. Several battalions of infantrymen surged forward, supported by artillery pieces and armored vehicles. The Tenth Panzer Division readied for the renewed assault, as noted in an action report: "Vehicle concentrations increasing in both of the enemy's main directions of advance."[9]

=====

Patton's next move to push through German defenses down Highway 15 kicked off at noon on March 30. General Harold Alexander had provided new direction for II Corps late the previous afternoon, but Patton was angry that his British superior commander had told him exactly how to position his troops for the next advance.

Colonel Clarence Benson, the white-haired fifty-one-year-old commander of the Thirteenth Armored Regiment, was tapped to lead the First Armored Division's push down Highway 15. His seven battalions included two battalions of Sherman tanks, an 899th Tank Destroyer Battalion with new M10s, a reconnaissance battalion, two battalions of artillery, a company of engineers, and the Third Battalion of the Thirty-Ninth Infantry, the latter moved in by trucks. Supported by artillery fire, Benson's armored force raced forward but made it only 5,000 yards before German artillery and mortar fire commenced. Anti-tank guns joined the barrage, and C Company of the 899th took the brunt of the initial punishment. Slowed by minefields, the company suffered at least three M10s knocked out.[10]

Captain Thomas Hawksworth of Idaho Falls, Idaho, moved his A Company forward from one wadi to the next until it began receiving heavy weapons fire. In short order, the scene became chaotic and casualties piled up. Hawksworth's Third Platoon leader, Second Lieutenant Robert Henderson, was killed by a projectile that sliced him in half. Near Hawksworth's command half-track, First Sergeant Barney Ruffatto was directing 899th soldiers where to take cover when a shell exploded against the front hub of the vehicle. When Hawksworth's men rolled him over, they found that a 75mm shell had passed through his leg, ripping away much of his shinbone.[11]

The tank destroyer crew administered first aid to Ruffatto until the shelling died down. Then Hawksworth's men lashed the bodies of Lieutenant Henderson, deceased, and Sergeant Ruffatto, injured, onto the broad, flat hood of a half-track for transport back to an aid station. The bloodstains across the hood of his armored vehicle served as a constant reminder to Hawksworth for days of his comrades' sacrifice. After depositing the casualties, he had his M10 return to the battlefield, where he rendezvoused with Colonel Benson for further orders.[12]

Other units of the 899 Tank Destroyer Battalion were racking up their own losses. Captain Clarence Heckethorn's C Company was hit hard early on. To the company's right, the destroyer commanded by Sergeant Herschel Floyd Briles was knocked out and set aflame. Briles kept his gunners actively firing even as the fuel in their vehicle burned, covering others as they escaped. Briles's actions would earn him the Silver Star.[13]

Another of Heckethorn's crews, that of Sergeant Werner Lefebre, was maneuvering under fire over a steep incline when its M10 rolled over. The men scrambled out, only to be met by an Italian captain and several infantrymen. Stunned to be confronted face-to-face, Lefebre—an American of Italian and Jewish ancestry who spoke fluent Italian and German—reached a temporary truce with his enemy. "Until we decide who is whose prisoner, let's go to our dugout and talk this over," the Italian captain said. Lefebre's M10 crew spent the night in a dugout with the Italian infantrymen. The next morning, when things looked dismal for the Axis forces, the Italian captain surrendered his men to Lefebre's armored crew. The next morning

Lefebre and his tank crew marched back to the Allied lines with a company of Italian prisoners in tow.[14]

Despite its losses, C Company claimed two tanks destroyed, another damaged, thirteen enemy guns destroyed by high-explosive fire, six light-machine-gun nests destroyed, and two German half-track infantry carriers blown up. But the 899th had gained no ground on March 30. Captain Hawksworth and his surviving A Company half-track crew were giving their updates to Colonel Benson when Lieutenant Colonel Maxwell Tincher, the 899th commander, arrived by jeep to report in.[15]

Benson, tugging on his corncob pipe, unleashed his full fury on Tincher. He called the 899th leader a disgrace to the Military Academy. Hawksworth was stunned to hear Benson dress him down in a manner more severe than a sergeant working over a recruit. Tincher was told that if he were not personally on the battlefield where his destroyers were burning by nightfall, he would be tried for cowardice. No charges were ever filed, but the fact remained that the Benson force had been stopped cold in its tracks by the Germans this day.[16]

———

Second Lieutenant Red Phillips was also frustrated by the lack of progress. For two days his M Company of the Forty-Seventh Infantry Regiment had endured Luftwaffe raids and persistent pounding from Germany artillery.

As acting platoon commander, Phillips tried to keep his men moving slowly forward when possible. Each pocket of heavy enemy resistance forced his machine gunners to work over the German strongholds until their firing was eliminated. Most of the firing was done from some distance, with little chance of seeing the enemy. But Phillips saw one dark-uniformed, white-scarfed Axis soldier rise up on Djebel Berda, only to be sent tumbling down the slope from his observation post as II Corps gunners found their mark.[17]

His M Company performed well, save one platoon sergeant who broke down under the pressure of constant bombardment. "The son of a bitch was yella," Phillips's first sergeant declared after the man in question was demoted to other duties far removed from direct combat.[18]

Colonel Benson's force, licking its wounds from the previous day, made ready for another advance on March 31. Lieutenant Colonel John Keeley, leading the Third Battalion of the Thirty-Ninth Infantry, pushed eastward at 0600 and succeeded in linking up with the Third Battalion of the Forty-Seventh Infantry. They captured 369 Italian prisoners from a well-developed position on Hill 290. In one more case of battlefield confusion, Colonel Randle's Forty-Seventh Infantry headquarters mistakenly reported that Hill 369 had been taken instead of Hill 290.[19]

George Patton was unsatisfied with the actions of the Benson force the previous day. "This morning, things look pretty bad," he wrote in his diary on March 31. "We seem to be stuck everywhere." He impatiently sent his aide Colonel Kent Lambert to Benson to stir things up, ordering him to expend a whole tank company, if necessary, to break through.[20]

Benson's armored forces had no such luck. Rolling forward shortly after midday on March 31 without waiting to make a coordinated attack with infantry, they again encountered blistering resistance from the German Panzers. The Second Battalion, First Armored Regiment, lost eight tanks, although four were later salvaged. In return, they claimed several destroyed 88mm and lighter anti-tank guns, plus a half dozen German tanks. Old Ironsides was forced to cling to its ground between the road and the foothills.[21]

The Axis forces would have to be ousted from their anti-tank positions by infantry and artillery before the armored division could move farther ahead. Patton's effort to have II Corps troops push through Tunisia to the sea had bogged down. But his army had lured two Panzer divisions away from the British Eighth Army's front. This had helped Field Marshal Montgomery break through at Mareth, capture Gabès, and engage the Axis forces at Wadi Akarit on the coast, due east of the Americans.[22]

Patton's patience was running thin. A report that Manton Eddy's Ninth Division was troubled by a phantom German battery on a ridge that could not be hit brought a sharp reply: "Find it and destroy it." He held a midday meeting with Major Generals Beetle Smith and Richard McCreery and Colonel Thomas Jefferson Davis. His subordinates were in favor of a battle plan that Patton had suggested the day before, one that had been put off due to orders from General Alexander. Patton informed Smith that such plans were too late at this point and asked him to speak to Alexander about issuing so many specific battalion-placement orders that limited the U.S. Army's effectiveness.[23]

Then Patton called the First Armored Division commander, Major General Pinky Ward, and ordered him to attack Maknassy to help the Benson force break free. Ward protested, saying the enemy's hold on the area was too great for any reasonable expectation of success. Irate, Patton ordered him forward, telling him to take up to 25 percent losses if necessary. Old Blood and Guts was disgusted that his valiant Old Ironsides armored division seemed reluctant to fight.

Writing in his diary from a position of safety, Patton admitted to feeling "quite brutal" ordering Ward to take losses. But he saw no other option: "Wars can only be won by killing and the sooner we start the better."[24]

=====

Charlie Scheffel was less than enthusiastic with his new orders. During his previous recon patrol against Hill 772, he had lost eight men. Now his Thirty-Ninth Infantry battalion commander had ordered him to take another patrol out to find a way through the German fortifications in the hills before them.

The second lieutenant was scared, but he dutifully gathered another dozen soldiers, each loaded with a light combat pack, one blanket, and rations for three days. After two days of traversing dry wadis, German minefields, and enemy positions, Scheffel's scouts found themselves pinned down in a canyon by a German machine-gun crew. One of his corporals was shot through the right leg and was too badly wounded to be moved. It was a gut-wrenching decision for Scheffel to leave the man behind in order to spare others. His patrol returned to report the enemy's position, but the lieutenant felt he had left part of himself in the canyon.[25]

He was much relieved to learn that his wounded man was recovered the following day. Scheffel's intelligence stressed the fact that the U.S. Army was facing an enemy force well entrenched in the hills of the El Guettar desert region. It would take the full participation of artillery, infantry, and armored vehicles to claim any fresh ground on this desolate battlefield.

Heavy fighting persisted throughout April Fool's Day as two battalions again assaulted Hill 772. General Alexander doggedly ordered another charge, believing the American infantrymen could bust open a gap for the First Armored Division to plow through. But heavy German machine-gun fire, combined with ample doses of mortar and artillery rounds, only ensured mounting American casualties.

Red Phillips and his heavy weapons platoon of the Forty-Seventh Infantry Regiment were assigned to take over the position of another company that had been fighting at Djebel Berda. Late on April 1 the lieutenant moved his men forward several hundred yards, along the battalion's left flank on a ridgeline. Phillips paused to gather the latest intelligence from the platoon commander he was replacing.

"They put a few mortar rounds in here every day about this time," the officer told him.[26]

The platoon leader offered a spare steel helmet to Phillips, who had recently lost his. Red was just placing the helmet on his bare head when Italian mortar rounds slammed into their position. One of the explosions struck Phillips in the back with enough force to pitch him down the slope. Stunned, he saw his freshly acquired helmet on the ground nearby, sporting a ragged hole through it. Red was only partially coherent, bleeding from shrapnel wounds to his skull and back.

To Sergeant Joe Smith, he muttered, "The platoon is yours."

Smith and a medic dragged their wounded lieutenant down the hill to a foxhole. Phillips passed out as the medic cut away his clothes to get to his wounds. He was transported that evening to a mobile army surgical hospital for operations on his head and back. The following day he was flown with other wounded to Oran for convalescence in a station hospital. Phillips would receive the Silver Star and Purple Heart for his actions at El Guettar, but he had been effectively removed from further immediate action.[27]

Patton endured his own pains on April Fool's Day. His Benson force had stalled in its advance. His British superior seemed intent on dictating his men's every move. And the loss of one of his trusted friends furthered the II Corps commander's anguish.

His aide Captain Dick Jenson had looked up to Patton as a father figure. The twenty-seven-year-old's family had been close to Patton's family back stateside in California. The lieutenant general referred to Jenson as being "the bravest and best." During the morning of April 1, Patton sent him forward with Major General Omar Bradley and several officers to inspect Colonel Benson's command post, located on a ridgeline twelve miles southwest of El Guettar.[28]

Shortly after Bradley's force arrived, a flight of a dozen Junkers 88 twin-engine bombers approached the command post at low altitude. Antiaircraft guns pockmarked the sky with black bursts as the German bombers circled. Staffers and soldiers alike dived into trenches as the Luftwaffe raiders commenced their attack runs. Five-hundred-pound bombs with instantaneous fuses exploded, ripping helmets from heads and peppering men with sand and shrapnel.

Several men were killed and others wounded, including British staffer Brigadier Charles Dunphie. Dick Jenson, taking cover in a trench, was killed by the concussion of a bomb blast, his neck apparently broken by the force of the blow against his helmet chin strap. His body was unscratched, but Jenson was dead. His watch stopped at the moment of impact, 1012.[29]

Patton was at his Gafsa headquarters early that afternoon when a jeep arrived carrying the body of his aide. In company with aide Hugh Gaffey, he later drove to the small French cemetery in the European section of town, where he found Jenson's body on a stretcher rolled up in a tent shelter half. Patton uncovered Jenson's face and knelt to say a prayer as tears streaked down his own face. Removing a small pair of scissors from his pocket, he clipped a lock of Jenson's hair and kissed him on the forehead as a proxy for his mother. Patton folded the lock into his wallet and drove silently back to his headquarters.[30]

He returned to the cemetery at 1600 with several from his staff to attend an Episcopal service for Jenson and other recent casualties. The corps chaplain read scripture as a trumpeter played "Taps." Four of the captain's friends, including Lieutenant Alex Stiller, lowered his body into the grave. Patton was still weeping after returning to his office, where he wrote to Jenson's mother, enclosing the locket of hair and telling her "how loyal and gallant he was."[31]

The loss of Jenson, coupled with the earlier capture of his son-in-law, further fueled the passion of George Patton to drive the Germans from Tunisia. His wrath toward all things that slowed this quest would not be long in emerging.

EIGHTEEN

"ATTACK AND DESTROY"

Grief-stricken by the loss of Captain Jenson, Patton took his frustration out on British leaders that afternoon. By his estimation, rather than patrolling the skies over his battlefield, Allied airmen had employed at least 1,000 planes to strike the German air force elsewhere. The RAF was at the time observing its twenty-fifth anniversary, and Patton believed the British were flexing their air muscles on April 1 to celebrate the milestone. Left without air protection through most of the day, his II Corps was pounded by the Luftwaffe. Fifteen men were killed and fifty-five more were wounded. "While the cat's away, the mice will play," Patton wrote in his diary.[1]

He reacted by writing a situation report from Gafsa that criticized the British: "Total lack of air cover for our units has allowed German air forces to operate almost at will." Late that night, Air Vice Marshal Arthur Coningham, the New Zealander who commanded the Allied tactical air forces, wrote a scathing reply to Patton's protest. Coningham's response, which even reached the U.S.

Pentagon, stated that 353 Allied fighters had flown on April 1, more than two-thirds of them over II Corps. The air vice marshal at first assumed Patton's report was something of an April Fool's Day joke. He claimed it was "inaccurate and exaggerated," even a "false cry of wolf." Coningham further fueled the fire by adding that Patton's soldiers must not be "battleworthy in terms of present operations."[2]

The following day, still unaware of Coningham's message, Patton reached out to General Harold Alexander. He implored his air command to assault the German tanks that his II Corps held under fire. Alexander told him that he could offer no extra air support at the moment, prompting Patton to push his complaints on up to General Eisenhower. His bitterness over lack of air support spilled into his diary entries: "Our air cannot fly at night, nor in a wind, nor support troops. The Germans do all three, and do it as the result of three years' experience in war."[3]

While Patton feuded with the Allied air command, a letter reached his office on April 2 from Alexander. Patton had just returned from placing flowers on the grave of Dick Jenson. Alexander's note requested that Major General Pinky Ward be relieved of his command of the First Armored Division. Patton, having already considered that decision himself, put in a call to Eisenhower. He asked Ike to recall Major General Ernie Harmon, recently returned to Morocco, to prepare to take over Old Ironsides within days.

Patton spent the following morning touring the front lines of the First and Ninth divisions and the command post of Colonel Clarence Benson. He noted that Major General Manton Eddy's Ninth had suffered heavy losses but had taken many German prisoners and more than three dozen 81mm mortars. He returned to his Gafsa headquarters to find Coningham's "outrageous telegram," one that "accused me of being a fool and of lying."[4]

The touchy affair with air command became even more volatile

at noon when a group of Allied air chiefs arrived at Patton's headquarters in hopes of soothing the tensions. Lieutenant General Carl
Spaatz—the commander of the Northwest African Air Forces—
arrived with Air Chief Marshal Sir Arthur Tedder, the commander
in chief of the Mediterranean Allied Air Forces, and another whom
Patton despisingly labeled "some boy wonder by the name of Kuter":
Brigadier General Laurence Kuter. He found the air commanders to
be clearly uncomfortable as they discussed the situation. In the
midst of his heated exchange with them, Patton was interrupted by
the whine of four German Focke-Wulf fighters roaring in at low altitude to strafe and bomb his command area.

Their final run resulted in a chunk of shrapnel ripping a hole
through the wall of the conference room, where the officers had taken
cover on the floor. Patton charged from the room to fire his trusted
Colts at the departing planes. He returned with his blood boiling.
Tedder casually inquired how the American commander had ar-
ranged such a perfect demonstration of the lack of aerial protection.[5]

"I'll be damned if I know," Patton said. "But if I could find the
sonsabitches who flew those planes, I'd mail each one of them a
medal!"

Fortunately, no one was injured. Patton logged in his diary that
the only casualty was a camel whose leg was dislocated while racing
from the explosions: "An Arab ran out and put it back, and the camel
bolted, pursued by all available Arabs." He gloated over the "good
effect" the enemy's bombing attack was in punctuating his complaints with the Allied air bosses.[6]

Coningham arrived at Patton's office the following day, April 4.
He was greeted by the American lieutenant general in rare form. His
offer to shake hands was ignored. His feeble attempt at an apology
only further inflamed Patton when his raised voice compelled the
American general to become more elevated in volume. "Pardon my

shouting," Patton snapped at one point, "but I too have pride and will not stand for having Americans called cowards." Patton hollered that he had requested an official investigation and concluded by saying, "If I had said half what you said, I would now be a colonel and on my way home."[7]

Coningham collected his composure and offered an apology. "What can I do to make amends?"

"If you will send a message specifically retracting your remarks about the lack of battle worthiness of our men, and send it to the same people to whom you sent the first message, I shall consider the incident closed," said Patton.

Coningham agreed. The pair shook hands, then headed to lunch together to bury the hatchet. Patton hoped his troops would benefit from stronger air support but privately doubted whether Eisenhower would allow the vice air marshal to submit the formal apology. In his diary Patton noted two particular British units he despised, hoping the Germans would "beat the complete life out of [them]. I am fed up with being treated like a moron by the British."[8]

Patton dispatched Omar Bradley to Maknassy that day to formally relieve Pinky Ward of his command of the First Armored Division. To his diary he confided that he should have made the changes by March 23 but had delayed doing so because of the active battle then raging at El Guettar. Bradley wasn't happy about carrying out the orders against one of his closest friends, but Ward took the news in stride. He would receive the Distinguished Service Cross for leading the battle at Djebel Naemia and would return within weeks to his Denver home, where he would assume command of the Army's tank destroyer and field artillery schools.[9]

Major General Ernie Harmon received an equally gruff reception from Patton upon his arrival at II Corps headquarters on April 5. He was ordered to proceed forty miles east to Maknassy to replace Ward. Harmon asked whether he should go on the attack or defend.

His query sent his new chief into a rage. "What have you come here for, asking me a lot of goddamned stupid questions?" Patton shouted. "Get the hell out of here and get on with what I told you to do, or I'll send you back to Morocco!"[10]

———————

Les Kness found ways to amuse himself at the expense of his commander in chief. A month earlier, the second lieutenant had been reamed out by Patton for not wearing a necktie. Now the Ranger platoon leader found himself in the unenviable position of guarding Patton's headquarters.

Lieutenant Colonel Bill Darby's First Ranger Battalion had been relieved of frontline duty on March 26 by elements of Manton Eddy's Ninth Infantry Division. Their primary combat role in Tunisia complete, Darby's soldiers had since been assigned various patrol duties. Two Ranger companies were placed at Madjene el Fedj, twenty-four miles north of Gafsa; two were stationed at Sidi Bou Zid; and another two companies, including Kness's E Company, were assigned to guard Gafsa and Patton's HQ.[11]

The battle in the mountains near El Guettar was still raging when Darby was summoned one afternoon to the small public building that served as Patton's headquarters. As the two stood on his upper balcony, Old Blood and Guts suddenly spotted a Ranger marching up the street, defiantly wearing a green beret instead of his required steel helmet.

"What the hell is that?" Patton barked. "Bring that officer to me at once. I'll kick his ass."[12]

"No, you don't," Darby said, with a nervous tremor in his voice. "That is our British chaplain, sir, and you have no right to discipline him." He explained that Father Albert Basil, who had proven himself in combat, was the only man assigned to his battalion not required to wear a steel helmet due to his role as a man of the cloth. Darby felt great relief when Patton cooled and burst into laughter.[13]

The feisty Basil, beloved by his Rangers, was crushed that the British Army now demanded his return to England for further assignment. In his last service at Gafsa, he expressed his sorrow at having to leave. He promised never to forget his fellow Rangers while asking them to remember him by never taking the Lord's name in vain. Darby's men collected enough money to buy Basil a silver chalice, its base engraved with "First Ranger Battalion."[14]

With the departure of the courageous priest, the Rangers settled into their duties of protecting Gafsa, Sidi Bou Zid, and Madjene el Fedj. Kness felt belittled by his platoon's role as Patton's headquarters guards. When the men saw him on the street, they mimed shooting at him, cutting the buttons off his coat, and shooting Patton's ivory-handled revolvers.

No one was immune to the lieutenant general's wrath. During noon mess one day, Major General Bradley quietly asked Kness to see his personal driver when he passed by the motor pool. "Tell him to get up here with my steel helmet before that crazy idiot fines me for not having it on," Bradley told him.[15]

One night, the last recon patrol led by Kness was sent eight miles into the desert. Two men moving along the left flank of his twenty-two-man platoon reported a pair of German sentries manning a fox-hole near the road leading to Gafsa. But when Kness led six Rangers back to ambush the position, the Germans were nowhere to be found. Upon his platoon's return to Gafsa, Kness's men alleviated their boredom by pulling pranks at the expense of George Patton.[16]

Sergeant Les Cook had similar ill memories of Patton screaming in his face a month before and slapping him with fines for being improperly dressed for frontline duty. During his time standing guard duty atop the general's headquarters, Cook and his fellow Rangers pilfered from Patton's unlocked private pantry on the building's first floor, liberating hams, sweeteners, and all kinds of goodies.[17]

Kness enjoyed a different form of entertainment with Patton's personal vehicle. Dispatched to the rear one afternoon by Darby to collect the battalion's payroll, Kness found darkness settling over the Tunisian desert by the time he had obtained the funds. Fortunately for him, a motor pool sergeant approached, asking if the Rangers officer could lend a hand with a fresh request: someone was needed to drive Patton's Buick back to Gafsa. Kness jumped at the chance. He offered a ride back to the battalion to a fellow Ranger freshly released from the hospital.[18]

Kness drove the Buick wide-open, roaring down the Tunisian highway, dodging potholes with the brights burning. Soldiers from other II Corps outfits they passed screamed at the "idiot" driver to turn out his lights, only to mutter quick apologies when they realized they were shouting at Patton's command car.

Darby's Rangers remained on sentry duty through mid-April, at which time they were recalled to Algeria to begin preparation for their upcoming role in the invasion of Sicily, code-named Operation Husky. By this point, Darby considered his men to be "battle-tested veterans, experienced in mountain and hit-and-run warfare." Major General Terry Allen penned a glowing letter of commendation for the Rangers' work during the El Guettar actions. A year later his words helped form the basis for the battalion's Presidential Unit Citation.[19]

––––––

Major General Harmon, the new commander of the First Armored Division, was quickly exposed to his II Corps leader's impatience. Harmon's tanks had gained some ground against the Germans on April 6, returning to the area of Faid Pass, where the U.S. Army had been manhandled in early 1943. But Patton remained unsatisfied with the progress as he toured the area in his scout car, ignoring the danger of Axis mines. Displeased with the slow advance of Brigadier General Ray McQuillin's Combat Command A, he replaced McQuillin with his own staff G-3, Colonel Kent Lambert.[20]

Major General Ted Roosevelt, second-in-command of the First Infantry Division, sensed the enemy was beginning to withdraw from the El Guettar area. The British Eighth Army launched a massive assault on April 6 along Wadi Akarit, fifty miles east of the First and Ninth Division front. Moving forward with 462 tanks against the Axis count of only 25, the Eighth took 5,000 Italian prisoners. The surviving Italian and German troops began falling back after dark. The British suffered 2,000 wounded and six hundred dead that day but failed to annihilate their enemy or prevent the survivors from escaping.[21]

General Alexander responded by ordering Patton's American forces to push forward the following morning, regardless of tank losses, in an attempt to ram the Axis flank. Patton was not feeling well, suffering from the effects of antimalarial medicine his staff had been issued. Finding that Major General Eddy's Ninth Division had been unable to take Hill 369, he ordered Benson's forces to attack the following morning. Surveying the situation at the colonel's command post, Patton ordered him to "succeed or else." He voiced his displeasure at the slow movement of the previous day and told Benson to push on until he found either a big fight or the ocean. Patton's order was simple. Ripping a page from his notebook, he scribbled to Benson: "Attack and destroy the enemy; act aggressively. G.S.P., Jr."[22]

Benson's force of armored vehicles and infantry pushed forward nearly thirty-five miles on April 7. Patton spent the morning visiting Colonel Randle's Forty-Seventh Infantry command post. From there, Patton perceived that Benson's advance was timid due to enemy minefields. He drove back east on the Gafsa road and found Benson taking a lunch break. He told Benson to stop eating and get out in front. To punctuate his point, he had his driver steer right through the minefield, shrugging off protests from other officers that he was going to get himself killed.[23]

The II Corps commander's brashness was contagious. Benson's

forward units had advanced far enough by afternoon to make contact with the Twelfth Lancers of the British Eighth Army. In its push toward the Tunisian coast, his force captured more than 1,000 Axis prisoners. Although 90 percent were Italian soldiers, the total haul of POWs secured by II Corps at El Guettar had reached 4,700.[24]

Operations continued in the II Corps' northern sector for the next few days as the First Armored Division cleared the Germans from the area east of Maknassy and around Faid Pass. From April 8 to April 12, the majority of the Tenth Panzer Division rolled northward toward Tunis while several of its units fought a furious rearguard action to allow the rest of the Italian First Army to escape to the Enfidaville Line, a mountainous region that marked the eastern end of the Axis last stand.

Oberleutnant Heinz Schmidt's Special Group 288 was pulled from the El Guettar valley during the second week of April. He felt fortunate to be alive, as his men were attacked by Allied aircraft throughout their retreat. Weeks later he received approval for a year-old request to take leave to get married. In time, he would learn the dismal fate of his unit, slowly whittled down as casualties and POWs mounted by early May. Schmidt escaped the closing weeks of the North Africa campaign with the same unplanned good fortune that had originally landed him on the staff of Erwin Rommel.[25]

Fighting in Tunisia would persist for a matter of weeks, but Patton could sense that the backbone of enemy resistance had been broken. From his headquarters on April 8, he issued a letter of commendation to Terry Allen and Ted Roosevelt's Big Red One. "For twenty-two days of relentless battle, you have never faltered," he wrote. "Over country whose rugged difficulty beggars description and against a veteran enemy cunningly disposed, you have pressed on. Undeterred by cold, by lack of sleep, and by continued losses, you have conquered. Your valorous exploits have brought fame to the soldiers of the United States."[26]

Allen forwarded Patton's words to his First Infantry Division, further praising the loyalty and discipline of his men under intense combat operation. "The German Army has learned to fear the 1st Infantry Division, just as it did in the last war," he wrote.[27]

On April 9, Patton went forward with Omar Bradley and surveyed the El Guettar area battlefields from the enemy side. He found that Allied artillery fire had been devastating, leaving acres of desert terrain littered with shell splinters and freshly dug graves. Most of the Italian ones had a bottle under the cross with the man's rosary inside. Patton found helmets, charred notebooks, and a Christmas card lying near the remains of a German anti-tank 75mm gun. "After seeing how strong the position was, I don't wonder that we took so long to take it," Patton wrote. "I wonder that we ever drove them out."[28]

He continued his tour of the front lines the following day, visiting Allen's First Division and taking lunch at Sbeitla with Major General Ernie Harmon's First Armored Division. During a four-week period, the First Infantry Division had sustained more than 1,301 casualties: 126 killed in action, 1,016 wounded, and 159 missing. Overall, II Corps listed 5,893 casualties for this period. Lieutenant Red Phillips's Forty-Seventh Infantry Regiment had suffered twice as many killed and wounded and evacuated—Red falling into the latter category—as had their sister regiment, the Thirty-Ninth Infantry. The Forty-Seventh had lost 868 men to all causes, or more than a quarter of its effective strength.[29]

Phillips believed that the untested U.S. Ninth Division emerged from the El Guettar campaign as an efficient fighting machine whose leaders had learned how to cohesively mesh all units. Lessons learned in the Tunisian conflict would pay dividends in terms of Allied performance in the upcoming invasions of Sicily and Normandy.

Patton's time in North Africa came to a close, and he passed the baton of leadership to Bradley for the final push. (Ironically, German records for the period of March–April 1943 give little indication they were even aware that George Patton was commanding U.S. Army forces.) Thousands more lives would be lost in the final weeks of fighting in Tunisia as the Axis army slowly succumbed to capture.

In a mere five weeks of command, Patton had turned the tide. He had achieved payback for the capture of his son-in-law and the death of his close friend Dick Jenson, and retribution for losses endured at Ousseltia and Kasserine Pass. After assuming command of II Corps on March 5, he had charted a course for victory, and had whipped an ill-prepared army into shape. His steering influence built character into the army he would oversee in Sicily in the year ahead.

———————

On April 14, Patton and Bradley flew to meet General Eisenhower at Haïdra, headquarters for the Eighteenth Army Group. Patton found Ike "all heated up" about Operation Husky, ready for Bradley to clean up in Tunisia while Patton planned for Sicily. "I said that if I was to go, today was the best time as it would permit Bradley to make arrangements for the next move," Patton wrote in his diary. Eisenhower agreed and issued an order to II Corps announcing the change. "I hate to quit a fight but feel that I had best do so as I fear that on the north flank, where Alexander has put us, there is no future," wrote Patton. "Also, the II Corps will be under the First British Army. I fear the worst."[30]

Patton flew back to Gafsa that afternoon and prepared to exit Tunisia. On the morning of April 15, he sent Lieutenant Stiller with his command jeep and three radio scout cars by road, along with most of his staff. Patton piled into his sedan with two staffers, departing at 0815 for Constantine. They stopped briefly at the cemetery, where the II Corps commander placed nasturtiums on the grave of Dick Jenson.

En route to Morocco, Patton detoured through the ancient city of Timgad, Algeria, once occupied by the Romans. In his diary he noted that Timgad had been founded by Trajan in the first century AD. He marveled at the Roman theater, the still-functioning Roman sewer system, and even a whorehouse with a sign on it. "I was tremendously impressed with this monument of a great and vanished race," he wrote. "Yet I have fought and won a bigger battle than Trajan ever heard of."

The war in Tunisia was unfinished, but Patton left his forces in an improved state. Order had been restored, and the road to Allied victory was being forged through miles of jagged djebels and craggy wadis in the North Africa desert. He reflected that even the greatest of leaders could be "wonderfully weak and timid. They are too damned polite."[31]

In reference to his own character, Patton wrote, "War is very simple, direct, and ruthless. It takes a simple, direct, and ruthless man to wage war." He was referring to himself.

EPILOGUE

Fifty-year-old Major General Omar Bradley went to work with a passion. He arrayed his divisions for the last phase of the Tunisian campaign as George Patton returned to his Operation Husky preparations. He was quick to repeal strict dress code requirements such as the necktie in desert operations that had been so unpopular. Strategically, Bradley decided that the key to driving the Germans to the coastal town of Bizerte was to move through the town of Mateur.

He ordered his commanders to avoid the "Mousetrap" along the course: the narrow Tine River valley, where he expected his forces to encounter another German ambush. He moved the Ninth Infantry Division north along the far-left flank toward the Mediterranean Sea, while the Thirty-Fourth and Terry Allen's Big Red One would attack farther south. His First Armored Division would drive toward Bizerte's coastal plains by taking advantage of any breakthroughs, with all of II Corps employing what Bradley termed "djebel hopping": taking the high grounds to avoid deadly bottlenecks.[1]

On April 23, II Corps kicked off its attack against German forces occupying the hills leading toward the coast. They were greeted by ten Axis divisions whose stiff resistance and pounding artillery resulted in hundreds of casualties among the American divisions. During Easter Week alone, 2,000 U.S. soldiers were wounded and another five hundred perished as Allen's First Infantry struggled to move south a few thousand yards a day. Hundreds of fresh graves were dug to bury those who died along the route to the Tunisian coast in their various fights to secure jagged hills known only by their numeric designations.[2]

Long weeks of battle in the Tunisian desert had taken its toll on the men of II Corps, even if Ted Roosevelt sensed that the Germans were breaking before them. He yearned for a bath and a night's sleep in a real bed. Writing home to family in late April, he encouraged them not to fret over his health: "The old iron man is still bumping along."[3]

Bradley recognized Djebel Tahent—known to the Americans as Hill 609—as the key point of General Hans-Jürgen von Arnim's entrenched forces. Hill 609 stood nearly 2,000 feet above sea level; Bradley considered it so important to his push that he ignored British directives to bypass the small mountain. He ordered Allen's forces forward. "Take it and no one will ever again doubt the toughness of your division," he told one commander.[4]

His II Corps pushed forward, taking several lesser hills, but sustained more than 2,400 casualties in the final days of April. For acting corporal Harley Reynolds, his Company B, First Battalion, of the Sixteenth Infantry would endure its greatest challenge on April 30 against Hill 523, another nameless butte a mile due east of Hill 609. Rising above the mostly desolate terrain, the limestone summit bristled with crevices that helped hide and protect defenders. Reynolds's battalion commander, Lieutenant Colonel Charles Denholm, was among the 150 soldiers captured by the Germans as Hill 523 changed hands several times within a twenty-four-hour period.

Second Lieutenant Frank Kolb had been freshly assigned to a rifle platoon of C Company, First Battalion. Stationed near his battalion's command post, Kolb became concerned as German fire knocked out their radios and severed two freshly laid telephone lines. Axis soldiers knocked out one platoon and then began picking off members of Kolb's unit. As potato-masher grenades rained down, Kolb and his platoon sergeant were soon overwhelmed, forced to surrender with Denholm.[5]

For Reynolds, the battle for Hill 523 was "the most courageous action" of the war he experienced. "Not a whimper did I hear on that hill," he said. Reynolds would endure fighting of greater magnitude on Omaha Beach during 1944's D-Day landings, but on Hill 523 he believed every man would go down fighting before the hill was captured. His forty-two-man machine-gun squad had just reached the base of the hill at daybreak when heavily entrenched German troops opened up on them.[6]

Many Sixteenth Infantry soldiers were killed and captured. The fighting on Hill 523 became hand-to-hand in places. Reynolds cut down one advancing German soldier with his pistol and dropped another with his machine gun. Comrades fell wounded all around him as the battle raged. Pinned down with a handful of comrades throughout the day, he passed grenades up to Sergeant Richard Swanger while jagged junks of shrapnel slammed into the steep slope near them. After nightfall, Reynolds and a dozen other men, many wounded, retreated from the hill and withdrew to the southeast.[7]

The next day, when Hill 523 was secured, Reynolds and the other dozen survivors from his battalion were visited by their Big Red One commanders, Terry Allen and Ted Roosevelt. They expressed their pride in how the surviving men had conducted themselves under the most severe conditions, and they promised that the First Battalion would be recommended for an award. Roosevelt shook hands with each man and said in his booming voice, "Anything you want, just ask, and if possible, I'll get it for you." One of the men, whose bare feet were raw, simply requested a clean pair of socks.[8]

Omar Bradley's combined infantry and armored task forces maintained the fight until German resistance began to crumble and Hill 609 was secured. Mateur had fallen by May 3, with the First Armored Division rumbling forward for the final push on Bizerte. *The rout is on,* thought Second Lieutenant Charlie Scheffel of the Thirty-Ninth Infantry as his forces pushed the Germans eastward. When they reached the Tunisian coast, he watched as Axis ships were bombed as they attempted to recover defeated Afrika Korps soldiers. Scheffel and one of his sergeants smeared mud on the swastika adorning a motorcycle's sidecar and took a joyride down the main Tunis–Bizerte highway. He felt like a conquering hero as the wind roared in his ears and whipped through his uniform.[9]

By May 9, Bradley's forces had secured the path from Tunis to Bizerte, effectively ending combat operations in Tunisia. German troops accepted the terms of unconditional surrender by the tens of thousands. Allied troops relished their victory by using German helmets to decorate their trucks and jeeps. Pockets of resistance would consume the next few days, but the Axis backbone had been broken. Scheffel marveled at the scores of defeated German soldiers who soon began surrendering, realizing he was viewing a beaten bunch of men who were glad to be finished with the war.[10]

Omar Bradley sent a cable to General Eisenhower on May 9 that read simply: "Mission accomplished." Four days later, after Generals von Arnim and Hans Cramer had surrendered with the last of their Afrika Korps caravan, General Alexander sent Prime Minister Winston Churchill the victorious news: "We are masters of the North African shores."[11]

———

Oberleutnant Wilhelm Reile was in the fight to the bitter end. He had been elevated to command of the Tenth Panzer Division's

Kradschützen-Bataillon 10 after his superior officer was wounded by an artillery barrage on May 8. His German forces dwindled during their retreat toward the Tunisian coast. His battalion was down to very few Panzers, which soon were depleted of fuel, and only two 88mm antiaircraft guns. Reile wrote that his enemy was "firing on anything that moves."[12]

By May 10, Reile's battalion was down to roughly 200 men from an original strength of 850. His force was a mixed bag of radio operators, drivers, and armored car personnel armed only with pistols. "The most powerful weapon was an infantry gun with little ammunition," he remembered. The division was ordered to burn unnecessary equipment and vehicles before surrendering over the next few days. General von Arnim passed word to his troops to prepare for the inevitable negotiations, hoping that the behavior of his soldiers in the Tunisian conflict "will have earned the respect of my opponent."[13]

Former Rommel driver Rudolf Schneider was among the hundreds of thousands of Axis soldiers taken prisoner on May 16, 1943. He would eventually be shipped to America, where he spent the balance of the war at Camp Swift, Texas, picking cotton for five cents an hour. His suffering did not end with the close of war. After he was transported back to Europe, the British learned that he had been a member of Rommel's *Kampfstaffel*. Only thirty-nine members of the elite guard unit, once numbering nearly four hundred, had survived the war. When his ship arrived in Liverpool, he was one of more than 400,000 Germans that Britain refused to repatriate. Schneider would spend three years working as a farm laborer in Staffordshire.[14]

It was not until 1948 that Schneider was allowed to return to East Germany. There, he happily married his childhood sweetheart, Alfreda, who had waited for him. He had kept her photograph with him through seven years of separation. Schneider and his wife raised three children as he pursued a career as an agricultural researcher. He avidly studied history for many years, and as of 2020 was believed to be the last surviving member of Rommel's elite protection and reconnaissance unit.[15]

Lieutenant Colonel John Waters, captured by the Germans at Sidi Bou Zid in February 1943, narrowly survived his ordeal. He was shot by a defending guard in 1945 as a secret task force set up by Patton attempted to liberate the prisoners in the Hammelburg POW camp. Waters was treated by Serbian doctors, and he and his camp were liberated by a U.S. armored division in April. He returned to active duty and rose to the rank of four-star general before retiring in 1966.

For many of the soldiers who had served under Waters and his father-in-law, Patton, the war in Tunisia was but the first of several Allied invasions they would endure during World War II. Infantryman Harley Reynolds fought with his battalion during its landings in Sicily and Normandy, rising to the rank of staff sergeant. He earned a second Bronze Star for his valor in capturing a German pillbox during the landings in Sicily, where his close friend Ivy Bradshaw died. In 1945, Reynolds declined an offer to be advanced to officer's rank. Instead, he used his service points to return to the United States for discharge on the Fourth of July. He started engineering school on the GI Bill and retired in Florida after more than four decades working for the same company.

Reynolds's First Battalion of the Sixteenth Infantry would receive the Presidential Unit Citation for its actions in Tunisia. He felt that II Corps infantrymen had been like firefighters during those desperate months, called forward on numerous occasions to put out the fires wherever needed. As their effective fighting numbers were whittled down, they were endlessly shifted from one djebel to another to engage the Germans and Italians. "I was sure we would run out of men before we got through all those mountains," Reynolds remembered.[16]

Henry "Red" Phillips was another who made it through the mountains of Tunisia and participated in the Ninth Infantry Division's campaigns in Sicily, France, and Germany. Commissioned into the U.S. Army following World War II, Phillips would retire as a lieutenant colonel in 1967. He earned degrees from the University of Maryland and Illinois while raising two daughters with his wife, Lee. In later years, Red published and edited his community's newspaper in Lake Wildwood, California.

Phillips was also a noted historian who authored several books on the Ninth Infantry Division and his heavy weapons company, and a biography of General Manton Eddy. He served as both president of the Ninth Infantry Division Association and as the division's official historian. Phillips passed away on August 19, 2011.

Charlie Scheffel of the Thirty-Ninth Infantry served during both the Operation Husky and Normandy invasions, achieving a battlefield commission as a captain along the way. Severely wounded in a leg and both hands near Belgium in September 1944, he would retire from the Army in January 1946, having earned two Purple Hearts, the Silver Star, a Bronze Star, and other awards for his service. He and his wife, Ruth, raised three children while building a successful insurance business in Oklahoma City. Scheffel passed away on June 24, 2011, one week after his ninety-second birthday.

Tom Morrison remained with the 601st Tank Destroyer Division following the injuries he sustained at El Guettar. His request to become a medic was approved in July 1943. He was wounded a second time during his service with the division's landings at Salerno and Anzio. Following the war, Morrison used the GI Bill to attend the Cleveland School of Art, where he met his future wife, Marian Gnant. He retired from General Motors in 1979 and passed away in Ohio on June 27, 2009. Today, Morrison's numerous drawings and memoirs are available both at the U.S. Army Heritage and Education Center in Carlisle, Pennsylvania, and at the Third Cavalry Museum at Ford Hood, Texas.

Lieutenant Colonel Bill Darby received the Distinguished Service Cross for his leadership of the First Ranger Battalion at El Guettar.

Only months later, in July 1943, he would earn a second DSC for extraordinary heroism during the Sicily campaign. Darby also took part in the Allied invasion of Italy and was promoted to full colonel in December. He lost his life to an artillery shell on April 30, 1945, just two days before all German forces in Italy surrendered.

The success of Darby's First Ranger Battalion brought about the creation of the Third Ranger Battalion, led by Major Herman Dammer, and the Fourth Ranger Battalion, led by Major Roy Murray. Lieutenant Les Kness, who had received his battlefield commission in North Africa, took command of A Company, Fourth Ranger Battalion. He served with distinction, earning a Silver Star and later rising to the position of operations officer for his battalion. He was wounded in Italy during November 1943 and eventually separated from Army service in 1946 with the rank of captain.

Kness pursued his education and operated a successful plumbing business for a quarter century in Des Moines. He was a dedicated member of Ranger battalion reunions and, among other accomplishments, was involved in manufacturing the Ketch-All mouse trap, which his father had invented. Kness passed away at age eighty-seven in 2006 at the VA Medical Center in Des Moines.

Kness's close friend Lester Cook continued to serve with the Rangers through the invasions of Sicily and Italy. He was nearly buried alive in his foxhole by the explosion of an Italian artillery shell. He was fortunate enough to have his helmet over his face, allowing him just enough air to survive until comrades dug him out. Cook, who rose to master sergeant, served as a paratrooper during the Korean War and was an advisor for the Seventy-Seventh Special Forces at the start of the Vietnam War. His awards included two Silver Stars and four Purple Hearts. Cook, like Kness, was later inducted into the Ranger Hall of Fame at Fort Benning, Georgia. Following the war, he went to work for the U.S. Postal Service and later retired in his home state of Iowa. He passed away on August 9, 2020, approaching the age of ninety-eight. Cook was the last surviving member of Darby's original 1942 First Ranger Battalion.

One of the last known living veterans of the Seventeenth Field Artillery was Hubert Edwards, who turned 101 in 2020. When visited at his home near Fort Bragg by the author in 2019, Hubert was still driving himself around, active in his community with his wife, Lynda, and full of energy. He spoke passionately about his many experiences in World War II, including the time he shot down a German aircraft from the back of his jeep during the battle of El Guettar. He returned to civilian life in North Carolina in 1945, having reached the rank of sergeant after nearly two years of frontline service.

His early impressions of George Patton mirrored those of other soldiers who helped "Old Blood and Guts" achieve glory through the shedding of their own blood. "Most of the people didn't like him," Edwards said in 2019. "But one thing you have to give him credit for: that sucker was a fighter!"[17]

During the Allied drive through France, Edwards had a chance encounter with Generals Patton and Eisenhower. The artillerymen had dug a small hole in the ground and were in the process of boiling coffee in a gallon can when they were startled by the sudden appearance of the U.S. command staff. Edwards jumped to his feet and called his men to attention, only to be ordered at ease. Ike casually chatted with the soldiers, adding, "With what I'm seeing, I think we can win this war. What do you think?"

The reply from Edwards shocked the brass. "I don't think so, sir."

Eisenhower and Patton were clearly taken aback momentarily before Edwards continued. "Sir, you say you think we're going to win this war and I disagree with you. I don't think we're going to win this war. I *know* we're going to win it."

Eisenhower smiled and said, "That's the best response I've heard all day."

The brash artilleryman would survive a long string of campaigns through North Africa, Sicily, France, and Central Europe, and receive the Silver Star and a collection of Bronze Stars. In 2016 the avid baseball fan was the guest of honor when his beloved Atlanta Braves played the Florida Marlins at Fort Bragg. It was the first time Edwards had attended a Major League Baseball game in person, so officials made sure he was able to meet all his favorite players before the game.

Even as he celebrated the centenarian mark in 2019, Edwards occasionally visited the North Carolina base at Fort Bragg to spend time in the field with paratroopers and to watch artillery fire from close range. He was impressed with the modern howitzers, a far cry from the World War I–vintage pieces he had fired in North Africa. Edwards insists that he plans to live to be 110 with the hope of being the last living World War II veteran.

The well-respected commanders of the Big Red One, Terry Allen and Ted Roosevelt Jr., continued as valiant leaders through the next invasions. Roosevelt stormed ashore on the beaches of Normandy, defiantly riding in his "Rough Rider" jeep as shells burst around him, imploring his men to fight hard. He died of a heart attack in France in July 1944 and was later recognized with a posthumous Medal of Honor for his heroism on the beaches of Normandy. Allen led his First Infantry Division through the Sicily campaign and commanded the 104th Infantry Division through tough European fighting in France, the Netherlands, and Germany.

"I don't know how any of the men who went through the thick of that hill-by-hill butchery could ever be the same again," war correspondent Ernie Pyle wrote of the North Africa campaign in 1943. His press articles, and those of his journalistic brothers-in-arms, helped Americans back home comprehend the magnitude of endurance and courage required of II Corps soldiers who fought the battles in little-known places like Ousseltia Valley, Kasserine Pass, and El Guettar.[18]

Wearing an armored corps jacket given to him by Major General Lloyd Fredendall, Pyle attached himself to the First Infantry Division during its final drive from Mateur toward the coast of Tunisia. He witnessed artillerymen like Edwards using their howitzers to create cauldrons of fire, smoke, and dirt in pulverizing Axis forces. He wrote that the U.S. Army had been "hardened and practiced by going through the flames" in Tunisia. But he was also aware that the campaign had been a warm-up for the bigger push through Europe, where "the worst was yet to come."[19]

For Pyle, his coverage of the war would continue until his life was finally taken by a bullet on Okinawa during the final push of the Pacific War. His gentle character, and his colorful descriptions of both regular GIs and commanding generals, had endeared him to millions of American readers. During his time in North Africa, he revered the deposed Fredendall as something of a father figure, a sentiment he did not have for Patton. In Pyle's 1943 book on the North Africa campaign, *Here Is Your War*, he never once included Patton's name. Pyle biographer James Tobin further notes that Patton's name never once appeared in a Pyle newspaper column due to the reporter's hatred of the general. The kindhearted journalist preferred to immortalize more modest generals like Omar Bradley while completely ignoring Patton due to his "bluster, show and complete disregard for the dignity of the individual."[20]

Lloyd Fredendall returned to the United States, where the press pronounced him to be "hero of the American landing at Oran in North Africa." On April 22 he was named commanding general of the Second Army. On June 1 he was promoted to lieutenant general, supervising training and field maneuvers of his widespread training army. Once very open to members of the press, he largely shunned them stateside after being stung by an April 12, 1943, *Time* magazine article that said he had become "the goat of the U.S. defeat" at Kasserine Pass. *Time* also reported, "His lines were extended so far it would have taken a week to send a postcard from one end to the other."[21]

Eisenhower did not publicly criticize Fredendall's command in North Africa but instead allowed him to continue his career with honor stateside. Fredendall served in largely a training role through the end of the war and retired on March 31, 1946. Although he was certainly stung by being replaced by Patton in North Africa, he remained quiet about it during his retirement. He avoided the media and did not participate in the Army's Senior Officer Oral History Program. Fredendall died in San Diego on October 4, 1963, and was interred at Fort Rosecrans National Cemetery at Point Loma in San Diego.

Patton's legend played out in the media, boosted by his success at El Guettar. The April 12, 1943, issue of *Time* magazine included his face—stern, with a hint of a smile—and an article about his fight against Rommel in Tunisia. But his fame skyrocketed later in 1943 after leading the successful campaign in Sicily. His face graced the covers of magazines and newspapers. In its July 26 issue, *Time* acknowledged the general's legend that had led to such nicknames as "Gorgeous George" and "Old Blood & Guts" but offered that he was more balanced. Aside from his spectacular impressions, Patton "was also a patient and careful and studious man, a field officer with a good staff mind."

During a break from the fighting in Sicily, he met with reporters, inviting one to return to the battlefields with him. "You had better come now, or my men will have killed all the bastards." *Time* shared another anecdote from Sicily where Patton had reportedly ordered a two-star general to the top of a hill "so that you can get shot at a bit." The general's brash reputation soared back home from rallying statements he made, such as "It makes no difference which part of Europe you kill Germans in."

But Patton's harshness, all too familiar to his troops, was exposed to a larger audience when he was temporarily removed from battle-field command during the Allied invasion of Sicily. The national controversy that ensued was the result of Patton slapping and verbally abusing two shell-shocked American soldiers, ordering both of the battle-fatigued men back to the front lines. Eisenhower reprimanded his subordinate in private, ordering Patton to make formal apologies to the two men and the field hospital staff who had witnessed the embarrassing events.

Bradley would take the helm during the next eleven months while the controversy played out in the press. It was not until January 1944 that Patton was returned to a combat command role in England, in charge of the newly formed U.S. Third Army. His status as a premier leader of men was cemented during a highly successful rapid armored drive across France in August 1944. Patton's biggest challenge came during the Battle of the Bulge, in the final offensives that pushed across Belgium, Luxembourg, and northeastern France. His Third Army's Fourth Armored Division reached Bastogne on December 26, prompting Patton to write of this relief as his most brilliant operation thus far. He declared the successful advance to be "the outstanding achievement of the war. This is my biggest battle."[22]

Patton's battle accomplishments helped him achieve his coveted fourth star when he was promoted to full general on April 14, 1945, during the Allied occupation of Germany. Following the end of hostilities in Europe, he enjoyed a brief visit with his family back home before returning to Europe to assume the appointment of military governor of Bavaria. Unhappy with this position, Patton made enough aggressive public statements against the Soviet Union and denazification that Eisenhower relieved him of command of the Third Army in October 1945.

In his final assignment, Patton commanded the U.S. Fifteenth Army in Europe for little more than two months. He was severely injured on December 9, 1945, while riding with his chief of staff, Major

General Hobart Gay, when their vehicle collided with an American army truck at low speed. Gay and the others were only slightly injured, but Patton's head struck the glass partition in the rear seat, causing him to suffer a broken neck and paralysis from the neck down. He survived nearly two weeks but died in his sleep on December 21, 1945, of pulmonary edema and congestive heart failure.

Patton's wife, Beatrice, wished for her husband's body to be returned for burial at West Point, but she was informed of Army policy that he must be buried on foreign soil just like the thousands of young men he had commanded. Representatives from nine countries were on hand as Patton's coffin was carried through Luxembourg to the American military cemetery. Ironically, Old Blood and Guts had once written that he hoped to one day have his body carried "between the ranks of my defeated enemy, escorted by my own regiment, and have my spirit come down and revel in hearing what people thought of me."[23]

President Franklin Roosevelt called Patton "our greatest fighting general." The *New York Times* opined, "He was not a man of peace." North Africa veteran Red Phillips wrote, "Patton estimated the situation at El Guettar and influenced his subordinate commanders before the battle." The U.S. forces became more close-knit in the Tunisian desert, where Patton and other great leaders like Omar Bradley, Manton Eddy, Terry Allen, and Ted Roosevelt learned valuable lessons in coordination and discipline.[24]

Phillips ably summed up the desert war's importance: "The battle was severe and went on long enough so that most of the weak links snapped or became casualties before it was over. At the end, what came out of the pot was pure gold, the quintessence of combat leadership."[25]

ACKNOWLEDGMENTS

With each of my previous books, I have generally started with a vision on a topic that captivated me. With this one, full credit is due to my longtime Caliber editor, Brent Howard. He suggested that I consider taking a fresh look at the 1943 North Africa campaign in World War II and how the leadership of Lieutenant General George Patton came to be. And so, my journey began.

As with other World War II manuscripts I have taken on, my first task has always been to interview as many living witnesses to the conflict as I can track down. In this case, that task was monumental, as our veterans from this era are departing so rapidly. But, thanks in large to several individuals who helped guide my quest, I was able to track down a handful of aging veterans, such as Earl Blassingame, Lester Cook, Hubert Edwards, Dale Jones, Tony Konopka, Harley Reynolds, and Lloyd Richards.

Family members of other veterans helped fill in key details

by providing letters, diaries, and manuscripts their fathers had penned years before. Those who assisted include Catherine Morrison Friedman, who shared memoirs and illustrations compiled by her father, Thomas, a veteran of the 601st Tank Destroyer Battalion. Enlightening details of Ranger Les Kness came from his children, Lee Kness, Wade Kness, and Kathy Kness Wauson. My thanks also go out to other children and relatives of North Africa veterans: Patricia Grayem, Christine Irving, John Irving, Thomas Mascari, Kathryn Phillips, Barbara Stima, Michael J. Stima, and John D. Yowell Jr.

I am in debt to accomplished authors who were kind enough to share some of their North Africa interview archives. Orr Kelly offered his Bruce Pirnie interview and fielded a number of my questions. Douglas Bekke provided a number of First Ranger Battalion documents, including photos and personal memoirs of Ranger Lester Kness. Victor "Tory" Failmezer offered several photos and key documents from veterans of the 601st Tank Destroyer Battalion. Liesl Bradner, author of Phil "Snapdragon" Stern's biography, guided me through various Ranger documents and helped me to establish personal contact with the last living World War II veterans of Darby's Rangers.

As my research continued into 2020 among the world-changing Covid pandemic, I found myself faced with archives and museums that had closed down to most researchers. Colonel Don Patton helped put me in touch with videographers Robert Barros and others from the Minnesota archives. Researcher Katie Rasdorf went out of her way to dig out source material and potential photos for use in this book. My friend Maarten de Jong from Belgium helped by contacting the Rudolf Schneider family and searching through German archives. Michael Fraticelli, an accomplished researcher who is compiling a video history of North Africa, helped steer much of my early research for this book. My agent, Jim Donovan, is greatly appreciated for his careful editorial review of this manuscript.

Again, I must thank the World War II veterans who took the time to meet personally or to answer my questions over the telephone. To them, and to the comrades they lost in action in North Africa, this book is dedicated.

NOTES

PROLOGUE

1. Atkinson, *An Army at Dawn*, 267–68.
2. Patton diary, March 2, 1943.
3. Ibid., March 3, 1943; D'Este, *Patton*, 40.
4. Patton diary, March 4, 1943.

CHAPTER 1: PURPLE HEART TANKER

1. Morrison, "The 601 Tank Destroyers in Tunisia, 1942–1943," 3; Morrison letter to L. L. Gill, November 16, 1984, 5.
2. Kelly, *Meeting the Fox*, 15; Atkinson, *An Army at Dawn*, 164.
3. Morrison, "The 601 Tank Destroyers in Tunisia, 1942–1943," 3.
4. Fletcher, *British Battle Tanks*, 5.
5. Smithsonian, *Tank*, 17–18.
6. Ogorkiewicz, *Tanks*, 12–13.
7. Wells, "The Land Ironclads"; Fletcher, *British Battle Tanks*, 4.
8. Zaloga, *Armored Thunderbolt*, 2–10.
9. Yeide, *The Tank Killers*, 3–6.
10. Josowitz, *An Informal History of the 601st Tank Destroyer Battalion*, 3.

11. Yeide, *The Tank Killers*, 11.
12. Morrison, Veterans History Project interview; Harper, Veterans History Project interview; Barron, *Patton's First Victory*, xiv.
13. Rottman, *M3 Medium Tank vs Panzer III*, 51–52.
14. Ibid., 53.
15. Morrison, Veterans History Project interview.
16. Failmezger, *American Knights*, 26–27.
17. Morrison, "The 601 Tank Destroyers in Tunisia, 1942–1943," 3.
18. Ibid., 4.
19. Ibid.
20. Morrison, Veterans History Project interview.
21. Morrison, "The 601 Tank Destroyers in Tunisia, 1942–1943," 4.
22. Harper and Marcus interviews, *Patton 360*, Episode 2: "Rommel's Last Stand," and Episode 1: "Blood and Guts."
23. Boyle, Harold V. "Fayetteville Lieutenant Makes Successful Dash," 1.
24. "Lawrence Marcus, Member of the Legendary Retailing Family, Dies at 96."
25. Morrison, "The 601 Tank Destroyers in Tunisia, 1942–1943," 5.
26. Morrison, Veterans History Project interview.
27. Ibid.
28. Ibid.
29. Boyle, "Fayetteville Lieutenant Makes Successful Dash," 1.
30. "Lawrence Marcus, Member of the Legendary Retailing Family, Dies at 96."

CHAPTER 2: "LLOYD'S VERY LAST RESORT"

1. Bennett, "Yanks Can 'Lick' Nazis, Says General," 1, 18.
2. Fredendall, order to Combat Command B.
3. Atkinson, *An Army at Dawn*, 304–305; Wheeler, *The Big Red One*, 163–64.
4. Atkinson, *An Army at Dawn*, 305.
5. Ossad, "Command Failure," 45–46.
6. Knopf, *These Are the Generals*, 227.
7. Kelly, *Meeting the Fox*, 21.
8. Atkinson, *An Army at Dawn*, 273.
9. Truscott, *Command Missions*, 90.
10. Ibid.
11. Taaffe, *Marshall and His Generals*, 62–63.
12. Atkinson, *An Army at Dawn*, 274–75.
13. Eisenhower, *Crusade in Europe*, 141.
14. Atkinson, *An Army at Dawn*, 270–71.
15. Ibid., 279–80.
16. Ibid., 306–307.

17. Ibid., 307.
18. Waters, "Reminiscences of General John K. Waters," 49–55.
19. Hirshon, *General Patton*, 211.
20. Zaloga, *George S. Patton*, 9; D'Este, *Eisenhower*, 172–75.
21. Jordan, *Brothers, Rivals, Victors*, 10–11.
22. Ibid., 12–14; Hirshon, *General Patton*, 156.
23. Hirshon, *General Patton*, 156–57.
24. Jordan, *Brothers, Rivals, Victors*, 11–15.
25. Axelrod, *Patton*, 73–74.
26. Hirshon, *General Patton*, 228–32.
27. Ibid., 235–37.
28. Jordan, *Brothers, Rivals, Victors*, 33.
29. Ibid., 40.
30. Hirshon, *General Patton*, 246–48.
31. Jordan, *Brothers, Rivals, Victors*, 40.
32. Ibid.; Hirshon, *General Patton*, 249–50.
33. Jordan, *Brothers, Rivals, Victors*, 40–41.
34. Bradley and Blair, *A General's Life*, 98.
35. Waters, "Reminiscences of General John K. Waters," 149–58.
36. Hirshon, *General Patton*, 258–61.
37. Ibid., 265–75.
38. Patton diary, October 21, 1942.
39. Ibid.
40. Hirshon, *General Patton*, 276–81.
41. Patton diary, December 1–15, 1942.
42. Patton, "Account of General Patton's Visit to the Tunisian Front," 50–55.
43. Hirshon, *General Patton*, 291.
44. Waters, "Reminiscences of General John K. Waters," 187–88.
45. Patton diary, January 28 and February 18, 1943.

CHAPTER 3: THE DESERT FOX'S REDEMPTION

1. Mortimer, "Inside Rommel's Afrika Korps," 50, 52.
2. Ibid., 52.
3. Ibid., 50, 56.
4. Schmidt, *With Rommel in the Desert*, 89.
5. Ibid., 89–90.
6. Mortimer, "Inside Rommel's Afrika Korps," 55.
7. Schmidt, *With Rommel in the Desert*, 161–73.
8. Mortimer, "Inside Rommel's Afrika Korps," 56; Niderost, "Trial by Fire at Kasserine Pass," 30.

9. Mortimer, "Inside Rommel's Afrika Korps," 56.
10. Niderost, "Trial by Fire at Kasserine Pass," 30.
11. Kelly, *Meeting the Fox*, 153.
12. Lindell-Hart, *The Rommel Papers*, 389–91; Niderost, "Trial by Fire at Kasserine Pass," 30.
13. Atkinson, *An Army at Dawn*, 319–20.
14. Niderost, "Trial by Fire at Kasserine Pass," 31.
15. Atkinson, *An Army at Dawn*, 322.
16. Rottman, *M3 Medium Tank vs Panzer III, Kasserine Pass 1943*, 17.
17. Jentz and Doyle, *Tiger 1 Heavy Tank, 1942–1945*, 19–20.
18. Hartmann, *Panzers in the Sand, Volume 2*, 26.
19. Ibid., 28, 31.

CHAPTER 4: FAID PASS SETBACKS

1. Reynolds, *How I Survived the Three First Wave Invasions*, 29.
2. Wheeler, *The Big Red One*, 148; Reynolds, *How I Survived the Three First Wave Invasions*, 19–20.
3. Reynolds, National WWII Museum interview video.
4. Reynolds, *How I Survived the Three First Wave Invasions*, 21.
5. Ibid., 23.
6. Ibid., 15.
7. Atkinson, *An Army at Dawn*, 307–308.
8. Frank Zuzock statement of 4 November 1948 from Individual Deceased Personnel File (IDPF) for Private Joseph E. Conway, Serial Number 12-023-106, Record Group 92: Records of the Office of the Quartermaster General, Washington Records Center (WNRC), Suitland, MD.
9. Statement of Corporal James F. Butler, 15 November 1948, in Private Joseph E. Conway IDPF file.
10. Statement of Harold L. Liddell, 2 December 1948, contained in Individual Deceased Personnel File (IDPF) for Corporal Robert J. Fullown, Serial Number 12-007-741, Record Group 92: Records of the Office of the Quartermaster General, Washington Records Center (WNRC), Suitland, MD.
11. Individual Deceased Personnel File (IDPF) for Staff Sergeant Habard T. Gladhill, Serial Number 6-848-366, and Corporal Thaddeus J. Thomas, Serial Number 13-022-189, Record Group 92: Records of the Office of the Quartermaster General, Washington Records Center (WNRC), Suitland, MD.
12. Blumenson, *Kasserine Pass*, 143; Atkinson, *An Army at Dawn*, 311.
13. Schick, *Combat History of the 10 Panzer-Division*, 457.
14. Ibid., 458.
15. Ibid., 460.

16. Ibid., 461.
17. Atkinson, *An Army at Dawn*, 313.
18. Ibid., 314–15.
19. Ibid., 316.
20. Morrison, "The 601 Tank Destroyers in Tunisia, 1942–1943," 6.
21. Atkinson, *An Army at Dawn*, 323–24.
22. Kelly, *Meeting the Fox*, 48; Pyle, *Here Is Your War*, 153; Brady, *His Father's Son*, 242.
23. Atkinson, *An Army at Dawn*, 324.
24. First Armored Division, *Kasserine Pass Battles*.
25. Atkinson, *An Army at Dawn*, 325.
26. Ibid., 327.
27. Waters, "Reminiscences of General John K. Waters," 190.
28. Ibid., 191.

CHAPTER 5: "WORKED OVER BY RANGERS"

1. Jeffers, *Onward We Charge*, 26–29.
2. Ibid., 29–34.
3. Sullivan, diary, June 8–26, 1942; Frederick, oral history interview with Bekke.
4. Stern and Bradner, *Snapdragon*, 18–19, 27.
5. Altieri, *The Spearheaders*, 97.
6. Stern and Bradner, *Snapdragon*, 159–61.
7. Sullivan, diary, March 4 and February 7, 1943.
8. Ibid., March 14, 1943.
9. "Kness Among Original Darby Rangers in WWII."
10. Ibid.
11. Wade Kness, telephone interview with author; Lester Kness recollections given to Douglas Bekke, March 1994, Richfield, Minnesota; Lee Kness, telephone interview with author.
12. "Kness Among Original Darby Rangers in WWII."
13. Cook, telephone interviews with author.
14. "Kness Among Original Darby Rangers in WWII"; Jeffers, *Onward We Charge*, 40–41.
15. Moen and Heinen, *Heroes Cry Too*, 92–93.
16. Wade Kness, telephone interview with author.
17. Moen and Heinen, *Heroes Cry Too*, 94.
18. O'Donnell, *Beyond Valor*, 10–11, 2–5.
19. Lehmann, "Ranger Captain Albert E. Basil"; also contained in Bahmanyar, *Darby's Rangers*, 25–27.

20. Stern and Bradner, *Snapdragon*, 162.
21. Cook, telephone interviews with author.
22. Darby and Baumer, *We Led the Way*, 56.
23. Ibid., 56–57.
24. Altieri, *The Spearheaders*, 197.
25. Ibid., 199.
26. Darby and Baumer, *We Led the Way*, 57.
27. Cook, telephone interviews with author.
28. Darby and Baumer, *We Led the Way*, 57–58.
29. Frederick, oral history interview with Bekke.
30. Cook, telephone interviews with author.
31. O'Donnell, *Beyond Valor*, 34.
32. Moen and Heinen, *Heroes Cry Too*, 120.
33. O'Donnell, *Beyond Valor*, 34.
34. Darby and Baumer, *We Led the Way*, 58; Altieri, *The Spearheaders*, 209.
35. Frederick, oral history interview with Bekke.
36. O'Donnell, *Beyond Valor*, 34; Edwin L. Dean Silver Star citation, www
    .valor.militarytimes.com/hero/53857; Joseph Dye Silver Star citation, www
    .valor.militarytimes.com/hero/538578; Owen E. Sweasey Silver Star citation,
    www.valor.militarytimes.com/hero/538576.
37. Moen and Heinen, *Heroes Cry Too*, 120–21.
38. Altieri, *The Spearheaders*, 211.
39. Darby and Baumer, *We Led the Way*, 58–59.
40. Ibid., 59.
41. O'Donnell, *Beyond Valor*, 34.
42. Altieri, *The Spearheaders*, 221.
43. Sullivan, diary, February 13–14, 1943; Darby and Baumer, *We Led the Way*,
    59; Moen and Heinen, *Heroes Cry Too*, 121–22.
44. Altieri, *The Spearheaders*, 224.
45. Stern and Bradner, *Snapdragon*, 178.
46. Altieri, *The Spearheaders*, 227; Darby and Baumer, *We Led the Way*, 59.

CHAPTER SIX: SPRING BREEZE FURY

1. Waters, "Reminiscences of General John K. Waters," 208.
2. Blumenson, *Kasserine Pass*, 140; Atkinson, *An Army at Dawn*, 343; Kelly,
   Meeting the Fox, 184.
3. Atkinson, *An Army at Dawn*, 331–32.
4. Ibid., 333.
5. Ibid., 333–34.
6. Rottman, *M3 Medium Tank vs Panzer III*, 59, 64.
7. Ibid., 339.

8. Kelly, *Meeting the Fox*, 189–90; Atkinson, *An Army at Dawn*, 340.
9. "Tour of Duty," 1.
10. Pirnie, interview with Kelly; "Tour of Duty," 1; Kelly, *Meeting the Fox*, 187.
11. "Tour of Duty," 1.
12. Atkinson, *An Army at Dawn*, 340.
13. Pirnie, interview with Kelly; "Tour of Duty," 1.
14. Jones, telephone interview with author.
15. "Tour of Duty," 1.
16. Hubert G. Edwards interview with author.
17. Heinz, "POW Memories Haunt Cody Man," 1.
18. Bickers, "The First Kriegies."
19. Heinz, "POW Memories Haunt Cody Man," 1.
20. Atkinson, *An Army at Dawn*, 341.
21. Niderost, "Trial by Fire at Kasserine Pass."
22. Rottman, *M3 Medium Tank vs Panzer III*, 65.
23. Ibid., 66.
24. "The Tank Battle at Sidi Bou Zid," B19.
25. Niderost, "Trial by Fire at Kasserine Pass," 33; Hightower, interview in "Tankers in Tunisia," 24.
26. Waters, "Reminiscences of General John K. Waters," 210.
27. Hains, Report of 11 March 1943; Waters, "Reminiscences of General John K. Waters," 212.
28. Waters, "Reminiscences of General John K. Waters," 212–13, 222.
29. "Tour of Duty," 1.
30. Kelly, *Meeting the Fox*, 187; Pirnie, interview with Kelly.
31. Kness, letter to Ivey, December 22, 1993, 1.
32. Darby and Baumer, *We Led the Way*, 60.
33. Ibid., 60–61.
34. Kness, letter to Ivey, December 22, 1993, 2.
35. Cook, telephone interviews with author.
36. Kness, letter to Ivey, December 22, 1993, 2.
37. Ibid.
38. Ibid.; Darby and Baumer, *We Led the Way*, 62.
39. Cook, telephone interviews with author.
40. "Kness Among Original Darby Rangers in WWII"; Kness, letter to Ivey, December 22, 1993, 2.
41. Ibid.

CHAPTER SEVEN: KASSERINE PASS

1. Wolff, "Tank Battle in Tunisia," 61.
2. Ibid.

3. Hartmann, *Panzers in the Sand, Volume 2,* 120.
4. Wolff, "Tank Battle in Tunisia," 61–62.
5. Ibid., 62.
6. Hartmann, *Panzers in the Sand, Volume 2,* 120.
7. Wolff, "Tank Battle in Tunisia," 62.
8. Hartmann, *Panzers in the Sand, Volume 2,* 120; Wolff, "Tank Battle in Tunisia," 62.
9. Zaloga, *Kasserine Pass 1943,* 42.
10. Niderost, "Trial by Fire at Kasserine Pass," 34; Pyle, *Here Is Your War,* 136–37.
11. Niderost, "Trial by Fire at Kasserine Pass," 34.
12. Atkinson, *An Army at Dawn,* 351.
13. Pyle, *Here Is Your War,* 139.
14. Newton, "Battle for Kasserine Pass," 54–55.
15. Ibid., 55.
16. Wolff, "Tank Battle in Tunisia," 62–63.
17. Schick, *Combat History of the 10. Panzer-Division,* 468.
18. Wolff, "Tank Battle in Tunisia," 63.
19. Hartmann, *Panzers in the Sand, Volume 2,* 120.
20. Liddell-Hart, *The Rommel Papers,* 398.
21. Schmidt, *With Rommel in the Desert,* 198–201.
22. Wolff, "Tank Battle in Tunisia," 63.
23. Niderost, "Trial by Fire," 34.
24. Atkinson, *An Army at Dawn,* 354.
25. Drake, *Kasserine Pass Battles,* 20; Sherwood, "Bloodied but Bruised," 44–45.
26. Ibid., 20.
27. Ibid., 21–22.
28. Niderost, "Trial by Fire," 34.
29. Schick, *Combat History of the 10. Panzer-Division,* 469; Atkinson, *An Army at Dawn,* 359.
30. Liddell-Hart, *The Rommel Papers,* 400.
31. Ibid.; Niderost, "Trial by Fire," 35.
32. Liddell-Hart, *The Rommel Papers,* 400–401; Atkinson, *An Army at Dawn,* 359–60.
33. Atkinson, *An Army at Dawn,* 360–61.
34. Pyle, *Here Is Your War,* 143.
35. Morrison, "The 601 Tank Destroyers in Tunisia, 1942–1943," 7.
36. Ibid.
37. Ibid., 7–8.
38. Atkinson, *An Army at Dawn,* 362.
39. Ibid., 363.

40. Morrison, "The 601 Tank Destroyers in Tunisia, 1942–1943," 8.
41. Ibid.
42. Failmezger, *American Knights*, 49–50.
43. Morrison, "The 601 Tank Destroyers in Tunisia, 1942–1943," 9.
44. Raymond, "Slugging It Out," 16.
45. Ibid.
46. Morrison, "The 601 Tank Destroyers in Tunisia, 1942–1943," 9.
47. Tobin, *Ernie Pyle's War*, 82–83.
48. Atkinson, *An Army at Dawn*, 366–67.
49. Niderost, "Trial by Fire," 35–36.
50. Ibid., 36.
51. Atkinson, *An Army at Dawn*, 369–70.
52. Liddell-Hart, *The Rommel Papers*, 402.
53. Atkinson, *An Army at Dawn*, 368–69. 21st Panzer Division War Diary, 19 February 1943, in Kasserine Pass Readings, Vol. I, Part II.
54. Schmidt, *With Rommel in the Desert*, 203–204.
55. Ibid., 205–207.
56. Niderost, "Trial by Fire," 36.
57. 21st Panzer Division War Diary, 19 February 1943, in Kasserine Pass Readings, Vol. I, Part II.
58. Niderost, "Trial by Fire," 34. Fredendall to Eisenhower, Feb. 19, 1943, Eisenhower Presidential Library, PP-pre (Pre-Presidential papers), box 42.
59. Liddell-Hart, *The Rommel Papers*, 404.
60. Niderost, "Trial by Fire," 36.
61. Martello, oral history interview with Lofton.
62. Niderost, "Trial by Fire," 37.
63. Ibid.
64. Liddell-Hart, *The Rommel Papers*, 404.
65. Niderost, "Trial by Fire," 37; Liddell-Hart, *The Rommel Papers*, 405.
66. Martello, oral history interview with Lofton.
67. Black, *The Ranger Force*, 105.
68. Kelly, *Meeting the Fox*, 233–34; Black, *The Ranger Force*, 105–106.
69. Stern and Bradner, *Snapdragon*, 188.
70. Ibid., 190.
71. Darby and Baumer, *We Led the Way*, 65.
72. Kness, letter to Ivey, December 22, 1993, 3.
73. Atkinson, *An Army at Dawn*, 379; Liddell-Hart, *The Rommel Papers*, 405.
74. Atkinson, *An Army at Dawn*, 380.
75. Liddell-Hart, *The Rommel Papers*, 406.
76. Atkinson, *An Army at Dawn*, 380.
77. Ibid., 381; Liddell-Hart, *The Rommel Papers*, 407.
78. Atkinson, *An Army at Dawn*, 385–87.

79. Rottman, *M3 Medium Tank vs Panzer III*, 69, 72.
80. Niderost, "Trial by Fire," 37; Blumenson, *Kasserine Pass*, 304; Atkinson, *An Army at Dawn*, 389.
81. Jordan, *Brothers, Rivals, Victors*, 123; Bradley and Blair, *A General's Life*, 128.

CHAPTER EIGHT: "YOU MUST HAVE A BETTER MAN"

1. Nowak, "World War II Memoirs of John Nowak," 1–2.
2. Ibid., 3.
3. Josowitz, *An Informal History of the 601st Tank Destroyer Battalion*, 12.
4. Ibid., 3, 12.
5. Atkinson, *An Army at Dawn*, 387.
6. Harmon and MacKaye, *Combat Commander*, 112.
7. Ossad, "Command Failure," 45–52.
8. Atkinson, *An Army at Dawn*, 400.
9. Ossad, "Command Failure," 50; Harmon and MacKaye, *Combat Commander*, 120.
10. Patton diary, February 22, 1943; Hirshon, *General Patton*, 310.
11. Patton diary, February 27–March 1, 1943.
12. Ibid., March 2, 1943.
13. Ibid., March 3, 1943.
14. Bradley, *A Soldier's Story*, 42.
15. Crosswell, *Beetle: The Life of General Walter Bedell Smith*, 391.
16. Patton diary, March 4, 1943.
17. Hirshon, *General Patton*, 240–41.
18. Patton, *War as I Knew It*, 376; Patton diary, March 5, 1943.
19. Hirshon, *General Patton*, 312–13.
20. Patton diary, March 5, 1943.
21. Phillips, *Heavy Weapons*, 30.
22. Ibid.
23. Phillips, telephone interview with author; Irving, personal interview with author.
24. Phillips, *Heavy Weapons*, 2.
25. Ibid., 18, 13.
26. Ibid., 31.
27. Ibid.

CHAPTER NINE: PATTON TAKES CHARGE

1. Bradley, *A Soldier's Story*, 43.
2. Hirshon, *General Patton*, 314; Patton diary, March 6, 1943.
3. Pyle, *Here Is Your War*, 153.

4. Patton diary, March 6, 1943; Hirshon, *General Patton*, 315.

5. Hirshon, *General Patton*, 244, 260.

6. Patton diary, March 7, 1943.

7. Kelly, *Meeting the Fox*, 259.

8. Bradley, *A Soldier's Story*, 45–46.

9. Patton diary, March 8, 1943; Hubert Edwards interview with author.

10. Patterson, "Starting Off on the Right Foot"; Howard, *Patterson for Alabama*, 9; Trest, *Nobody but the People*, 72.

11. Patton diary, March 8, 1943.

12. Kness, letter to Ivey, December 22, 1993, 3.

13. Darby and Baumer, *We Led the Way*, 65.

14. Sullivan, diary, March 6–10, 1943.

15. Stern and Bradner, *Snapdragon*, 190.

16. Sullivan, diary, March 10–11, 1943; Stern and Bradner, *Snapdragon*, 191.

17. Bradley, *A Soldier's Story*, 44; Patton, *War as I Knew It*, 377.

18. Patton diary, March 9, 1943.

19. Phillips, *Heavy Weapons*, 31.

20. Patton diary, March 10, 1943.

21. Bradley, *A Soldier's Life*, 162–63.

22. Marcus interview, *Patton 360*, Episode 2: "Rommel's Last Stand."

23. Hawksworth, "Gafsa and El Guettar," 107.

24. Patton diary, March 10, 1943; Hirshon, *General Patton*, 320.

25. Patton diary, March 11, 1943.

26. Barron, *Patton's First Victory*, 11–12.

27. Liddell-Hart, *The Rommel Papers*, 412.

28. Ibid., 415–16.

29. Von Luck, *Panzer Commander*, 143–44.

30. Schmidt, *With Rommel in the Desert*, 231–32.

31. Atkinson, *An Army at Dawn*, 411.

32. Patton diary, March 12, 1943.

33. Ibid.

34. Ibid.

CHAPTER TEN: "TOTAL SURPRISE"

1. Patton diary, March 13, 1943.

2. Ibid.

3. Ibid.

4. Kness, letter, August 24, 1990, 1.

5. Ibid.

6. Frederick, oral history interview with Bekke; Lehmann, "Ranger Captain Albert E. Basil."

7. Kness, letter, August 24, 1990, 1.
8. Cook, telephone interviews with author.
9. Kness, letter, August 24, 1990, 2; Patton diary, March 13, 1943.
10. Kness, letter, August 24, 1990, 2.
11. Ibid., 2–3.
12. Black, *The Ranger Force*, 107; Kness, letter, August 24, 1990, 3.
13. Stern and Bradner, *Snapdragon*, 191–93.
14. Reynolds, *How I Survived the Three First Wave Invasions*, 35.
15. United States Army, *Our Battalion*, 17–18.
16. Patton diary, March 16, 1943.
17. Hubert Edwards interview with author.
18. Patton diary, March 16, 1943.
19. Wheeler, *The Big Red One*, 173.
20. Patton diary, March 17, 1943.
21. Black, *The Ranger Force*, 109.
22. Darby and Baumer, *We Led the Way*, 69.
23. Ibid., 69.
24. Patton diary, March 19, 1943.
25. Ibid.
26. Ibid.
27. Ibid.
28. Evans, interview with Holland; Moen and Heinen, *Heroes Cry Too*, 122–23.
29. Street, "The Operations of the First Ranger Battalion, El Guettar, 21–26 March 1943," 10.
30. Yeide, *Fighting Patton*, 159.
31. Patton diary, March 20, 1943.
32. Barron, *Patton's First Victory*, 30.
33. Street, "The Operations of the First Ranger Battalion, El Guettar, 21–26 March 1943," 8.
34. Ibid., 12.
35. Ibid., 13; Kness, letter, August 24, 1990, 3.
36. Darby and Baumer, *We Led the Way*, 71; Kness, letter, August 24, 1990, 3.
37. Darby and Baumer, *We Led the Way*, 72; Kness, letter, August 24, 1990, 3.
38. Kness, letter, August 24, 1990, 3; Cook, telephone interviews with author.
39. Street, "The Operations of the First Ranger Battalion, El Guettar, 21–26 March 1943," 13.
40. Darby and Baumer, *We Led the Way*, 73.
41. Morris, "Rangers Come Home," 4.
42. Kness, letter, August 24, 1990, 3.
43. Street, "The Operations of the First Ranger Battalion, El Guettar, 21–26 March 1943," 13; Moen and Heinen, *Heroes Cry Too*, 123; Kness, letter, August 24, 1990, 4.

44. Street, "The Operations of the First Ranger Battalion, El Guettar, 21–26 March 1943," 13.
45. Darby and Baumer, *We Led the Way*, 74.
46. Street, "The Operations of the First Ranger Battalion, El Guettar, 21–26 March 1943," 15.
47. Kness, letter, August 24, 1990, 4; Street, "The Operations of the First Ranger Battalion, El Guettar, 21–26 March 1943," 15.
48. Stern and Bradner, *Snapdragon*, 202.
49. Atkinson, *An Army at Dawn*, 438.

CHAPTER ELEVEN: PUSHING FORWARD

1. Barron, *Patton's First Victory*, 39.
2. Brady, *His Father's Son*, 245; Patton diary, March 21, 1943.
3. Patton diary, March 21, 1943.
4. Carter, "The Operations of the 1st Battalion," 13.
5. Barron, *Patton's First Victory*, 44–46.
6. Morrison, "Gafsa-Gabès Road" letter, 3.
7. Harper interview, *Patton 360*, Episode 2: "Rommel's Last Stand."
8. Marcus interview, *Patton 360*, Episode 2: "Rommel's Last Stand."
9. Barron, *Patton's First Victory*, 47; Morrison, "Gafsa-Gabès Road" letter, 3.
10. Patton diary, March 22, 1943.
11. Barron, *Patton's First Victory*, 56.
12. Ibid., 57–58.
13. Carter, "The Operations of the First Battalion," 15.
14. Ibid., 17.
15. Ibid.; Barron, *Patton's First Victory*, 60–62.
16. Ibid., 62–63; Trest, *Nobody but the People*, 74.
17. Patton diary, March 22, 1943.
18. Barron, *Patton's First Victory*, 63.
19. Baker, "Tank Destroyer Combat in Tunisia," 17; Baker, "Battle Operations Report."
20. Statement of Sgt. John J. Conway, Co. A, 601st T-D Bn., 26 March 1943.
21. Morrison, "Gafsa-Gabès Road" letter, 4, 5.
22. Stima, statement, March 23, 1943, 1; Yowell, "Battle Operations of Lt. John D. Yowell," 1.
23. Sundstrom, statement, 27 March 1943, 1.
24. Nowak, "World War II Memoirs of John Nowak," 3.
25. Atkinson, *An Army at Dawn*, 166.
26. Barron, *Patton's First Victory*, 52–53.
27. Ibid., 54; Schick, *Combat History of the 10. Panzer-Division*, 499.
28. Barron, *Patton's First Victory*, 55.

CHAPTER TWELVE: TANK DUEL IN "DEATH VALLEY"

1. Edwards, telephone interview with author, April 13, 2019.
2. Edwards, personal interview with author, May 3, 2019.
3. Carter, "The Operations of the First Battalion," 17.
4. Morrison, "Gafsa-Gabès Road" letter, 5–6.
5. Gioia, statement, 23 March 1943.
6. Baker, "Battle Operations Report."
7. Carter, "The Operations of the First Battalion," 17.
8. Sundstrom, statement, 27 March 1943; Yowell, "Battle Operations of Lt. John D. Yowell," 1.
9. Stima, statement statement, March 23, 1943.
10. Lambert, statement, 27 March 1943.
11. Ritchie, statement, 27 March 1943.
12. Stima, statement, March 23, 1943; Yowell, "Battle Operations of Lt. John D. Yowell," 1.
13. Raymond, statement, 27 March 1943.
14. Sundstrom, statement, 27 March 1943, 1.
15. Raymond, statement, 27 March 1943; Yowell, "Battle Operations of Lt. John D. Yowell."
16. Yowell, "Battle Operations of Lt. John D. Yowell." 1.
17. Paulick, "Battle Operations Report," 23 March 1943.
18. Luthi, statement, 22 March 1943.
19. Stima, statement, March 27, 1943.
20. Hamel, statement, 27 March 1943.
21. Yowell, "Battle Operations of Lt. John D. Yowell," 1.
22. Nowak, "World War II Memoirs of John Nowak," 3.
23. Cook, statement, 27 March 1943.
24. Nowak, "World War II Memoirs of John Nowak," 4.
25. Futuluychuk, statement, 27 March 1943.
26. Yowell, "Battle Operations of Lt. John D. Yowell," 2.
27. Carter, "The Operations of the First Battalion," 18.
28. Ibid., 19.
29. Barron, *Patton's First Victory*, 97.
30. Ibid., 97–99.
31. Ibid., 114.
32. Atkinson, *An Army at Dawn*, 438–40.
33. Smith, "Operations of the 3rd Battalion."
34. Marshall, *Proud Americans: Men of the 32nd Field Artillery*, 83.
35. Barron, *Patton's First Victory*, 104, 115.
36. Liebling, "Find 'Em, Fix 'Em, and Fight 'Em," 28.
37. Ibid., 26–27.

38. Barron, *Patton's First Victory*, 116.
39. Trest, *Nobody but the People*, 74–75.
40. Edwards, telephone interview with author, April 13, 2019.
41. Baker, "Battle Operations Report."
42. Morrison, "Gafsa-Gabès Road" letter, 2.
43. Morrison, Veterans History Project interview.
44. Harper interview, *Patton 360*, Episode 2: "Rommel's Last Stand."
45. Barron, *Patton's First Victory*, 82.
46. Stark, statement, 27 March 1943.
47. Lambert, statement, 27 March 1943.
48. Ritso, statement, 27 March 1943.
49. Ritchie, statement, 27 March 1943.
50. Charles Munn, statement, 27 March 1943.
51. Heckethorn, account of Gafsa and El Guettar, 2.
52. Ibid.; Hawksworth, "Gafsa and El Guettar," 109.
53. Hawksworth, "Gafsa and El Guettar," 109–11.
54. Barron, *Patton's First Victory*, 121–22.
55. Report of Combat, 899th TD Battalion, Period March 15, 1943, to April 11, 1943. Report dated April 15, 1943.
56. Brady, *His Father's Son*, 246; Atkinson, *An Army at Dawn*, 441.
57. Liebling, "Find 'Em, Fix 'Em, and Fight 'Em," 28.
58. Street, "The Operations of the First Ranger Battalion, El Guettar, 21–26 March 1943," 16; Kness, letter, August 24, 1990, 4.
59. Black, *The Ranger Force*, 112–13; Stern and Bradner, *Snapdragon*, 206.
60. Stern and Bradner, *Snapdragon*, 206.
61. Ibid., 208.
62. Schick, *Combat History of the 10. Panzer-Division*, 499.
63. Barron, *Patton's First Victory*, 102.
64. Schick, *Combat History of the 10. Panzer-Division*, 500.

CHAPTER THIRTEEN: "IT WAS LIKE MOWING HAY"

1. Patton diary, March 23, 1943.
2. Edwards, telephone interview with author, April 13, 2019.
3. Morrison, "Gafsa-Gabès Road" letter, 1–2.
4. Baker, "Battle Operations Report," 4.
5. Ibid., 5.
6. Ibid.
7. Morrison, "Gafsa-Gabès Road" letter, 6–7.
8. Barron, *Patton's First Victory*, 132.
9. Ibid., 133.

10. Moran, "Recollections, 17th Field Artillery"; Trest, *Nobody but the People*, 74.
11. Edwards, telephone interview with author, April 13, 2019.
12. Morrison, Veterans History Project interview.
13. Morrison, "Gafsa-Gabès Road" letter, 5–6.
14. Morrison, Veterans History Project interview.
15. Ibid.
16. Ibid.; Morrison, "Gafsa-Gabès Road" letter, 8.
17. Baker, "Battle Operations Report," 5; Baker, "Tank Destroyer Combat in Tunisia."
18. Ibid.
19. Barron, *Patton's First Victory*, 143.
20. Darby and Baumer, *We Led the Way*, 75; Kness, letter, August 24, 1990, 4.
21. Paulick, "Battle Operations Report," 23 March 1943; Otis, statement, 27 March 1943.
22. Baker, "Tank Destroyer Combat in Tunisia."
23. Edwards, telephone interview with author, April 13, 2019; Moran, "Recollections, 17th Field Artillery."
24. Moran, "Recollections, 17th Field Artillery."
25. Trest, *Nothing but the People*, 77.
26. Barron, *Patton's First Victory*, 150.
27. Ibid., 153–55.
28. Edwards, personal interview with author, May 3, 2019; Carter, "The Operations of the First Battalion," 22–23.
29. Barron, *Patton's First Victory*, 159.
30. Patton diary, March 23, 1943.
31. Baker, "Tank Destroyer Combat in Tunisia."
32. Kness, letter, August 24, 1990, 4.
33. Nowak, "World War II Memoirs of John Nowak," 4.
34. Ibid.
35. Failmezger, *American Knights*, 62.
36. Nowak, "World War II Memoirs of John Nowak," 5.

CHAPTER FOURTEEN: "GET MORE OFFICERS KILLED"

1. Kness, letter, August 24, 1990, 4.
2. Ibid., 5.
3. Ibid.
4. Barron, *Patton's First Victory*, 161; Yeide, *Fighting Patton*, 170.
5. Patton diary, March 24, 1943.
6. Moran, "Recollections, 17th Field Artillery."
7. Patton diary, March 24, 1943; Barron, *Patton's First Victory*, 169.

8. Barry, "Battle-Scarred and Dirty," 234; Lang, "Report on the Fighting of Kampfgruppe Lang (10th Pz Div) in Tunisia," Part II, 5–8.
9. Patton diary, March 22, 1943; Atkinson, *An Army at Dawn*, 445–46.
10. Atkinson, *An Army at Dawn*, 446.
11. Ibid., 447.
12. Lang, "Report on the Fighting of Kampfgruppe Lang (10th Pz Div) in Tunisia," Part II, 6.
13. Ibid., 6–8; Atkinson, *An Army at Dawn*, 447.
14. Atkinson, *An Army at Dawn*, 448.
15. Lang, "Report on the Fighting of Kampfgruppe Lang (10th Pz Div) in Tunisia," Part II, 9–10.
16. Atkinson, *An Army at Dawn*, 449.
17. Ibid.
18. Patton diary, March 24, 1943.
19. Atkinson, *An Army at Dawn*, 450.
20. Patton diary, March 24, 1943; Atkinson, *An Army at Dawn*, 450.
21. Patton diary, March 27, 1943.
22. Ibid., March 28, 1943.
23. Kness, letter to Ivey, January 28, 1994, 1.
24. Street, "The Operations of the First Ranger Battalion, El Guettar, 21–26 March 1943," 17.
25. Barron, *Patton's First Victory*, 171–72.
26. Ibid., 172–73; Carter, "The Operations of the First Battalion," 23.
27. Barron, *Patton's First Victory*, 176.
28. Street, "The Operations of the First Ranger Battalion, El Guettar, 21–26 March 1943," 17; Kness, letter to Ivey, January 28, 1994, 1.

CHAPTER FIFTEEN: THE FIGHT FOR HILL 772

1. Street, "The Operations of the First Ranger Battalion, El Guettar, 21–26 March 1943," 17.
2. Darby and Baumer, *We Led the Way*, 76.
3. Street, "The Operations of the First Ranger Battalion, El Guettar, 21–26 March 1943," 18.
4. Kness, letter to Ivey, January 28, 1994, 1.
5. Street, "The Operations of the First Ranger Battalion, El Guettar, 21–26 March 1943," 18.
6. Mercuriali, "In His Own Words," 63.
7. Barron, *Patton's First Victory*, 179.
8. Darby and Baumer, *We Led the Way*, 77.
9. Barron, *Patton's First Victory*, 181.
10. Atkinson, *An Army at Dawn*, 453.

11. Ibid., 455.
12. Schick, *Combat History of the 10. Panzer-Division*, 501.
13. Schmidt, *With Rommel in the Desert*, 244–49.
14. Patton diary, March 27, 1943.
15. Scheffel, National WWII Museum interview.
16. Scheffel and Basden, *Crack! and Thump*, 49.
17. Ibid., 49–50.
18. Ibid., 50.
19. Reynolds, National WWII Museum interview video; Reynolds, telephone interviews with author.
20. Phillips and Irving, *El Guettar: Crucible of Leadership*, Location 545 of 1858.
21. Phillips, *Heavy Weapons*, 19–20; Phillips and Irving, *El Guettar: Crucible of Leadership*, Location 417 of 1858.
22. Phillips, *Heavy Weapons*, 20.
23. Phillips and Irving, *El Guettar: Crucible of Leadership*, Location 545 of 1858.

CHAPTER SIXTEEN: "ALL HELL BROKE LOOSE"

1. Phillips and Irving, *El Guettar: Crucible of Leadership*, Location 535 of 1858.
2. Ibid., Location 572 of 1858.
3. Phillips, *Heavy Weapons*, 32; Phillips and Irving, *El Guettar: Crucible of Leadership*, Location 579 of 1858.
4. Phillips, *El Guettar: Crucible of Leadership*, Location 559 of 1858.
5. Ibid., Location 599 of 1858.
6. Ibid., Location 622 of 1858.
7. Ibid., Location 642–74 of 1858.
8. Ibid., Location 768 of 1858.
9. Phillips, *Heavy Weapons*, 36–37.
10. Phillips and Irving, *El Guettar: Crucible of Leadership*, Location 814 of 1858.
11. Phillips, *Heavy Weapons*, 34.
12. Ibid., 35.
13. Phillips and Irving, *El Guettar: Crucible of Leadership*, Location 861 of 1858.
14. Atkinson, *An Army at Dawn*, 456.
15. Scheffel and Basden, *Crack! and Thump*, 50.
16. Ibid., 51.
17. Ibid., 51–52.
18. Ibid.

19. Reynolds, *How I Survived the Three First Wave Invasions*, 30.
20. Wheeler, *The Big Red One*, 183; Reynolds, *How I Survived the Three First Wave Invasions*, 30.
21. Eddy, "3 Who Came Back," 44.
22. Reynolds, *How I Survived the Three First Wave Invasions*, 30.
23. Wheeler, *The Big Red One*, 183.
24. Reynolds, *How I Survived the Three First Wave Invasions*, 30.
25. Ibid., 31.
26. Eddy, "3 Who Came Back," 45.
27. Ibid.
28. Reynolds, *How I Survived the Three First Wave Invasions*, 30–31.
29. Finke, *No Mission Too Difficult*, 112.
30. Eddy, "3 Who Came Back," 45; Reynolds, *How I Survived the Three First Wave Invasions*, 31.
31. Patton diary, March 28, 1943.
32. Ibid.
33. Phillips and Irving, *El Guettar: Crucible of Leadership*, Location 255 of 1858.
34. Ibid., Location 889 of 1858.
35. Shockley, *Random Chance*, 26.
36. Patton diary, March 28, 1943.
37. Shockley, *Random Chance*, 26.
38. Phillips and Irving, *El Guettar: Crucible of Leadership*, Location 974–79 of 1858.
39. Atkinson, *An Army at Dawn*, 456.
40. Phillips and Irving, *El Guettar: Crucible of Leadership*, Location 1018 of 1858.
41. Eddy, "3 Who Came Back," 133.
42. Reynolds, telephone interviews with author; Reynolds, *How I Survived the Three First Wave Invasions*, 32.
43. Eddy, "3 Who Came Back," 133.
44. Atkinson, *An Army at Dawn*, 457.
45. Finke, *No Mission Too Difficult*, 112–13; Pyle, *Here Is Your War*, 216; Theodore Antonelli would later advance to the rank of major general before his retirement in 1979.
46. Pyle, *Here Is Your War*, 216–17.
47. Patton diary, March 29, 1943.
48. Ibid.
49. Scheffel and Basden, *Crack! and Thump*, 53.
50. Ibid., 56.
51. Scheffel, National WWII Museum interview.
52. Scheffel and Basden, *Crack! and Thump*, 56–57.

53. Ibid., 57.
54. Scheffel, National WWII Museum interview.
55. Scheffel and Basden, *Crack! and Thump*, 58.
56. Ibid.
57. Ibid., 60.

CHAPTER SEVENTEEN: "STUCK EVERYWHERE"

1. Reynolds, *How I Survived the Three First Wave Invasions*, 34.
2. Ibid.
3. Ibid.; Eddy, "3 Who Came Back," 133.
4. Ibid., 135.
5. Joseph S. Manak IDPF file, Serial Number 6690882.
6. Reynolds, *How I Survived the Three First Wave Invasions*, 32.
7. Schick, *Combat History of the 10. Panzer-Division*, 502.
8. Barron, *Patton's First Victory*, 157.
9. Schick, *Combat History of the 10. Panzer-Division*, 502.
10. United States Army, *Our Battalion*, 21.
11. Hawksworth, "Gafsa and El Guettar," 113–14.
12. Ibid., 114.
13. Heckethorn, account of Gafsa and El Guettar, 4.
14. Ibid., 3–4.
15. Report of Combat, 899th TD Battalion, Period March 15, 1943, to April 11, 1943, 4.
16. Hawksworth, "Gafsa and El Guettar," 115.
17. Henry Phillips oral history, National WWII Museum; Phillips, *Heavy Weapons*, 34–36.
18. Phillips, *Heavy Weapons*, 41.
19. Phillips and Irving, *El Guettar: Crucible of Leadership*, Location 1219–43 of 1858.
20. Patton diary, March 31, 1943.
21. Howe, *Northwest Africa*, 571.
22. Atkinson, *An Army at Dawn*, 459.
23. Patton diary, March 31, 1943.
24. Ibid.
25. Scheffel and Basden, *Crack! and Thump*, 61–64.
26. Phillips, *Heavy Weapons*, 36.
27. Ibid.
28. Hymel, "The Bravest and Best," 31–32.
29. Ibid., 33–36; Patton diary, April 1, 1943.
30. Hirshon, *General Patton*, 328; Bradley, *A Soldier's Story*, 61–62.
31. Patton diary, April 1, 1943; Hirshon, *General Patton*, 328.

CHAPTER EIGHTEEN: "ATTACK AND DESTROY"

1. Patton diary, April 1, 1943; Hirshon, *General Patton*, 330.
2. Atkinson, *An Army at Dawn*, 459–60.
3. Patton diary, April 2, 1943.
4. Ibid., April 3, 1943.
5. Atkinson, *An Army at Dawn*, 460.
6. Patton diary, April 3, 1943.
7. Ibid., April 4, 1943.
8. Ibid.; Atkinson, *An Army at Dawn*, 461.
9. Hirshon, *General Patton*, 332.
10. Ibid., 333.
11. Darby and Baumer, *We Led the Way*, 77.
12. Jeffers, *Onward We Charge*, 123.
13. Ibid., 123; Darby and Baumer, *We Led the Way*, 77.
14. Jeffers, *Onward We Charge*, 124.
15. Kness, letter to Ivey, January 28, 1994, 3. Patton's handguns were actually ivory handled, not pearl.
16. Ibid., 1–2.
17. Cook, telephone interviews with author.
18. Kness, letter to Ivey, January 28, 1994, 2–3.
19. Darby and Baumer, *We Led the Way*, 77–78.
20. Hirshon, *General Patton*, 333.
21. Atkinson, *An Army at Dawn*, 464.
22. Patton diary, April 7, 1943; Atkinson, *An Army at Dawn*, 464.
23. Patton diary, April 7, 1943.
24. Atkinson, *An Army at Dawn*, 464.
25. Schmidt, *With Rommel in the Desert*, 252–55.
26. Patton diary, April 8, 1943.
27. Ibid.
28. Ibid., April 9, 1943.
29. Phillips and Irving, *El Guettar: Crucible of Leadership*, Location 1644 of 1858.
30. Patton diary, April 14, 1943.
31. Ibid., April 15, 1943.

EPILOGUE

1. Atkinson, *An Army at Dawn*, 486.
2. Ibid., 500–502.
3. Brady, *His Father's Son*, 252.
4. Atkinson, *An Army at Dawn*, 503–506.

5. Finke, *No Mission Too Difficult*, 116.
6. Reynolds, telephone interviews with author; Reynolds, *How I Survived the Three First Wave Invasions*, 51–52.
7. Reynolds, *How I Survived the Three First Wave Invasions*, 46–49.
8. Ibid., 51.
9. Scheffel and Basden, *Crack! and Thump*, 90.
10. Pyle, *Here Is Your War*, 273; Scheffel and Basden, *Crack! and Thump*, 91.
11. Atkinson, *An Army at Dawn*, 523–29.
12. Schick, *Combat History of the 10. Panzer-Division*, 537–39.
13. Ibid., 541–46.
14. Mortimer, "Inside Rommel's Afrika Korps," 52.
15. Ibid., 56.
16. Reynolds, *How I Survived the Three First Wave Invasions*, 55.
17. Edwards interview with author, 2019.
18. Pyle, *Here Is Your War*, 244–45.
19. Ibid., 238.
20. Tobin, *Ernie Pyle's War*, 110–11.
21. "Fredendall Expected to Succeed Lear as Second Army Chief," A-4.
22. McNeese, *Great Battles Through the Ages: Battle of the Bulge*, 79.
23. O'Reilly, *Killing Patton*, 306–308.
24. Patton, *War as I Knew It*, xi; Phillips and Irving, *El Guettar: Crucible of Leadership*, Location 1546 of 1858.
25. Phillips and Irving, *El Guettar: Crucible of Leadership*, Location 1805 of 1858.

BIBLIOGRAPHY

ORAL HISTORIES/PERSONAL INTERVIEWS

Blassingame, Earl C. Telephone interview with author, February 5, 2020.

Cook, Lester B. Telephone interviews with author, February 5 and 22, 2020.

Edwards, Hubert G. Personal interview with author, May 3, 2019, and telephone interview, April 13, 2019.

Evans, Warren. Interview with James Holland, November 26, 2002.

Frederick, Donald S. Oral history interview with Douglas Bekke, July 13, 2005, Minnesota Historical Society.

Friedman, Catherine Morrison. Telephone interview with author, February 6, 2020, and subsequent correspondence, February 6–March 15, 2019.

Grayem, Patricia L. (daughter of Orion C. Shockley). Telephone interview with author, March 24, 2019, and subsequent correspondence.

Harper, Bill R. Veterans History Project interview, undated.

Irving, Christine L. (Phillips). Personal interview with author, January 12, 2020.

Irving, John. Telephone interview with author, December 30, 2019. Personal interview with author, January 12, 2020.

Jones, Dale W. Telephone interview with author, November 12, 2019.

Kness, Lee. Telephone interview with author, February 2, 2020.

Kness, Lester. Select papers, courtesy of Douglas Bekke. Kness letter, August 24, 1990.

Kness, Wade. Telephone interview with author, February 1, 2020.

Martello, Dominic J. Oral history interview with Thomas Lofton, August 28, 2008, National WWII Museum, New Orleans.

Mascari, Thomas. Telephone interview with author, February 5, 2020.

Morrison, Thomas E. Interview with Thomas Swope, July 29, 2001. Veterans History Project, American Folklife Center. Washington, DC: Library of Congress.

Nowak, John. "World War II Memoirs of John Nowak." Edited by Norma Nowak and Linda Nowak. Courtesy of Victor Failmezger.

Phillips, Henry. Oral history interview, National WWII Museum, New Orleans.

Phillips, Kathryn. Telephone interview, January 12, 2020. Email correspondence from January 12 to April 2, 2020.

Pirnie, Bruce. Interview with Orr Kelly, March 6, 2000. Courtesy of Orr Kelly.

Reynolds, Harley. Telephone interviews with author, April 28, June 11, and October 12, 2019.

Richards, Lloyd. Telephone interview with author, May 11, 2019.

Scheffel, Charles. National WWII Museum interview, http://www.ww2online .org/view/charles-scheffel.

Stima, Barbara. Telephone interview, October 12, 2019.

Stima, Michael J. Telephone interview and email correspondence, October–November 2019.

Sullivan, Thomas. Diary and letters, January 1942 to August 1943. bbc.co.uk /history/ww2peopleswar/stories/13/a2020113.shtml.

Wauson, Kathy Kness. Telephone conversations, October 2019; email correspondence, November 6, 2019.

Yowell, John D., Jr. Telephone interview, October 2019.

ARTICLES/LETTERS/MEMOIRS/OFFICIAL STATEMENTS

Baker, Herschel D. "Tank Destroyer Combat in Tunisia." *Tank Destroyer School*, 117, January 1944, 17 (TIS Library). tankdestroyer.net/images/stories/Articles PDFs/TD_Combat_in_Tunisia_Jan_1944.pdf.

——. "Battle Operations Report." March 28, 1943. tankdestroyer.net/images /stories/ArticlesPDFs/601st_Battle_Operations_Report_El_Guettar_Mar _23_1943–10_pages.pdf.

Barry, Steven T. "Battle-Scarred and Dirty: US Army Tactical Leadership in the Mediterranean Theater, 1942–1943." Doctoral dissertation, The Ohio State University, 2011.

Bennett, Lowell, "Yanks Can 'Lick' Nazis, Says General," *Lowell (MA) Sun*, December 18, 1941, 1, 18.

Bickers, James F. "The First Kriegies," unpublished article about his POW experience; courtesy of Thomas R. Kurtz, 17th Field Artillery Association.

Boyle, Harold V. "Fayetteville Lieutenant Makes Successful Dash for Freedom After Being Trapped by Germans in Central Tunisia." *Newark Times*, January 1943, 1.

Carter, Sam. "The Operations of the 1st Battalion, 18th Infantry (1st Division) at El Guettar, Tunisia, 17–25 March, 1943." Advanced Infantry Officers Course, 1947–1948, General Subjects Section, Academic Department, The Infantry School, Fort Benning, Georgia, 13.

Conway, Sgt. John J. Company A, 601st Tank Destroyer Battalion. Operation Report, 26 March 1943. tankdestroyer.net/images/stories/ArticlePDFs/601st _Op_Statements_Co_A_Mar._26_1943–3pages.pdf.

Cook, Cpl. Leo G. Company C, 601st Tank Destroyer Battalion. Statement, 27 March 1943. tankdestroyer.net/images/stories/ArticlePDFs/601st_Op _Statements_Co_C_Mar._27_1943–17_pages.pdf.

Dragon, Sgt. Michael H. Company B, 601st Tank Destroyer Battalion. Statement, 27 March 1943. tankdestroyer.net/images/stories/ArticlePDFs/601st _Op_Statements_Co_B_Mar._27_1943–15pages.pdf.

Drake, Colonel Thomas C. Report of 168th Infantry, February 7–17, 1943; in *Kasserine Pass Battles, Readings, Volume I, Part I.* U.S. Army Center of Military History. Washington, DC: Government Printing Office, 1995.

Eddy, Don. "3 Who Came Home." *American Magazine*, November 1943, 44–45, 130.

First Armored Division, Report of Operations, Sbeitla, Tunisia, February 3–18, 1943; in *Kasserine Pass Battles, Readings, Volume I, Part I.* U.S. Army Center of Military History. Washington, DC: Government Printing Office, 1995.

"Fredendall Expected to Succeed Lear as Second Army Chief." *Evening Star* (Franklin, Indiana), April 1, 1943.

Fredendall, Major General Lloyd R. Order to Combat Command B, January 1943; from "Report of Ousseltia Valley Campaign, 19–29 January 1943," Record Group 47, Entry 427, National Archives and Records Administration, College Park, MD.

Futuluychuk, Sgt. Steve. Company C, 601st Tank Destroyer Battalion. Statement, 27 March 1943. tankdestroyer.net/images/stories/ArticlePDFs/601st _Op_Statements_Co_C_Mar._27_1943–17_pages.pdf.

Gioia, 1st Lt. Joseph A. Recon Company, 601st Tank Destroyer Battalion. "Battle Operations Report," 23 March 1943. tankdestroyer.net/images/stories/Article PDFs/601st_Op_Statements_Recon_Co_Mar._23_1943–5_pages.pdf.

Hains, Peter C., III. Report of 11 March 1943, in *Kasserine Pass Battles, Readings, Vol. 1, Part 1.* U.S. Army Center of Military History. Washington, DC: Government Printing Office, 1995.

Hamel, Cpl. Victor T. Company B, 601st Tank Destroyer Battalion. Statement, 27 March 1943. tankdestroyer.net/images/stories/ArticlePDFs/601st_Op _Statements_Co_B_Mar._27_1943–15pages.pdf.

Hawksworth, Capt. Thomas A. "Gafsa and El Guettar," 107; personal narrative of the North Africa campaign; tankdestroyer.net/images/stories/ArticlePDFs2 /899th-Gafsa_and_El_Guettar_43-Hawksworth-16_pg.pdf.

Heckethorn, Captain Clarence W. Account of Gafsa and El Guettar, Tunisia, 1943, 2. tankdestroyer.net/images/stories/ArticlePDFs2/899th-El_Guettar _43_Heckethorn-4pg.pdf.

Heinz, Mark. "POW Memories Haunt Cody Man." *Cody Enterprise*, February 13, 2013.

Hightower, Louis. Interview, March 1, 1943, in "Tankers in Tunisia," article contained in *Kasserine Pass Battles, Doctrines and Lessons Learned, Vol. II, Part 4,* Carlisle, PA: U.S. Army Center of Military History, 24.

Hudel, Major, and Paul Robinett. "The Tank Battle at Sidi Bou Zid," B19; in *Kasserine Pass Battles, Readings, Volume I, Part 1.* U.S. Army Center of Military History. Washington, DC: Government Printing Office, 1995.

Hymel, Kevin M. "The Bravest and Best: Patton and the Death of Capt. Richard Jenson in North Africa." *Army History,* no. 91 (Spring 2014): 31–32.

"Kness Among Original Darby Rangers in WWII." *Union-Republican* (Albia, IA), November 7, 2013.

Lambert, 1st Lt. Francis X. Company B, 601st Tank Destroyer Battalion. Statement, 27 March 1943. tankdestroyer.net/images/stories/ArticlePDFs/601st _Op_Statements_Co_B_Mar._27_1943–15pages.pdf.

Lang, Oberst Rudolf. "Report on the Fighting of Kampfgruppe Lang (10th Pz Div) in Tunisia," Part II. College Park, MD: National Archives, NARA M1035, Record Group 338, 5–8.

"Lawrence Marcus, Member of the Legendary Retailing Family, Dies at 96." *Dallas Morning News,* November 1, 2013.

Lehmann, Carl. "Ranger Captain Albert E. Basil." secondworldwar.nl/ranger -basil.php.

Liebling, A. J. "Find 'Em, Fix 'Em, and Fight 'Em." *New Yorker,* May 1, 1943, 28.

Luthi, 1st Lt. Robert A. Company B, 601st Tank Destroyer Battalion. Statement, 27 March 1943. tankdestroyer.net/images/stories/ArticlePDFs/601st_Op _Statements_Co_B_Mar._27_1943–15pages.pdf.

Mercuriali, Gino. "In His Own Words," article from Ranger Battalions Association 2006 reunion book, *A Gathering of Heroes.* Willow Run Publishing, Lawrence, Kansas, 2006, 63.

Miner, 1st Lt. Frederick C. Company A, 601st Tank Destroyer Battalion. Operation Report, 26 March 1943. tankdestroyer.net/images/stories/ArticlePDFs /601st_Op_Statements_Co_A_Mar._26_1943–3pages.pdf.

Moran, Sergeant James F. "Recollections, 17th Field Artillery, 1st Battalion, Battery B." Provided to the 17th Artillery Regiment Association by Michael Neal, courtesy of Tom Kurtz to author.

Morris, Sgt. Mack. "Rangers Come Home." *Yank: The Army Weekly,* August 4, 1944, 4.

Morrison, Thomas E. "Gafsa-Gabès Road" letter. tankdestroyer.net/images /stories/ArticlePDFs2/601st-Pers_Narr_T._Morr_Gafsa_Rd.pdf.

——. "The 601 Tank Destroyers in Tunisia, 1942–1943." Personal battle recollections, courtesy of Morrison's daughter, Catherine Morrison Friedman.

——. Letter to L. L. Gill, November 16, 1984, 5, from www.tankdestroyer.net website.

Mortimer, Gavin. "Inside Rommel's Afrika Korps." *History of War*, August 2016, 48–56.

Munn, 2nd Lt. Charles N. Company C, 601st Tank Destroyer Battalion. Statement, 27 March 1943. tankdestroyer.net/images/stories/ArticlePDFs/601st _Op_Statements_Co_C_Mar._27_1943–17_pages.pdf.

Munn, First Lieutenant Kenneth B. Company B, 601st Tank Destroyer Battalion. Statement, 27 March 1943. https://tankdestroyer.net/images/stories /ArticlePDFs/601st_Op_Statements_Co_B_Mar._27_1943–15_pages.pdf.

Newton, Robert. "Battle for Kasserine Pass: 1st Armored Division Were Ambushed by the Afrika Korps at Sidi Bou Zid." *World War II*, September 2002, 54–56.

Niderost, Eric. "Trial by Fire at Kasserine Pass." *World War II Tank Battles*, Spring 2019, 30.

Ossad, Steven L. "Command Failure: Lessons Learned from Lloyd R. Fredendall." *Army*, March 2003, 45–52.

Patterson, John. "Starting Off on the Right Foot." *Field Artillery Journal*, October 1990: 31–34.

Patton, George Smith. Personal diary.

Paulick, Capt. Michael. Recon Company, 601st Tank Destroyer Battalion. "Battle Operations Report," 23 March 1943. tankdestroyer.net/images/stories /ArticlePDFs/601st_Op_Statements_Recon_Co_Mar._23_1943–5 _pages.pdf.

Raymond, Maj. Edward A., F.A. "Slugging It Out." *Field Artillery Journal*, vol. 34, no. 1, January 1944, 16.

Raymond, Sgt. Adolph I. Company B, 601st Tank Destroyer Battalion. Statement, 27 March 1943. tankdestroyer.net/images/stories/ArticlePDFs/601st _Op_Statements_Co_B_Mar._27_1943–15pages.pdf.

Ritchie, Cpl. Harry J. Company B, 601st Tank Destroyer Battalion. Statement, 27 March 1943. tankdestroyer.net/images/stories/ArticlePDFs/601st_Op _Statements_Co_B_Mar._27_1943–15pages.pdf.

Ritso, Sgt. John C. Company B, 601st Tank Destroyer Battalion. Statement, 27 March 1943. tankdestroyer.net/images/stories/ArticlePDFs/601st_Op _Statements_Co_B_Mar._27_1943–15pages.pdf.

Rogers, First Lieutenant Otis R. Reconnaissance Company, 601st Tank Destroyer Battalion. Statement, 27 March 1943.

Sherwood, Christopher Eric Jacob, Sr. "Bloodied but Bruised: How the World War II American Army at Kasserine Pass Grew Up in North Africa." MA thesis, Florida State University, 2013.

Smith, Herbert A. "Operations of the 3rd Battalion, 18th Infantry (First Infantry Division) at El Guettar, 17–23 March, 1943, (Tunisian Campaign), Personal Experiences of Executive Officer, Heavy Weapons Company," 1948–1949.

Stark, 1st Lt. Kenneth B. Statement, Company B, 601st Tank Destroyer Battalion. https://tankdestroyer.net/images/stories/ArticlePDFs/601st_Op_State ments_Co_B_Mar._27_1943–15_pages.pdf.

Stima, S/Sgt. Michael W. Company B, 601st Tank Destroyer Battalion. Statement, 27 March 1943. tankdestroyer.net/images/stories/ArticlePDFs/601st _Op_Statements_Co_B_Mar._27_1943–15pages.pdf.

Street, Jack. "The Operations of the First Ranger Battalion, El Guettar, 21–26 March 1943."

Sundstrom, Capt. Herbert E. Company C, 601st Tank Destroyer Battalion. Statement, 27 March 1943. tankdestroyer.net/images/stories/ArticlePDFs /601st_Op_Statements_Co_C_Mar._27_1943–17_pages.pdf.

Wallis, Frank. "Tour of Duty: Gunner Recalls Battle of Kasserine Pass." *Baxter Bulletin* (Mountain Home, AR), March 7, 2011, 1.

Waters, John K. Papers. "Reminiscences of General John K. Waters." Carlisle, PA: U.S. Army Heritage and Education Center.

Wolff, Kurt. "Tank Battle in Tunisia." Article originally appeared in *Das Reich*, April 11, 1943. Translated at the Command and General Staff School, Fort Leavenworth, Kansas. Published in *Command and General Staff School Military Review*, vol. 23, no. 6, September 1943.

Yowell, 1st Lt. John D. Platoon Commander, 1st Platoon, Company B, 601st Tank Destroyer Battalion. "Battle Operations of Lt. John D. Yowell," 27 March 1943. tankdestroyer.net/images/stories/ArticlePDFs/601st_Op_Statements _Co_B_Mar._27_1943–15pages.pdf.

VIDEO

Harper, Bill R. Interviews from *Patton 360*, Episode 2: "Rommel's Last Stand," and Episode 1: "Blood and Guts."

Marcus, Lawrence. Interviews from *Patton 360*, Episode 2: "Rommel's Last Stand," and Episode 1: "Blood and Guts."

Reynolds, Harley. "A Reason to Join." National WWII Museum interview. https://www.ww2online.org/view/harley-reynolds.

BOOKS/UNIT HISTORIES

Altieri, James. *The Spearheaders: A Personal History of Darby's Rangers.* Annapolis, MD: Naval Institute Press, 2014.

Atkinson, Rick. *An Army at Dawn: The War in North Africa, 1942–1943.* New York: Picador, 2002.

Axelrod, Alan. *Patton: A Biography*. London: Palgrave Macmillan, 2006.

Bahmanyar, Mir. *Darby's Rangers, 1942–1945*. Oxford, UK: Osprey Publishing, 2003.

Barron, Leo. *Patton's First Victory: How General George Patton Turned the Tide in North Africa and Defeated the Afrika Korps at El Guettar*. Lanham, MD: Stackpole, 2018.

Black, Robert W. *The Ranger Force: Darby's Rangers in World War II*. Mechanicsburg, PA: Stackpole, 2009.

Blumenson, Martin. *Kasserine Pass: Rommel's Bloody, Climatic Battle for Tunisia*. New York: Cooper Square Press, 2000. Reprint of 1966 edition.

Bradley, Omar N. *A Soldier's Story*. New York: Holt, 1951.

Bradley, Omar N., and Clay Blair. *A General's Life: An Autobiography by General of the Army Omar N. Bradley*. New York: Simon & Schuster, 1983.

Brady, Tim. *His Father's Son: The Life of General Ted Roosevelt, Jr*. New York: Berkley, 2017.

Crosswell, D. K. R. *Beetle: The Life of General Walter Bedell Smith*. Lexington: University Press of Kentucky, 2010.

Darby, William O., and William H. Baumer. *We Led the Way: Darby's Rangers*. San Rafael, CA: Presidio Press, 1980.

D'Este, Carlo. *Eisenhower: A Soldier's Life*. New York: Henry Holt and Co., 2002.
———. *Patton: A Genius for War*. New York: HarperPerennial, 1995.

Eisenhower, Dwight D. *Crusade in Europe: A Personal Account of World War II*. New York: Doubleday, 1948.

Failmezger, Victor. *American Knights: The Untold Story of the Men of the Legendary 601st Tank Destroyer Battalion*. Oxford, UK: Osprey Publishing, 2015.

Finke, Blythe Foote. *No Mission Too Difficult! Old Buddies of the 1st Division Tell All About World War II*. Chicago: Contemporary Books, 1995.

Fletcher, David. *British Battle Tanks: The First World War*. Oxford, UK: Osprey Publishing, 2016.

Harmon, William Ross, and Milton MacKaye. *Combat Commander: Autobiography of a Soldier*. Upper Saddle River, NJ: Prentice Hall, 1970.

Hartmann, Bernd. *Panzers in the Sand: The History of Panzer-Regiment 5. Volume 2, 1942–45*. Barnsley, UK: Pen & Sword Military, 2011.

Hirshon, Stanley P. *General Patton: A Soldier's Life*. New York: HarperCollins, 2002.

Howard, Gene L. *Patterson for Alabama: The Life and Career of John Patterson*. Tuscaloosa: University of Alabama Press, 2008.

Howe, George F. *Northwest Africa: Seizing the Initiative in the West (United States Army in World War II: The Mediterranean Theater of Operations)*. Norwalk, CT: Easton Press, 1995.

Jeffers, H. Paul. *Onward We Charge: The Heroic Story of Darby's Rangers in World War II*. New York: NAL Caliber, 2007.

Jentz and Doyle, *Tiger 1 Heavy Tank, 1942–1945*. Oxford, UK: Osprey Publishing, 1993.

Jordan, Jonathan W. *Brothers, Rivals, Victors: Eisenhower, Patton, Bradley, and the Partnership That Drove the Allied Conquest in Europe*. New York: Dutton Caliber, 2011.

Josowitz, Edward L. *An Informal History of the 601st Tank Destroyer Battalion*. Salzburg: 1945.

Kelly, Orr. *Meeting the Fox: The Allied Invasion of Africa, from Operation Torch to Kasserine Pass to Victory in Tunisia*. New York: John Wiley, 2002.

Knopf, A. A. *These Are the Generals*. New York: Curtis Publishing, 1943.

Liddell-Hart, B. H., ed. *The Rommel Papers*. New York: Da Capo Press, 1953.

Marshall, Malcolm, ed. *Proud Americans: Men of the 32nd Field Artillery Battalion in Action, World War II, as Part of the 18th Regimental Combat Team*. Privately published, 1994.

McNeese, Tim. *Battle of the Bulge (Great Battles Through the Ages)*. Broomall, PA: Chelsea House, 2003.

Moen, Marcia, and Margo Heinen. *Heroes Cry Too: A WWII Ranger Tells His Story of Love and War*. Middletown, CA: Meadowlark Publishing, 2002.

O'Donnell, Patrick. *Beyond Valor: World War II's Ranger and Airborne Veterans Reveal the Heart of Combat*. New York: Touchstone, 2002.

Ogorkiewicz, Richard. *Tanks: 100 Years of Evolution*. Oxford, UK: Osprey Publishing, 2015.

O'Reilly, Bill. *Killing Patton: The Strange Death of World War II's Most Audacious General*. New York: St. Martin's Griffin, 2014.

Patton, George S. "Account of General Patton's Visit to the Tunisian Front, December 9, 1942" in *George S. Patton Papers: Diaries, 1910 to 1945*. Library of Congress. https://www.loc.gov/collections/george-s-patton-diaries/about-this-collection.

Patton, George S., and Paul D. Harkins (editor). *War as I Knew It*. Boston: Houghton Mifflin, 1995.

Phillips, Henry Gerard. *Heavy Weapons*. Grass Valley, CA: Privately published, 2007.

———. *Remagen: Springboard to Victory*. Penn Valley, CA: Privately published, 1995.

———. *Sedjenane: The Pay-Off Battle*. Penn Valley, CA: Privately published, 1993.

———, and John Irving. *El Guettar: Crucible of Leadership*. Grass Valley, CA: Privately published, 2010.

Pyle, Ernie. *Here Is Your War: Story of G. I. Joe*. Cleveland, OH: World Publishing, 1945.

Reynolds, Harley. *How I Survived the Three First Wave Invasions: North Africa, Sicily, Omaha Beach*. Minneapolis: Mill City Press, 2008.

Rottman, Gordon L. *M3 Medium Tank vs Panzer III: Kasserine Pass 1943*. Oxford, UK: Osprey Publishing, 2008.

Scheffel, Captain Charles, with Barry Basden. *Crack! and Thump: With a Combat Officer in World War II*. Llano, TX: Camroc Press, 2007.

Schick, Albert. *Combat History of the 10. Panzer-Division, 1939–1943*. Winnipeg, Manitoba, Canada: J. J. Fedorowicz, 2013.

Schmidt, H. W. *With Rommel in the Desert: In Victory and Defeat with the Commander of the Afrika Korps*. New York: Ballantine, 1967.

Shockley, Orion. *Random Chance: One Infantry Soldier's Story*. Bloomington, IN: Trafford Publishing, 2007.

Smithsonian. *Tank: The Definitive Visual History of Armored Vehicles*. New York: DK Publishing, 2017.

Stern, Phil, and Liesl Bradner. *Snapdragon: The World War II Exploits of Darby's Ranger and Combat Photographer Phil Stern*. Oxford, UK: Osprey Publishing, 2018.

Taaffe, Stephen R. *Marshall and His Generals: U.S. Army Commanders in World War II*. Lawrence: University Press of Kansas, 2011.

Tobin, James. *Ernie Pyle's War: America's Eyewitness to World War II*. New York: Free Press, 1997.

Trest, Warren A. *Nobody but the People: The Life and Times of Alabama's Youngest Governor*. Montgomery, AL: NewSouth Books, 2008.

Truscott, Lt. Gen. Lucian K., Jr. *Command Missions: A Personal Story*. Mount Pleasant, SC: Arcadia Press, 2017.

United States Army. *Our Battalion: 899th Tank Destroyer Battalion History*. Munich: Knorr & Hirth, 1945.

Von Luck, Hans. *Panzer Commander: The Memoirs of Hans von Luck*. Barnsley, UK: Frontline Books, 2013.

Wells, H. G. "The Land Ironclads." Redditch, Worcestershire, UK: H. G. Wells Library/Read Books Ltd., 2016.

Wheeler, James Scott. *The Big Red One: America's Legendary 1st Infantry Division from World War I to Desert Storm*. Lawrence: University Press of Kansas, 2007.

Yeide, Harry. *Fighting Patton*. Minneapolis: Zenith Press, 2011.

———. *The Tank Killers: A History of America's World War II Tank Destroyer Force*. Havertown, PA: Casemate, 2005.

Zaloga, Steven. *Armored Thunderbolt: The U.S. Army Sherman in World War II*. Mechanicsburg, PA: Stackpole, 2008.

———. *George S. Patton: Leadership, Strategy, Conflict*. Oxford, UK: Osprey Publishing, 2010.

INDEX

Note: Page numbers in *italics* refer to maps.

ABOUT THE AUTHOR

Stephen L. Moore, a sixth-generation Texan, graduated from Stephen F. Austin State University in Nacogdoches, Texas, where he studied advertising, marketing, and journalism. He is the author of twenty-one previous books on World War II and Texas history, including *Battle Stations: How the USS* Yorktown *Helped Turned the Tide at Coral Sea and Midway.* Parents of three children, Steve and his wife, Cindy, live north of Dallas in Lantana, Texas.